T5-CRS-187

NONVERBAL COMMUNICATION

ADVANCES IN THE STUDY OF
COMMUNICATION AND AFFECT

Volume 1

NONVERBAL COMMUNICATION

Edited by

Lester Krames, Patricia Pliner, and Thomas Alloway
Erindale College
University of Toronto
Mississauga, Ontario
Canada

PLENUM PRESS · NEW YORK AND LONDON

Library of Congress Cataloging in Publication Data

Symposium on Communication and Affect, 3d, Erindale College, 1973.
  Nonverbal communication; [proceedings]

  (Advances in the study of communication and affect, v. 1)
  Includes bibliographies.
  1. Nonverbal communication. I. Krames, Lester, ed. II. Pliner, Patricia, ed.
III. Alloway, Thomas, ed. IV. Title. [DNLM: 1. Nonverbal communication—
Congresses. HM258 E68n 1973]
BF637.C45S9   1973   156'.3   74-6325
ISBN 0-306-35901-4

Proceedings of the Erindale Campus Symposium on Communication and Affect
held in Mississauga, Ontario, March 15-17, 1973

© 1974 Plenum Press, New York
A Division of Plenum Publishing Corporation
227 West 17th Street, New York, N.Y. 10011

United Kingdom edition published by Plenum Press, London
A Division of Plenum Publishing Company, Ltd.
4a Lower John Street, London WIR 3PD, England

Printed in the United States of America

List of Contributors

W. J. CARR
Beaver College, Glenside, Pennsylvania

VICTOR H. DENENBERG
Department of Biobehavioral Sciences, University of Connecticut, Storrs, Connecticut

PETER MARLER
Professor and Director, Center for Field Research in Ethology and Ecology, The Rockefeller University, New York, New York

ROBERT E. MILLER
Department of Psychiatry, University of Pittsburgh, Pittsburgh, Pennsylvania

HOWARD A. MOSS
Child Research Branch, National Institute of Mental Health, Bethesda, Maryland

JAMES H. REYNIERSE
Department of Psychology, Hope College, Holland, Michigan

WILLIAM N. TAVOLGA
Department of Animal Behavior, American Museum of Natural History, New York, and Department of Biology, City College of the City University of New York, New York

ADRIAN M. WENNER
Department of Biological Sciences, University of California, Santa Barbara, Santa Barbara, California

Contents

CHAPTER 6

ADRIAN M. WENNER

CHAPTER 7

HOWARD A. MOSS

CHAPTER 8

VICTOR H. DENENBERG

NONVERBAL
COMMUNICATION

CHAPTER 1

Communication Elements Constraining Animal Learning and Performance

James H. Reynierse

Department of Psychology
Hope College
Holland, Michigan

Over 20 years ago, comparative psychology was sharply criticized by Beach (1950) for excessive use of the albino rat and by Lorenz (1950) for not being properly comparative. More recently, comparative psychology has again been criticized, this time for not being sufficiently behavioral, biological, or evolutionary as well as for holding an inadequate phylogeny (Hodos and Campbell, 1969; Lockard, 1971; Wilcock, 1972). Such criticism identifies limits of the American behavioristic tradition, particularly of typical psychological investigations of animal learning and motivation.

There are, however, a number of current developments in animal learning psychology that are broadly biological and that call attention to ecologically adaptive and evolutionarily significant patterns of behavior. While relatively old compared to recent research and theorizing, the Brelands' classic paper, "The Misbehavior of Organisms" (Breland and Breland, 1961), as well as later development of their thinking (Breland and Breland, 1966) was undoubtedly a primary stimulant for and precursor of more contemporary efforts. At the very least, the breakdown of reinforcement contingencies that they reported with several, nonlaboratory species could neither be disregarded nor resolved within a strictly psychological framework. More recently, the autoshaping experiment (Brown and Jenkins, 1968), investigations of poison avoidance learning by Garcia, Revusky, Rozin, and their associates (e.g., Revusky and Garcia, 1970; Rozin and Kalat, 1971; Garcia *et al.*, 1972), the role of species-specific defense reactions in escape–avoidance learning (Bolles, 1970, 1971), adaptive interim activities and the superstition experiment (Staddon and Simmelhag, 1971), ethological displacement activities during response prevention and extinction (Reynierse, 1970, 1971a; Reynierse et al., 1970), competing species-specific response systems and learning in sticklebacks (Sevenster, 1968), a continuum of behavioral preparedness (Seligman, 1970), and stimulus relevance (Shettleworth, 1972a) all represent a significant synthesis of psychological and biological considerations within laboratory investigations of animal learning. Such approaches that emphasize an organism's evolutionary history and genetic endowment can be organized under the broad topic of biological constraints on learning (Shettleworth, 1972b) or biological boundaries of learning (Seligman and Haber, 1972). The same general approach has been taken by Razran (1971), who has recently published a particularly systematic analysis of learning based on a consistently biological and evolutionary point of view.

There is another, less well known body of literature that also fits the biological constraints model of animal learning. This research identifies communication elements in animal learning in which odors produced through nonreward may influence performance on appetitive learning tasks while visually mediated postures related to agonistic behavior may appear and have effects on performance for aversive learning tasks.

Odor of Nonreward

A major stimulant for a series of research projects on the odor of nonreward was the incidental finding of McHose and Ludvigson (1966) that in a discrimination learning situation, involving two distinctive runways, control animals which received the same reward in both runways exhibited discriminated, patterned responding when their training trials were interspersed with trials of experimental animals which received different reward magnitudes in the same two runways. A similar effect was obtained by Spear and Spitzner (1966).

In two experiments, McHose and Ludvigson (1966) used two parallel straight alleys, one black and the other white, in which rats received different magnitudes of reward at different delays within the goal box. Under the S+ condition, discrimination rats received either one 45-mg pellet at 0 sec delay, ten pellets at 0 sec delay, or ten pellets at 10 sec delay; under the S− conditions in the other straight alley, all discrimination rats received one pellet at 10 sec delay. Nondiscrimination control rats were not treated differentially in the two alleys but received a small, one-pellet reward at 10 sec delay in both of them. In a second experiment, magnitude of reinforcement was a constant three pellets. Discrimination rats under S+ conditions received reinforcement after either 0 or 15 sec delay while under

S— conditions reinforcement was delivered after 30 sec delay. Nondiscrimination control rats were reinforced following 30 sec delay in both alleys.

Exactly as in other studies that employed an explicit external cue (e.g., Bower, 1961), the discrimination groups ran faster under S+ than under S— conditions. But it was the performance of the nondiscrimination control groups which did not receive differential reinforcement that yielded the interesting data. Considering the S+ and S— alleys for the discrimination subjects but plotting the performance of nondiscrimination controls clearly indicated that controls ran significantly faster in the S+ than in the S— alley, even though the S+ and S— functions represented only differential reinforcement for other animals run in the same squad. McHose and Ludvigson interpreted these results as suggesting that discrimination rats exuded qualitatively or quantitatively different odors on S+ and S— trials and that the persistence of these odor trails influenced performance in control subjects. The evidence now available indicates that this effect is probably due entirely to odors of nonreward (S— trials). In this regard, the McHose and Ludvigson (1966) study and more recent related investigations share stimulus conditions that produce frustration and conflict, the general state that usually produces scent marking in mammals under natural conditions (Ralls, 1971).

Function of Odors

Assuming for the moment that McHose and Ludvigson's interpretation is essentially correct, we might inquire about the potential roles of odors of nonreward. There are at least three such roles in which the odor may serve a discrimination, cue, or pheromone function. A discrimination interpretation implies that the organism can detect a difference, i.e., that there is a perceptual difference between two or more odorous stimuli. Ideally, the defining operations for such an interpretation require a psychophysical experiment. A cue interpretation implies that a detected stimulus has a signal function that is associated with some specific environmental state. It implies that there is a learned association in which the detected stimulus exerts stimulus control. Ideally, this requires a learning experiment as the defining operation in which the stimulus cue (CS) is consistently paired with reinforcement. It should be noted that discrimination learning experiments include both discrimination and cue functions, employing at least two discriminably different values of a stimulus dimension. In the general form of the experiment, one of the stimuli, the S^D, is consistently associated with reinforcement, while the other, the S^Δ, is consistently associated with the absence of reinforcement. In a variation, the different stimulus cues may signal higher and lower magnitudes of reward.

Since pheromones refer to a general class of chemical substances that are secreted to the external environment and have an intraspecific communication function (Gleason and Reynierse, 1969), a pheromone interpretation is complex and ideally demands considering biological and chemical factors as well as behavioral factors. In addition, the specific responses produced by pheromones are presumably unconditioned and species specific. The methodological implication of this for demonstrating a pheromonal function is that several defining experiments are required. Minimally, operations are required that implicate a chemical stimulus mediated by olfaction, which indicate that one individual is transmitting a message, i.e., is communicating with another member of the species, and that the activities of both sender and receiver are unconditioned patterns of behavior.[1] That there is some ambiguity about demonstrating that a behavior pattern is unlearned (e.g., Jensen, 1961; Lorenz, 1965) as well as an unusually large number of different approaches to the concept of communication (Burghardt, 1970) suggests that any experimental manipulation will be somewhat unsatisfactory for these complex issues. In any event, a choice or preference test, examining the reactions of a receiving animal toward the odors of a sending animal, may best satisfy this social, communication function. Requiring that test animals be reared in isolation where experiences with odors can be carefully controlled and then later using a choice or preference test may permit determining whether responses to odors are unconditioned. Such a combined approach was used by Carr et al. (1970) in investigating the reactions of mice to odors induced by defeat during controlled agonistic encounters and by Rottman and Snowdon (1972) in investigating the reactions of mice to experimental stress. Finally, the chemical nature of pheromones ideally requires isolating the chemical substance, identifying the source of the odor in donor, sender animals, and demonstrating that any resulting behavior in receiver animals is mediated by olfaction. A word of caution is necessary at this point since both surgical anosmia and behavioral controls also have implications for the discrimination and cue functions of odors. As a consequence, olfaction is a necessary but not a sufficient condition for a pheromone interpretation. Similarly, a pheromone interpretation presupposes that animals can detect olfactory stimulation and make appropriate olfactory discriminations. Nevertheless, the ability to make olfactory discriminations is not a sufficient condition for a pheromone interpretation.

[1] It is clearly undesirable to resurrect fruitless debate regarding learning versus instinct, and such an emphasis is unintended. However, when pheromones mediate intraspecific interactions, there is a chemically coded message in which the sender and receiver share the code. How the code was acquired, whether through ecological, ontogenetic, or genetic mechanisms, either alone or in combination, is not essential for the present methodological distinctions. On the other hand, while learning or conditioning experiments can identify cue functions of chemical stimuli, they are unsatisfactory preparations for demonstrating pheromone functions.

Returning to the results obtained by McHose and Ludvigson (1966), a satisfactory analysis of their data must determine whether their results reflect discrimination and cue effects or whether scent marking by rats during learning tasks can communicate information to other rats about the reward and nonreward conditions in effect.

Generality of Discrimination and Cue Effects

Although most of the experimental research has concentrated on the runway behavior of albino rats in a straight alley, examining running speed (e.g., Wasserman and Jensen, 1969), single alternation patterning effects (e.g., Amsel *et al.,* 1969), or double alternation patterning effects (e.g., Ludvigson and Sytsma, 1967), the general effect has also been obtained in other learning situations and with additional animal species. Thus, related effects have been obtained using a bar-press response in a Skinner box (Valenta and Rigby, 1968) and choice responses in a T-maze (Morrison and Ludvigson, 1970; Means *et al.,* 1971) or Y-maze (Bowers and Alexander, 1967). At this time, such effects are restricted to rodents, including mice (Davis, 1970; Bowers and Alexander, 1967) and gerbils (Topping and Cole, 1969) as well as laboratory rats.

Table I

Daily Schedules of Reward (R) and Nonreward (N) and Order of Trials[a]

Group	S	Trial							
		1	2	3	4	5	6	7	8
P	S1	R1	R2	N1	N2	R1	R2	N1	N2
(homogeneous)	S2	R1	R2	N1	N2	R1	R2	N1	N2
	S3	R1	R2	N1	N2	R1	R2	N1	N2
	S4	R1	R2	N1	N2	R1	R2	N1	N2
	S5	R1	R2	N1	N2	R1	R2	N1	N2
	S6	R1	R2	N1	N2	R1	R2	N1	N2
	S7	R1	R2	N1	N2	R1	R2	N1	N2
NP	S1	R1	R2	N1	N2	R1	R2	N1	N2
(heterogeneous)	S2	R	N1	N2	R1	R2	N1	N2	R
	S3	N1	N2	R1	R2	N1	N2	R1	R2
	S4	N	R1	R2	N1	N2	R1	R2	N
	S5	R1	R2	N1	N2	R1	R2	N1	N2
	S6	R	N1	N2	R1	R2	N1	N2	R
	S7	N1	N2	R1	R2	N1	N2	R1	R2

From Ludvigson and Sytsma (1967).
[a] S1 through S7, in that order, received trial 1, then trial 2, etc. Numbers following R and N designate first and second events of the doublets for which data were summarized. Thus trials 1 and 8 for *S2, S4,* and *S6* of group NP were excluded from the data.

Discrimination and cue effects have been demonstrated often and appear to be straightforward and unambiguous. Ludvigson and Sytsma (1967) gave rats eight trials per day of rewarded (R) and nonrewarded (N) trials in a straight alley according to a double alternation pattern of rewarded and nonrewarded trials. Within both groups, all rats completed a given trial before receiving the next trial, and groups were simply differentiated by whether this between-subjects trial sequence was homogeneous (all R or all N trials) or heterogeneous (a double alternation pattern). The schedules are summarized in Table I. Thus if rats produce differential odor cues on N as opposed to R trials, they receive a consistent olfactory cue in the homogeneous trial schedule condition but an inconsistent cue in the heterogeneous schedule. Based entirely on the

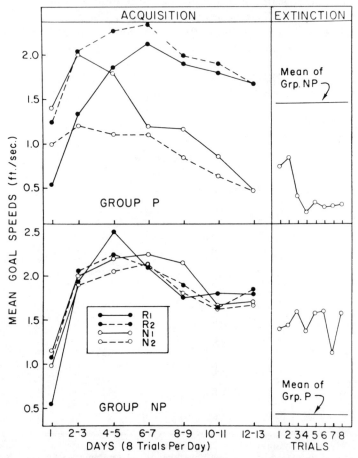

Fig. 1. Mean goal speeds during acquisition and extinction. From Ludvigson and Sytsma (1967).

consistency of rewarded and nonrewarded trials in preceding rats, Ludvigson and Sytsma (1967) found patterning, i.e., faster times on reinforced than on nonreinforced trials, an effect that was confined to running speed in the goal section of the alley for the homogeneous olfactory cue group. Rats ran fast on all trials in the noncue condition. These results are summarized in Fig. 1. Similar patterning to a consistent odor cue based on the order of rewarded and nonrewarded trials in preceding rats was obtained by Ludvigson (1969).

In another investigation in which the cue function of odors was specifically separated from any unconditioned pheromone effects, Morrison and Ludvigson (1970) gave either rewarded or nonrewarded trials to odorant donor rats at the choice point of a T-maze and then examined whether other experimental rats could use the odors of reward or nonreward as cues for making the correct turning response. Cue odors were provided by placing a hungry odorant rat into the choice area for 30 sec either with an abundant supply of food or without food. A neutral, clean floor odor cue was established by pulling clean paper across the maze floor. Two of the "odors" were used in each group, one as a cue for correctly turning left in the maze and one for turning right. All experimental rats received six training trials per day, three trials with each of the two odor cue conditions. In one group, "odor" of reward was a cue for turning into one arm of the maze while "odor" of nonreward was a cue for turning into the other arm. A second group received "odor" of reward as one cue and the neutral clean floor as the other. In a third group, "odor" of nonreward and the clean floor were the cues, while the fourth group was a baseline control in which all trials took place on a clean floor. Evidence for discriminated responding occurred only in the two groups having "odor" of nonreward as a cue.

Amsel et al. (1969), using a within-subjects design with training at one trial per day, confirmed the patterning effects obtained by Ludvigson and Sytsma (1967). More importantly, by altering the presentation of N and R trials during different stages of training, they were able to produce strong patterning when a homogeneous set of odor cues (all N or all R trials) were administered across all subjects but to completely disrupt patterning by mixing the within-day presentation of odors produced by N and R trials. They too found that patterning effects were confined to running speed in the goal area. Additional studies supporting an olfactory cue interpretation of patterned runway performance include McHose (1967), McHose et al. (1967), Davis et al. (1970), and Prytula et al. (1972, 1973).

Several studies have shown that rodents can discriminate odors associated with a variety of physiological or social conditions and use them as cues in discrimination learning. Bowers and Alexander (1967) found that mice quickly learned discriminations based on sex, species, or individual odors. Similarly, normal and castrated male rats learned a discrimination based on the odors of receptive versus nonreceptive females, while normal and ovariectomized female rats were trained to discriminate between the odors of normal and castrated males (Carr and Caul, 1962).

Valenta and Rigby (1968) obtained air samples from stressed rats which had received electric shock and unstressed rats which had not been shocked and demonstrated that other rats could respond differentially to these odors. Food-deprived rats were initially trained to make bar-press responses on a variable-interval (VI-1) partial reinforcement schedule for a sucrose solution reward. Discriminative punishment training was then superimposed on the VI-1 schedule such that any bar presses that occurred when air samples from stressed rats were introduced into the learning compartment produced 0.3 sec of scrambled footshock. However, when air from unstressed rats was introduced, every other bar-press response was effective in producing the sucrose solution. Under these conditions, latency to bar press was significantly longer when odors of stressed animals ($\bar{X} = 8.49$) were the cue compared to when odors of unstressed ($\bar{X} = 1.59$) animals were introduced.

Generality of Pheromonal Effects

The experimental data providing unambiguous support for discrimination or cue functions of hypothesized odors also provide some indirect evidence for a pheromonal interpretation. For example, the most common finding in straight-alley studies is that behavioral effects are restricted, at least during acquisition, to running speed in the goal area (Ludvigson and Sytsma, 1967; Ludvigson, 1969; Amsel et al., 1969). Within a pheromone framework, the goal area is the place where unconditioned marking responses should occur and where odors produced in response to reward or nonreward conditions should be maximized.

Additional indirect evidence for a pheromone interpretation is the typical finding that only "odor" of nonreward serves as an effective cue for learning, an effect clearly demonstrated by Morrison and Ludvigson (1970), Wasserman and Jensen (1969), and Collerain and Ludvigson (1972). On the other hand, Means et al. (1971) concluded that the odor trails of reinforced rats provided a weak cue for learning a discrimination. In their study, donor rats traversed a T-maze and were forced to turn either right or left but in any event were always reinforced with four 45-mg pellets on entering the goal area. Experimental rats were reinforced only if they chose the path of the donor animal, while control rats were reinforced randomly with respect to the odor trails and arm of the maze entered by donor animals. Under these conditions, frequency of correct choices increased significantly, reaching about 80% correct responding after 100 trials for experimental rats, but remained at chance levels for control animals. Such results provide convincing evidence that the "odor" serves a consistent cue function. More importantly, however, even though donor rats were always rewarded, these results do not yield any compelling evidence for a distinct "odor" of reward as the significant olfactory cue. Rather, since their procedures included pairing one donor rat with one experimental and one control rat for the duration of the experiment, it is quite likely that individual recognition (Bowers and Alexander, 1967), and not "odor" of reward, mediated learning.

There is some indication that odor of reward may have a weak, temporary effect (Morrison and Ludvigson, 1970; Wasserman and Jensen, 1969). In a recent study, Mellgren et al. (1973) used a three-compartment box in which the middle compartment contained paper that had been present earlier when a donor rat had been either rewarded with a water reinforcer, or nonrewarded (extinction), or had only entered the compartment but had never received a water reward in the apparatus. The two end compartments always contained clean paper. Experimental recipient rats were run following the appropriate donor rat but never received any reward in the apparatus. Using a measure of latency to entering and escaping from the middle compartment, they found that recipient rats take a relatively long time to enter a compartment when it contains the odor of rats that have just received a nonrewarded extinction trial and, once there, tend to leave that compartment relatively quickly. Both effects are entirely congruent with the idea that rats emit odors associated with nonreward and that these odors are broadly aversive. More importantly, they also demonstrated that recipient rats enter a compartment relatively quickly when it contains the odor of rats that have been rewarded there and leave this area relatively slowly. This study provides the best available evidence that rats may emit odors associated with reward and that these odors are broadly attractive. While particularly sensitive procedures may indicate that rats respond to an odor of reward, the cumulative evidence available suggests that odor of nonreward is primary. Within the boundaries of learning experiments, rodent behavior is controlled to a considerable extent by odor of nonreward while odor of reward tends to yield minimal, temporary effects.

One interpretation of the fact that only nonreward conditions routinely produce effects is that odors are generated only when aversive or frustrating conditions are introduced within learning situations. Such an interpretation is entirely consistent with the evidence for alarm substances as pheromones (Gleason and Reynierse, 1969; Carr et al., 1970; Rottman and Snowdon, 1972), with the established finding that electric shock can generate olfactory cues that facilitate later escape-avoidance learning (King, 1969), and with the evidence that territorial marking in natural environments is also generated by broad sources of frustration (Ralls, 1971) and quite possibly even that olfactory signals associated with active territorial exclusion by territory-dominant animals may reinforce avoidance behavior directed toward other established territorial boundaries (Thiessen and Dawber, 1972). Similarly, it is also consistent with latent extinction effects, i.e., the decrement in running speed during extinction when an animal is placed in an empty goal that previously had been associated with reward. In this regard, Pratt and Ludvigson (1970) demonstrated that the "odor" of nonreward may account for the latent extinction effect, since goal speeds during extinction in their study were significantly slower following placement in an empty goal box relative to a control condition where placements were made in a neutral compartment. More importantly, goal speeds were slower following placement in an empty goal box when odor cues were present relative to a control (placement in empty goal box) where odor cues were removed.

Direct evidence for a pheromone interpretation requires reference to the unconditioned, chemical communication function of implicated chemical stimuli. Rottman and Snowdon (1972) stressed communicator donor mice by intraperitoneal injections of 0.3 ml saline solution and then examined the preference behavior of unstressed receiver mice to air samples obtained from stressed animals. For the preference test, the experimental chamber containing the receiver animal was divided in half, a side nearest the air input and a side farthest from the air input. Under these conditions, receiver rats preferred the side of the compartment farthest from air input when the air carried the odor of a stressed mouse but not when it carried the odor of the same mouse but under unstressed conditions. Although they did not employ a learning experiment to establish the cue value of an odor associated with stress, they did use both social isolation and anosmia manipulations in subsequent experiments. The results of the isolation study were equivocal, as isolated mice emitted the odor when stressed but behaved inappropriately in that they showed a preference rather than an aversion to the odor of stressed mice. The anosmia manipulation clearly demonstrated an olfactory component, as surgical destruction of the olfactory mucosa produced mice which were indifferent to odors of stressed animals. In a particularly interesting series of experiments, Carr *et al.* (1970) showed that mice could make an unlearned discrimination based on odors associated with victims or victors in agonistic encounters. Furthermore, it is clear that odors associated with a stressed victim which had been subjected to defeat are the effective cue. Thus male mice showed a clear preference for odors from isolates rather than odors from victims, indicating that they could detect the different olfactory conditions. In contrast, they showed no discrimination and preference for the odors from isolates and victors. That there is a greater odor effect for stressed victims is a result that exactly parallels the asymmetrical olfactory effects associated with odors of nonreward. Unfortunately, evidence for a pheromone interpretation such as that provided by both Rottman and Snowdon (1972) and Carr et al. (1970) is less systematic for the effects of "odor" of nonreward on performance of instrumental learning tasks.

Although effective chemical substances have not yet been isolated or identified and the source of the odor in sender, donor animals is still in doubt, there is considerable evidence implicating an odor of nonreward in which animals previously rewarded in a goal box mark an empty goal box with a distinctive olfactory stimulus. Almost every investigation has specifically included procedural precautions that would maximize olfactory stimulation in experimental conditions and minimize olfactory stimulation in control groups. Apparatus has routinely been carefully cleaned with water or a disinfectant to minimize odors (Bowers and Alexander, 1967; Ludvigson and Sytsma, 1967; Ludvigson, 1969; Pratt and Ludvigson, 1970; Seago et al., 1970; Davis and Ludvigson, 1969). Removable paper on the floor or interior walls of apparatus has been replaced after each trial in order to minimize odors but retained from one trial to the next in order to maximize odors (Wasserman and Jensen, 1969; Morrison and Ludvigson, 1970; Collerain and Ludvigson, 1972). Similarly, odors have been maximized by introducing an absorbent desk blotter or pad on the floor of the straight alley or in the goal box (Pratt and Ludvigson, 1970). Prytula et al. (1972, 1973) have developed a straight-alley runway with an odor exhaust duct underneath the runway and extending from the start to the goal box. An odor exhaust system consists of a quiet ducted fan located underneath the goal box but continuous with the tunnel forming the exhaust duct. In their investigations, blocking the fan maximized goal box odors while in the unblocked conditions odors were exhausted and minimized. Since odors are airborne, delivery of odor-loaded and clean air samples to a receiver animal (e.g., Valenta and Rigby, 1968; Bowers and Alexander, 1967) has been another viable way of controlling olfactory stimuli.

Seago et al. (1970) replicated the homogeneous reward and nonreward cue conditions of Ludvigson and Sytsma (1967) and Ludvigson (1969) using normal and anosmic rats. All rats received eight trials per day in which the double alternation pattern of reward and nonreward consisted of a sequence of RRNNRRNN trials. Four groups consisted of normal controls, sham-operated controls, and two groups of anosmic experimental animals. Anosmia was achieved surgically by removing the olfactory bulbs and connecting olfactory tracts with an aspirator. That this procedure was successful was confirmed by visual examination of each rat's brain on completion of the study. Although both groups of anosmic experimental rats should not show response patterning to differential olfactory cues associated with R and N trials, after 14 days of training one anosmic group was given a consistent visual cue in which a lamp was lighted on R trials but darkened on N trials and these visual cue conditions were maintained for the remainder of acquisition training. The results of this study are clear, as marked patterning, i.e., fast running speeds on R trials but slow speeds on N trials, occurred in intact controls while both anosmic experimental groups failed to show any patterning (Fig. 2). Furthermore, with the introduction of consistent visual cues, appropriate patterning also appeared in anosmic rats (Fig. 3). In both cases, such patterning appeared for running speed in both the goal and the runway sections of the alley.

The olfactory hypothesis also suggests that as successive rats receive the same nonrewarded trial in the goal box, odor of nonreward should accumulate. Accordingly there should be a correlation between the position of a rat in the group running order, i.e., the number of immediately preceding rats experiencing the same nonreward goal event, and the

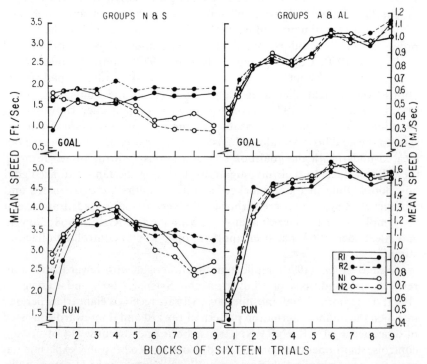

Fig. 2. Group mean run and goal speeds, expressed in both meters and feet per second, over the 18 days of acquisition for groups N (normal control) and S (sham control) combined and groups A and AL (anosmic) combined. From Seago *et al.* (1970).

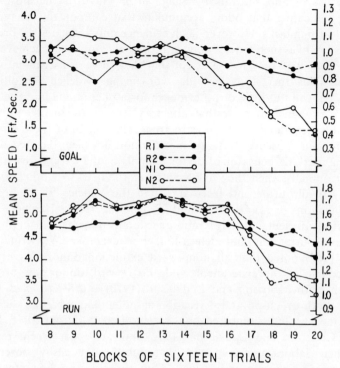

Fig. 3. Mean run and goal speeds over the last 25 days of acquisition for group AL (anosmic), during which time the lamp cue was operative. From Seago *et al.* (1970).

magnitude of response patterning. In this regard, Seago *et al.* (1970) found that for intact controls the patterning effect increased as the position of rats in the running order increased. However, anosmic rats utilizing a light cue that should not show such a between-trials accumulation effect did not show a relationship between magnitude of patterning and running position within the group. Strictly interpreted, their data indicate only that this increased patterning is the result of similar goal experiences. Their data do not implicate a sequence of between-subjects rewarded or nonrewarded trials since they only attended to the combined effects of reward and nonreward, examining the mean difference in running speeds between rewarded and nonrewarded trials as a function of each rat's position within the fixed group running order. However, the mass of available evidence clearly indicates that there is an odor only on nonreward and it is this odor that undoubtedly accounts for the increased patterning effects when odor systematically accumulates in the goal area.

The use of anosmic rats by Seago *et al.* (1970) is the most direct evidence indicating that odors accumulate that can control behavior on runway learning tasks. However, such evidence only indicates the presence of odors. While such odors may control behavior, they achieve such behavioral control only to the extent that they serve a discriminative cue function. Thus this study provides convincing evidence for olfactory stimulus control but little or no evidence for a pheromone interpretation.

Even though it is clear that olfactory stimuli are involved and are presumably generated on nonreward trials, the source of these olfactory stimuli remains obscure. Little or no attention has been directed toward either the marking behavior of donor animals or the natural reactions of recipient animals when they first encounter the marks of other rodents. Similarly, while urine and feces are often the vehicles for pheromonal communication (e.g., Gleason and Reynierse, 1969; Hediger, 1950) there is insufficient, usually only anecdotal, information implicating the role of urination and defecation. For example, Wasserman and Jensen (1969) noted that all nonreward extinction donor rats urinated in the course of the experiment while no reward, donor rats urinated. However, both Morrison and Ludvigson (1970) and Seago *et al.* (1970) discount both urination and defecation as potential sources of the odors since urine and feces appeared only rarely after the initial trials. In this regard, Collerain and Ludvigson (1972) indicated that recent research from their laboratory suggested that subtle, not easily observable, quantities of urine may be involved. Thus emissions are apparent under ultraviolet light that are not apparent under ordinary light. Although identification of these emissions is currently equivocal, it is instructive to note that rat urine does fluoresce under ultraviolet light (H. W. Ludvigson, personal communication).

The strongest evidence indicating that odor of nonreward has unconditioned effects comes from studies showing the suppressing effects of odors on performance in learning tasks where odors do not function as discriminative cues. Wasserman and Jensen (1969) trained rats to traverse a runway for food reward in which the apparatus floor was either clean paper, paper recently traversed by a reinforced rat, or paper recently traversed by an unreinforced, frustrated rat. The start times and running speeds of consistently reinforced rats were significantly slower when they ran on a paper floor used by donor rats which had received an unreinforced extinction trial (Figs. 4 and 5). Similarly, Courtney *et al.* (1968) found that straight-alley running speed was suppressed when rats were exposed to the odor of rats which had been shocked in the goal box. Another indication that odor of nonreward is inherently aversive is the finding of Collerain and Ludvigson (1972) that rats given free-choice test trials in a T-maze consistently avoided an odor of nonreward, entering a clean goal

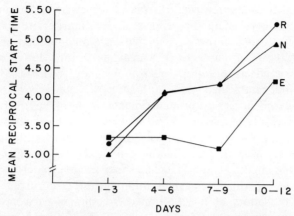

Fig. 4. Mean starting speeds for recipient paper subjects over 12 days of testing. Trials were conducted on new paper (N), extinction-traversed paper (E), and reward-traversed paper (R). From Wasserman and Jensen (1969).

box instead. On the other hand, rats were indifferent toward goal boxes in which donor rats had previously been rewarded.

Although such suppression and free-choice avoidance behavior are consistent with the idea that odor of nonreward elicits an unconditioned alarm reaction, there remains the possibility that any novel or unanticipated odor might elicit competing, exploratory behavior (Pratt and Ludvigson, 1970) or neophobic avoidance reactions. If odor associated with aversive

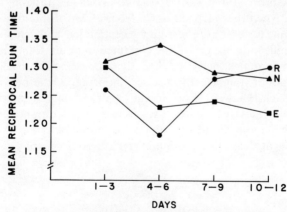

Fig. 5. Mean running speed for recipient paper subjects over 12 days of testing. Trials were conducted on new paper (N), extinction-traversed paper (E), and reward-traversed paper (R). From Wasserman and Jensen (1969).

conditions such as nonreward, frustration, or electric shock could also produce excitatory, energizing effects under appropriate experimental conditions, such an alternative explanation would be considerably less attractive. Although such evidence is unavailable for odor of nonreward, the energizing effects of alarm pheromones for avoidance learning is reasonably well established.

In an excellent series of experiments, King (1969) gave rats 35 inescapable pairings of a light CS and shock US in the shock compartment of a hurdle-jump one-way avoidance box. In a postconditioning test, he clearly demonstrated that the elimination of the odors of shocked rats suppressed the latency to run from the shock compartment to a safe box. In subsequent experiments, postconditioning testing occurred either with or without the odors of a conditioned rat, and in each case response latencies were significantly faster when olfactory stimuli were present, presumably because olfactory stimuli present in the feces and urine of shocked rats have an important fear arousal function. In a conceptually similar study, Kimbrell *et al.* (1970) showed that goldfish acquired a shuttle avoidance response more rapidly if an alarm pheromone released by epidermal damage was present in the aquarium water where training occurred. Fish trained in plain water achieved the acquisition criterion in 65.5 trials, while fish trained in water in which a freshly decapitated goldfish had been scaled reached criterion in 45.5 trials. Interestingly, the unconditioned behavior of naive goldfish to the pheromone solution consisted of agitated, nondirectional, jerky movements with fins fully erected, and all fish remained in the corner farthest away from where the pheromone solution had been dumped.

Finally, Sprott (1969) used a passive avoidance task in which mice were shocked when they stepped down from a platform onto a grid floor. Conditioned mice were more resistant to extinction and remained on the platform significantly longer if their extinction trials followed a donor mouse which had just been shocked than if extinction trials followed nonshocked donor animals. Even more importantly, the performance of naive mice which followed donor animals shocked only during acquisition but were never shocked themselves suggests an unconditioned, facilitation effect since they spent about the same time on the platform as the conditioned mice spent there during original training over an equivalent number of trials.

Agonistic Postures

Taken together, the research related to odor of nonreward indicates that odors may have pheromonal, communication functions within animal learning investigations. Nevertheless, odors have usually functioned as discriminative cues controlling behavior rather than as pheromones. Both discriminative cues and the less frequent pheromone effects are relatively unambiguous and noncontroversial. In contrast, the idea that visually mediated postures related to agonistic behavior may be relevant for aversive learning tasks is highly speculative.

Behavior elicited by electric shock in laboratory rats has been examined previously (Kimble, 1955; Trabasso and Thompson, 1962; Reynierse *et al.,* 1970) but has largely consisted of motor movements rather than social postures. With the delivery of shock, rats exhibit unconditioned responses such as jumping, running, or flinching, depending on shock intensity, but with the termination of shock, rats usually remain motionless and assume passive postures. That these postures may be related to social postures is indirectly supported by Baenninger and Grossman's (1969) report of dominance–subordination interactions in pain-elicited aggression and Logan and Boice's (1969) report of such interactions when rats were paired during an avoidance learning task. In addition, Reynierse (1971*b*) confirmed the Baenninger and Grossman (1969) report of dominance and systematically recorded the occurrence of threat and submissive postures during pain-elicited aggression.

The topography and functional significance of aggressive postures in social situations have been described in detail for a number of rodent species. Thus agonistic behavior has been investigated in inbred laboratory mice (Scott and Fredericson, 1951; Grant and Mackintosh, 1963) and wild mice (Eisenberg, 1962), laboratory (Grant, 1963; Grant and Mackintosh, 1963; Reynierse, 1971*b*) and wild rats (Barnett, 1958, 1963, 1967; Logan and Boice, 1969), guinea pigs and hamsters (Grant and Mackintosh, 1963), gerbils (Reynierse, 1971*c*) ground squirrels (Turner *et al.,* 1973), and voles (Clarke, 1956). These studies clearly indicate that there are both aggressive and defensive moods that are characterized by aggressive and submissive movements and postures, respectively. Thus intraspecific aggression involves complex aspects of social behavior in which behavioral acts and postures serve important intraspecific communication functions.

Species-specific defense reactions involving flight are complicated in many species by the availability of two pathways of flight behavior. In one, the organism simply turns or runs aways, and, if attempts at escape are blocked, it crouches (Chance, 1962). In this way, it physically removes itself from the presence of the other animal. It is presumably this pathway of flight that Bolles (1969, 1970, 1971) refers to in his analysis of the role of species-specific defense reactions as effective avoidance responses in escape–avoidance learning. Such an analysis is consistent with aversively motivated behavior such as prey–predator relationships that lack a social, intraspecific communication function. There is also a social pathway that permits an animal to remain in physical contact with its opponent while the defensive postures that occur remove that animal from the sight of the other animal. Such defensive postures are called *cut-off postures* since they cut off the animal's vision of the offensive opponent (Chance, 1962). Such cut-off postures occur in many species, including rats (Chance, 1962; Grant, 1963). In defensive and submissive postures in rats, the submissive rat cannot see the other rat by virtue of the way in which the head is turned up and back, and in many cases these postures are also accompanied by eye closure (Chance, 1962). Such cut-off postures may be relevant responses within avoidance learning.

Ulrich and Azrin (1962) reported that rats occasionally learn to avoid footshock by lying on their backs rather than making the required instrumental response such as a bar-press or shuttle-running response. As a solution, they suggested applying Nair, a commercially available hair remover. Since hair is a sufficient insulator to eliminate or drastically reduce the shock stimulation, removing the hair eliminates the possibility that a rat could avoid shock by lying on its back. But what is particularly interesting here is that the full submissive posture of rats involves the animals' lying flat on their backs (Grant and Mackintosh, 1963), and it is presumably this full submissive posture that laboratory rats exploit when they lie flat on their backs and avoid shock.

The full submissive posture is a rare event that occurs only infrequently in escape–avoidance learning situations. I have never observed it in a one-way box and only a few times in a shuttlebox. However, social postures related to dominance–subordinance relationships have been observed when rats were paired during an avoidance learning task (Logan and Boice, 1969; Logan, 1971). Interestingly, the vast number of escape and avoidance responses are made by the subordinate member of a pair, and such pairing usually results in a profound reduction in avoidance performance and a gradual decrement for animals which were performing efficiently when in the apparatus alone.

A preliminary study by students[2] in my laboratory has used different social postures as the escape and avoidance response. In this study, four groups of rats were distinguished only by the nature of the escape–avoidance response. Since social postures require an opponent animal for orientation, for fulfilling the response contingency each posture was reduced to its nonorientation components. Although some obvious judgments were required, in general the posture classes were unambiguous and easily identified. The classes were as follows:

---

[2] Gretchen Cooper, Terry Reen, and Michael Stevenson were student participants in the social postures study.

Upright boxing—Rearing on hind legs with front paws raised in front of the eyes or chest.

Low crouch—A flat crouch in which the head was oriented toward the grids with the belly down on the grids.

Elevated crouch—Similar to the low crouch but with the back and the belly elevated above the grids.

Eye Closure—Complete closure of both eyes.

The apparatus was a clear plexiglass observation chamber, 24 by 18 by 18 inches, with a grid floor. A tone CS (85 db, 2800 cps) overlapped with a 1.3-mA scrambled shock US, with each new trial initiated after a constant 2-min intertrial interval.

Since shock itself elicits behavioral acts such as jumping, running, or flinching rather than social postures, the conventional delayed conditioning procedure with the shock US on continuously until response terminated seemed undesirable. Accordingly, a special delayed conditioning arrangement was used in which the tone CS was on continuously for up to 2 min, while short, 1-sec pulses of shock were delivered at 5-sec intervals. The procedure, illustrated in Fig. 6, resembles Sidman avoidance with a shock–shock interval of 5 sec but under signaled rather than unsignaled conditions. The occurrence of the appropriate posture immediately terminated the CS-US arrangement such that a posture occurring during the initial 5-sec CS-US interval resulted in an avoidance while postures occuring during the 5-sec intervals between shocks produced an escape. If the appropriate posture failed to occur within 120 sec of CS onset, that trial was terminated noncontingently. Termination of the CS-US sequence was always achieved manually by the observer.

The results of this initial investigation were relatively clear. Qualitatively, during the shock–shock interval, rats reliably exhibited the boxing, low crouch, and elevated crouch postures. Eye closure also occurred, but less frequently. Similarly, when the upright boxing, low crouch, and elevated crouch postures contingently terminated the CS and US, the rat tended to maintain the effective posture throughout the intertrial interval, thereby perseveratively producing an avoidance on the next trial. In contrast, eye closure only rarely perseverated into the intertrial interval.

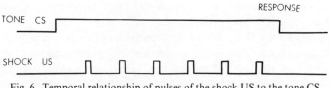

Fig. 6. Temporal relationship of pulses of the shock US to the tone CS.

During the early stages of any trial, rats successively made the upright boxing, low crouch, and elevated crouch postures until they succeeded in terminating the shock, after which the successful posture was usually maintained throughout the intertrial interval. During the shock–shock interval, it appeared as if rats were sampling activities from the repertoire of responses that might be appropriate under aversive conditions, since all animals showed the same stereotyped postures at this time. While eye closure was relatively infrequent, postures frequently included head-down elements that may have effectively blocked any classically conditioned offending visual stimuli, e.g., the apparatus itself, from the sight of the rat. Such cut-off postures may be more frequent than complete eye closure, particularly in a visually ambiguous situation where a clear visual referent is not present.

Because postures tended to perseverate, avoidances cannot be interpreted in the same anticipatory sense as occurs in conventional escape–avoidance learning. Accordingly, for purposes of quantitative analysis we did not distinguish escape from avoidance responses, conservatively considering that an animal reached criterion if the required posture occurred on any nine out of ten consecutive trials. The mean number of trials to reach this criterion was 11.8 for boxing, 10 for low crouch, 10 for elevated crouch, and 21.3 for eye closure. An analysis of variance was significant ($F = 5.76$, df $= 3/30$, $p < 0.01$), indicating that while each posture was effective at least as an escape response, eye closure was less efficient than each of the other three postures. While these results are encouraging and suggestive, additional research is required that permits unambiguous interpretation of the results, particularly in terms of a procedure that can generate unequivocal, anticipatory avoidance postures.

A Concluding Comment

Performance on several appetitive learning tasks is clearly constrained by odors associated with nonreward, an effect that parallels ecologically adaptive behavior of animals in the wild. The role of "odor" of reward as well as that of agonistic postures during escape–avoidance learning tasks remains equivocal and requires further empirical evidence. The material reviewed joins a growing collection of evidence indicating the influence of broadly biological factors on learned performances.

It seems to me there are two potential dangers inherent in a broadly biological approach that applies terms such as "preparedness," "biological constraints," or "biological boundaries" to learning experiments. On one hand, such terms may be invoked uncritically and used as explanations for incompletely understood phenomena. On the other hand, these terms and their behavioral referents may be simply dismissed as complications introduced when laboratory control is inadequate. Alternatively, and properly, one can make assumptions about the evolutionary significance of behavior. Operating with the explicit assumption that all organisms have a specific evolutionary history has profound implications for the design of learning experiments that will express itself in the questions asked and the variables manipulated. The entire strategy of a program of research will be affected by the assumptions an investigator chooses to make about the evolutionary significance of behavior. Whether or not a broadly biological emphasis that assumes the ecological adaptiveness and evolutionary significance of behavior has any value for the psychology of learning is an empirical question. Ultimately, such an approach must demonstrate that it yields a clearer articulation of crucial questions and a more successful organization of relevant behavioral events than alternative approaches that make different assumptions.

References

Amsel, A., Hug, J. J., and Surridge, C. T., 1969, Subject-to-subject trial sequence, odor trails, and patterning at 24-hour ITI, *Psychon. Sci.* **15**: 119–120.

Baenninger, R., and Grossman, J. C., 1969, Some effects of punishment on pain-elicited aggression, *J. Exptl. Anal. Behav.* **12**: 1017–1022.

Barnett, S. A., 1958, An analysis of social behaviour in wild rats, *Proc. Zool. Soc. Lond.* **130**: 107–152.

Barnett, S. A., 1963, *The Rat,* Aldine, Chicago.

Barnett, S. A., 1967, Rats, *Sci. Am.* **216**: 78–85.

Beach, F. A., 1950, The snark was a boojum, *Am. Psychologist* **5**: 115–124.

Bolles, R. C., 1969, Avoidance and escape learning: Simultaneous acquisition of different responses, *J. Comp. Physiol. Psychol.* **68**: 335–358.

Bolles, R. C., 1970, Species specific defense reactions and avoidance learning, *Psychol. Rev.* **77**: 32–48.

Bolles, R. C., 1971, Species specific defense reactions, in: *Aversive Conditioning and Learning* (F. R. Brush, ed.), Academic Press, New York.

Bower, G. H., 1961, A contrast effect in differential conditioning, *J. Exptl. Psychol.* **62**: 196–199.

Bowers, J. M., and Alexander, B. K., 1967, Mice: Individual recognition by olfactory cues, *Science* **158**: 1208–1210.

Breland, K., and Breland, M., 1961, The misbehavior of organisms, *Am. Psychologist* **16**: 681–684.

Breland, K., and Breland, M., 1966, *Animal Behavior,* Macmillan, New York.

Brown, P. L., and Jenkins, H. M., 1968, Autoshaping of the pigeon's key peck, *J. Exptl. Anal. Behav.* **11**: 1–8.

Burghardt, G. M., 1970, Defining "communication," in: *Advances in Chemoreception,* Vol. 1: *Communication by Chemical Signals.* (J. W. Johnson, Jr., D. G. Moulton, and A. Turk, eds.), Appleton-Century-Crofts, New York.

Carr, W. J., and Caul, W. F., 1962, The effect of castration in rats upon the discrimination of sex odours, *Anim. Behav.* **10**: 20–27.

Carr, W. J., Martorano, R. D., and Krames, L. , 1970, Responses of mice to odors associated with stress, *J. Comp. Physiol. Psychol.* **71:** 223–228.

Chance, M. R. A., 1962, An interpretation of some agonistic postures; the role of "cut-off" acts and postures, in: *Symposium No. 8 of the Zoological Society of London,* pp. 71–89.

Clarke, J. R., 1956, The aggressive behavior of the vole, *Behaviour* **9:** 1–24.

Collerain, I., and Ludvigson, H. W., 1972, Aversion of conspecific odor of frustrative nonreward in rats, *Psychon. Sci.* **27:** 54–56.

Courtney, R. J., Reid, L. D., and Wasden, R. E., 1968, Suppression of running times by olfactory stimuli, *Psychon. Sci.* **12:** 315–316.

Davis, S. F., 1970, Conspecific odors as cues for runway behavior in mice, *Psychon. Sci.* **19:** 169–170.

Davis, S. F., and Ludvigson, H. W., 1969, The "depression effect" and the problem of odor control, *Psychon. Sci.* **14:** 93–94.

Davis, S. F., Crutchfield, W. P., Shaver, J., and Sullivan, T., 1970, Interspecific odors as cues for runway behavior, *Psychon. Sci.* **20:** 166–167.

Eisenberg, J. F., 1962, Studies on the behavior of *Peromyscus maniculatus gambelii* and *Peromyscus californicus parasiticus, Behaviour* **19:** 117–207.

Garcia, J., McGowan, B. K., and Green, K. F., 1972, Biological constraints in conditioning, in: *Classical Conditioning II: Current Research and Theory* (A. H. Black and W. F. Prokasy, eds.), Appleton-Century-Crofts, New York.

Gleason, K. K., and Reynierse, J. H., 1969, The behavioral significance of pheromones in vertebrates, *Psychol. Bull.* **71:** 58–73.

Grant, E. C., 1963, An analysis of the social behaviour of the male laboratory rat, *Behaviour* **21:** 260–281.

Grant, E. C., and Mackintosh, J. H., 1963, A comparison of the social postures of some common laboratory rodents, *Behaviour* **21:** 246–259.

Hediger, H., 1950, *Wild Animals in Captivity,* Butterworth, London.

Hodos, W. and Campbell, C. B. G., 1969, *Scala naturae:* Why there is no theory in comparative psychology, *Psychol. Rev.* **76:** 337–350.

Jensen, D. D., 1961, Operationism and the question "Is this behavior learned or innate?" *Behaviour* **17:** 1–8.

Kimbrell, G. McA., Weinrott, M. R., Morris, E. K., Scheid, J., and Sangston, D., 1970, Alarm pheromone and avoidance conditioning in goldfish, *Carassius auratus, Nature* **225:** 754.

Kimble, G. A., 1955, Shock intensity and avoidance learning, *J. Comp. Physiol. Psychol.* **48:** 281–284.

King, M. G., 1969, Stimulus generalization of conditioned fear in rats over time: Olfactory cues and adrenal activity, *J. Comp. Physiol. Psychol.* **69:** 590–600.

Lockard, R. B., 1971, Reflections on the fall of comparative psychology: Is there a message for us all? *Am. Psychologist* **26:** 168–179.

Logan, F. A., 1971, Dominance and aggression, in: *Experimental Psychopathology: Recent Research and Theory* (H. D. Kimmel, ed.), Academic Press, New York.

Logan, F. A., and Boice, R., 1969, Aggressive behaviors of paired rodents in an avoidance context, *Behaviour* **34:** 161–183.

Lorenz, K., 1950, The comparative method in studying innate behaviour patterns, *Symp. Exptl. Biol.* **4:** 221–268.

Lorenz, K., 1965, *Evolution and Modification of Behavior,* University of Chicago Press, Chicago.

Ludvigson, H. W., 1969, Runway behavior of the rat as a function of intersubject reward contingencies and constancy of daily reward schedule, *Psychon. Sci.* **15:** 41–42.

Ludvigson, H. W., and Sytsma, D., 1967, The sweet smell of success: Apparent double alternation in the rat, *Psychon. Sci.* **9:** 283–284.

McHose, J. H., and Ludvigson, H. W., 1966, Differential conditioning with nondifferential reinforcement, *Psychon. Sci.* **6**: 485–486.

McHose, J. H., Jacoby, L. L., and Meyer, P. A., 1967, Extinction as a function of number of reinforced trials and squad composition, *Psychon. Sci.* **9**: 401–402.

Means, L. W., Hardy, W. T., Gabriel, M., and Uphold, J. D., 1971, Utilization of odor trails by rats in maze learning, *J. Comp. Physiol. Psychol.* **76**: 160–164.

Mellgren, R. L., Fouts, R. S., and Martin, J. W., 1973, Approach and escape to conspecific odors of reward and nonreward in rats, *Anim. Learn. Behav.* **1**: 129–132.

Morrison, R. R., and Ludvigson, H. W., 1970, Discrimination by rats of conspecific odors of reward and nonreward, *Science* **167**: 904–905.

Pratt, L. K., and Ludvigson, H. W., 1970, The role of odor in latent extinction, *Psychon. Sci.* **20**: 189–190.

Prytula, R. E., Bridges, C. C., Anderson, H. R., and Hayes, L. C., 1972, Partial reinforcement effect under odor control, *Psychol. Rep.* **30**: 215–221.

Prytula, R. E., Cox, T. P., and Bridges, C. C., 1973, Acquisition and extinction of a runway response as a function of a between- or within-subjects odor condition, *Psychol. Rep.* **32**: 367–373.

Ralls, K., 1971, Mammalian scent marking, *Science* **171**: 443–449.

Razran, G., 1971, *Mind in Evolution,* Houghton Mifflin, Boston.

Revusky, S., and Garcia, J., 1970, Learned associations over long delays, in: *The Psychology of Learning and Motivation,* Vol. 4, (G. H. Bower, ed.), Academic Press, New York.

Reynierse, J. H., 1970, A conflict and ethological theory of extinction, Paper presented at the Psychonomic Society Meetings, San Antonio, Texas.

Reynierse, J. H., 1971a, Displacement activities during psychological extinction: Empirical results and theorical implications, Paper presented at the XIIth International Ethological Conference, Edinburgh, Scotland.

Reynierse, J. H., 1971b, Submissive postures during shock-elicited aggression, *Anim. Behav.* **19**: 102–107.

Reynierse, J. H., 1971c, Agonistic behavior in Mongolian gerbils, *Z. Tierpsychol.* **29**: 175–179.

Reynierse, J. H., Scavio, M. J., and Ulness, J. D., 1970, An ethological analysis of classically conditioned fear, in: *Current Issues in Animal Learning* (J. H. Reynierse, ed.), University of Nebraska Press, Lincoln, Neb.

Rottman, S. J., and Snowdon, C. T., 1972, Demonstration and analysis of an alarm pheromone in mice, *J. Comp. Physiol. Psychol.* **81**: 483–490.

Rozin, P., and Kalat, J., 1971, Specific hungers and poison avoidance as adaptive specializations of learning, *Psychol. Rev.* **70**: 459–486.

Scott, J. P., and Fredericson, E., 1951, The causes of fighting in mice and rats, *Physiol. Zool.* **24**: 273–309.

Seago, J. D., Ludvigson, H. W., and Remley, N. R., 1970, Effects of anosmia on apparent double alternation in the rat, *J. Comp. Physiol. Psychol.* **71**: 435–442.

Seligman, M. E. P., 1970, On the generality of the laws of learning, *Psychol. Rev.* **77**: 406–418.

Seligman, M. E. P., and Haber, J., 1972, *Biological Boundaries of Learning,* Appleton-Century-Crofts, New York.

Sevenster, P., 1968, Motivation and learning in sticklebacks, in: *The Central Nervous System and Fish Behavior* (D. Ingle, ed.), University of Illinois, Chicago.

Shettleworth, S. J., 1972a, Stimulus relevance in the control of drinking and conditioned fear responses in domestic chicks (*Gallus gallus*), *J. Comp. Physiol. Psychol.* **80**: 175–198.

Shettleworth, S. J., 1972b, Constraints on learning, in: *Advances in the Study of Behavior,* Vol. 4 (D. S. Lehrman, R. A. Hinde, and E. Shaw, eds.), Academic Press, New York.

Spear, N. E., and Spitzner, J. H., 1966, Simultaneous and successive contrast effects of reward magnitude in selective learning, *Psychol. Monogr.* **80:** Whole No. 618.

Sprott, R. L., 1969, "Fear communication" via odor in inbred mice, *Psychol. Rep.* **25:** 263–268.

Staddon, J. E. R., and Simmelhag, V. L., 1971, The "superstition" experiment: A reexamination of its implications for the principles of adaptive behavior, *Psychol. Rev.* **78:** 3–43.

Thiessen, D. D., and Dawber, M., 1972, Territorial exclusion and reproductive isolation, *Psychon. Sci.* **28:** 159–160.

Topping, J. S., and Cole, J. M., 1969, A test of the odor hypothesis using Mongolian gerbils and a random trials procedure, *Psychon. Sci.* **17:** 183–184.

Trabasso, T. R., and Thompson, R. W., 1962, Supplementary report: Shock intensity and unconditioned responding in a shuttlebox, *J. Exptl. Psychol.* **63:** 215–216.

Turner, J. L., Boice, R., and Powers, P. C., 1973, Behavioral components of shock-elicited aggression in ground squirrels (*Citellus tridecemlineatus*), *Anim. Learn. Behav.* **1:** 254–262.

Ulrich, R. E., and Azrin, N. H., 1962, Elimination of undesired escape from footshock, *J. Exptl. Anal. Behav.* **5:** 72.

Valenta, J. G., and Rigby, M., 1968, Discrimination of the odor of stressed rats, *Science* **161:** 599–601.

Wasserman, E. A., and Jensen, D. D., 1969, Olfactory stimuli and the "pseudo-extinction" effect, *Science* **166:** 1307–1309.

Wilcock, J., 1972, Comparative psychology lives on under an assumed name—psychogenetics, *Am. Psychologist* **27:** 537–538.

CHAPTER 2

Animal Communication

Peter Marler

Center for Field Research in Ethology and Ecology
The Rockefeller University
New York, New York

One hears the view that communication is a purely human prerogative and that, to the extent there is anything remotely similar in animals, the divergence is so great as to constitute a difference in kind rather than just in degree. Yet we take completely for granted the continuity that exists in morphology and physiology. Much of experimental medicine is predicated on that assumption. Why are we so reticent about accepting an equivalent degree of communality at the behavioral level? There are many things for a biologist to wonder at in our language and in many other aspects of human behavior, but I believe we delude ourselves if we think that a complete discontinuity separates us from other animals.

To undertake a search for what man has in common with other animals need in no sense demean our appreciation of those human attributes that are unique. Each species is uniquely different from all others in some respects, and we are no exception. Our appreciation of those traits that are distinctive can only be heightened if we understand how they arose in the course of evolution, and how much or how little of our behavioral makeup is held in common with our relatives. If this is not yet obvious, I believe it stems from the fact that we still know so little about the behavior of animals, especially of a social nature, their societies, and the processes of communication by which social structure is underlain.

As a biologist, I approach animal communication by attempting to understand how it works. Because it so often helps in understanding the working of a biological process, I also strive to gain some appreciation for how it has evolved and the forces that have shaped its present structure. The establishment of correspondence or contrast between animal communication systems and human language is not my primary aim. Nevertheless, I find myself repeatedly impressed by both similarities and contrasts with the human condition.

Some Primordia for Communication

There has been controversy, some rather sterile, about where to draw the line between animal actions that are truly communicative and others that are not. All biologists who have studied the problem agree that those species which show some degree of social cooperation in their behavior, however primitive, also display the primordia for communication. But there are many cases which, equally fascinating, fall on the borderline, hence the argument. Some of these marginal cases have been the object of force is not the critical issue. We intuitively require some degree of system of communication.

Cherry (1966) placed a finger firmly on one requirement when he said that to tell a man to jump off a bridge is an act of communication; to push him is not. To carry this improbable analogy a little further, if I cause a man to lose his balance by driving my car too close to him, even though I do not touch him, this is not the same as a spoken command. Thus use of force is not the critical issue. We intuitively require some degree of specialization of the communicative act for the function it is to serve; accidental epiphenomena hardly qualify as communicative.

Where do we find stimuli from one organism to another, qualifying as specialized signals, that do not necessarily satisfy other criteria for a communicative act? They are many and varied, and by no means restricted to interactions between members of the same species. Recent biochemical research reveals a wealth of animal secretions that are highly specialized for the function of chemical repulsion of predators (Eisner, 1970). Some are nonspecific, highly volatile toxicants of low molecular weight that cause irritation or pain when they contact the skin or mucous membranes. Eisner, the discoverer of many such compounds used against predators, points out that some of these secretions are "for all intents and purposes natural imitations of histological fixatives, as for instance the spray of a whip scorpion, which contains 84% acetic acid." Aliphatic acids, aldehydes, aromatic compounds, quinones, and terpenes, sometimes virtually pure, are often present in remarkably high concentrations in insects. Predators as disparate as mice and toads are effectively repelled on the discharge of such compounds by intended insect prey. The affected area may be rubbed and wiped in an effort to remove the offensive stimulus. The predator retreats and, its lesson learned, is less likely henceforth to treat this kind of insect as prey. Thus the effectiveness of these defensive secretions in repelling predators, either on contact or at a distance, is demonstrable. They work not only with vertebrates but also with arthropod predators such as ants and beetles. Their specialization for the particular function is obvious, yet we are hardly tempted to label them as signals for communication.

Signal specialization can occur in a relationship between organisms that are by no means close relatives. Both within their tissues and as excretions shed into the environment, plants have long been known to produce an enormous variety of chemicals. Some are vital to the plant's metabolism, but many have been regarded as without biological significance other than as by-products or waste material that the plant must somehow get rid of. Only in the last few years have we begun to realize that many of these chemical excretions provide the basis for what is coming to be known as chemical ecology (Whittaker, 1970).

Some plant secretions inhibit the germination, growth, or survival of other plants. The sparseness of undergrowth in a grove of walnut trees is attributable to their production of hydroxyjuglone in leaves, fruits, and twigs of the walnut. Carried down from the leaves by rain, it is released into the soil in the oxidized form, juglone, which then inhibits growth of many other species. The fragance of the vegetation type in California known as chaparral is attributable to another set of compounds with allelopathic effects. In this case, the terpenes, produced by sagebrush and salvia, are not carried by rain but are volatile. Absorbed on soil particles, they inhibit the growth of plant competitors.

Some of these compounds exert effects not so much on other plants as on animals that eat them. Other chemical plant defenses are contained within the tissues and exert their effect only after contact. In addition to the obvious effects on herbivorous arthropods and vertebrates, there are suggestions of more subtle defenses against fungal infections and perhaps even against bacteria and viruses. The classical example is, of course, penicillin, evolved by a fungus as protection against bacteria. The ecological dynamics of plant communities may involve many such specialized chemical products.

Brower (1970) has discovered a marvelously intricate sequence by which butterflies gain protection. They sequester chemicals from the food plants of the larvae, chemicals that must have originated as a defense against plant-eating insects, now used to nauseate a bird which eats the butterfly. When such a butterfly, repugnant to birds because of these plant-derived poisons, becomes in turn the model for other harmless butterfly mimics, their appearance thus constituting a highly specialized set of visual signals designed to deter bird predators, we begin to appreciate how complex the interactions within plant and animal communities can become.

As R. H. Whittaker (1970) points out eloquently, "Man's use of alkaloids for flavor, mild stimulation, medicinal effect, or pleasurable self-destruction should not obscure a common theme: They are probably, though not necessarily in all cases, repellents and toxins, evolutionary expressions of quiet antagonism of the plant to its enemies." Yet such are the powerful dynamics of adaptation, some such compounds become the key stimuli by which highly specialized phytophagous insects locate their food plants after evolving a tolerance for them. According to Dethier (1970), "There are very few convincing experiments demonstrating that the choice of a plant by an individual is in fact directed by the nutrient characteristics of that plant." Instead, plant-eating insects rely heavily on cues provided by these secondary plant substances. The specialization extends even to the neurophysiology of their chemical receptors, some times tuned to be especially responsive to the compounds that identify their particular host plant, perhaps originally evolved as a means of defense.

Perhaps the ultimate specialized chemical defense is the evolution by some plants of replicas or mimics of insect hormones, withdrawal of which is necessary for the larva to metamorphose to adulthood. Like so many great biological discoveries, this one derived from perceptive analysis of an accidental discovery. Attempts to raise moth larvae to maturity failed using chambers lined with a particular kind of handtowel paper. It was then found that the most potent inhibitors are papers derived mainly from pulp of the balsam fir (*Abies balsamea*). The tree presumably evolved a chemical for its own defense that survives the papermaking process. According to discoverer Carrol Williams (1970), "Present indications are that certain plants and more particularly the ferns and evergreen trees have gone in for an incredibly sophisticated self-defense against insect control that we are just beginning to comprehend."

I have dwelt on these recent biochemical discoveries at some length to emphasize that the specialization of chemical signals evoking a particular response in other species may go to remarkable extremes. The participants may be as phylogenetically remote from one another as an insect and a tree. Thus signal specialization, one component of a communicative system, is widespread. But in true communicative behavior we expect to see evidence of mutual evolutionary specialization in both sender and receiver, lacking in such cases as these.

Mutualism as a Criterion for Communication

The mutualism that characterizes a true communication system, seen with its richest manifestations in interactions within a species, also recurs in those interspecific relationships where symbiotic interplay can be discerned. We find illustrations in the relationship between plants and those animals which pollinate their flowers or disperse their fruits, with gain to both plant and animal.

The bright coloration of many fruits has evolved as a signal perceptible at a distance to animals which disperse them. There are fascinating ramifications to the adaptations of flowers to particular pollinators. Basic and recurring patterns that seem best to attract certain types of pollinators are obviously adapted to the visual physiology of the pollinator. Flowers pollinated by hummingbirds are generally red, evidently an attractive color to them (Grant and Grant, 1968). This color recurs in some flowers pollinated by butterflies but is less common in those pollinated by bees. A comparison of the physiology of the eye in these two insects reveals a fundamental difference. While butterflies see colors much as we do, bees do not see red, but are able to see into the ultraviolet. Blue and yellow are more common colors in bee-pollinated flowers, and many that appear white to us are actually ornamented with ultraviolet designs. Although invisible to us, these designs are visible to bees as distinctively colored and lead them to pollen and nectar. Scent is another signal effective at a distance that attracts many insect pollinators but is not pronounced in those flowers pollinated by birds. It may be present again in flowers specialized for bat pollination, more of a stench than a scent to us, but evidently to bats' liking.

If such general considerations dictated all characteristics of the specialized signals produced for their pollinators, one might expect flowers of many plants to be similar. But there is an element of competition between flowering plants for the favors of pollinators that are in demand, and this generates a trend toward diversity in flower design. It either encourages particular pollinating species to become specialists in that relationship, or it induces more catholic pollinators to remain faithful to flowers of one type at least for a time, whether a season or an hour of the day. This trend toward diversity is evident in the botanical use of flower characteristics in taxonomy. If you make lists of plants pollinated by birds or bees and then compare flowers pollinated by wind or water, or by unspecialized insects, the taxonomic characteristics of the former lean much more heavily on the flowers. The latter depend more on other parts of the plant, their flower structure being much less varied.

Embarking on the path of specialization to encourage a particular pollinator, the plant will often evolve a floral structure that restricts visits by other pollinators, thus insuring for the chosen symbiont a supply of nectar in return for the benefit of pollination. This tendency for adaptation to diverse pollinators can be detected even within a closely related group such as the phlox family, with corresponding variations in the characteristics of the flowers (Grant and Grant, 1965).

The orchid family contains far more species than any other family of flowering plants, and the competition for pollinators is intense. Orchids have almost gone to excess in encouraging specialization by particular pollinators. Closely related orchids differ not only in flower structure but also in chemical composition of their scents known to attract particular species of euglossine bees (Dodson, 1970). Other orchids, pollinated only by the males of certain bees, have gone so far as to mimic the female bee in the construction of their flowers, inducing the insect to go through mating movements with the flower and thereby pollinating it. Most remarkable of all, the flowers mimic not only the appearance of the female but also her distinctive odor, varying with the species of bee. Such is the intricacy of the relationship between plant and pollinator, here essentially a parasitic one, but often mutualistic in the sense that it has called forth adaptations in both partners, bringing us another step closer to true communication.

Genetics of Social Cooperation

Cooperation and competition are the warp and woof of the cloth from which societies are made. Communication in the true sense is cooperative. Sometimes this is obvious, when one animal gives an alarm call that aids another to escape, perhaps even altruistically sacrificing its own life in the process. It is perhaps less obvious in other kinds of interaction such as aggressive display, less obvious, that is, until one reflects that the alternative to aggressive display is combat, with inevitable damage to both participants. Both winner and loser gain something in the long run if the contest becomes a tournament. Both survive unharmed physically, if not psychologically.

One aim of modern research in ethology is to gather facts that will help us to understand how the delicate balance is set between competition and cooperative forces in an animal species so that they can evolve into distinct patterns of social organization, as different as those of the social lion and the solitary leopard, the wolf and the fox, the solitary and social bees. Theorizing has made little progress thus far, but one aspect has been illuminated by the thinking of population geneticist William D. Hamilton (1971). He points out the importance of particular genetic considerations in the evolution of animal communication.

The degree of similarity between two organisms is an important issue in predicting the likelihood that they will compete. The more alike two animals are, the more they are prone to depend on similar resources—food obtained in the same ways at the same time, similar hiding and nesting places, and so on. Thus resource competition will be more acute between species that are close relatives than between two that are more distant relatives. It will be especially acute within a species, aided and abetted in varying degress by stealing, hostile behavior, and other forms of what ecologists are prone to call "interference" competition. There is a great deal of genetic diversity within species, and competition among the many genotypes represented must be responsible for much of the dynamic nature of the speciation process.

Notwithstanding genetic variability within a species, we can find animals living in groups that consist of very close relatives indeed, with much the same genotype. One obvious example is a group of parents and offspring. In this situation, in spite of the inevitability of eventual resource competition, evolutionary pressures will encourage a shift in the balance to favor maximal cooperation. Aggressive or "interference" competition will tend to be reduced to a minimum as far as this is possible. If we are right in thinking of communication as instrumental in effecting cooperative interaction, some of its most advanced accomplishments should be found in animals with societies so constructed that groups of very close genetic relatives live together.

Where should we look, then, but among the social insects? Entire colonies of many thousands of insects may be derived from a single mother, the queen, as in that acme of sociality, the honey bee. The male or drone, being produced from an unfertilized egg, is homozygous, reducing the genetic variability contributed by the father, although this is admittedly countered somewhat by the mating of a queen with several drones. And we must add the fact that a majority of the operations within the hive are performed by a group consisting of one sex, the sterile females or workers. Thus the genetic conformity is extreme, and we should not be surprised in hindsight that the great German zoologist Karl von Frisch (1954) discovered one of the most remarkable examples of social communication in the dancing behavior of the honeybee (see also Lindauer, 1961). Almost as remarkable are some of the elaborate chemical communication systems to be found in ants (Wilson, 1970).

We know so little about the genetic structure of natural populations of vertebrates that it is hard to know where to look for examples comparable to the social insects. This gap in our knowledge is a serious hindrance to theorizing about the origin of vertebrate social behavior. The need to fill it is urgent. There are hints that some vertebrates also live in social groups which are quite inbred, if not as genetically homogeneous as a bee colony. This is the case with house mice and some other rodents, and may be true of some birds, and of primates—there is evidence that a troop of baboons, for example, may show a degree of inbreeding. This is just the situation in which we should look for the elaboration of vertebrate communication systems.

I have begun to suspect that a great deal of the social behavior of animals is concerned with the development and maintenance of a genetic substructure, establishing what may be basic units on which natural selection operates. Song dialects in birds may have such a function, and it is not inconceivable that the troop organization of some primates is of similar consequence. Careful long-term studies are needed of natural populations in which individual histories are documented. This is a stringent requirement but one that must be met if vertebrate sociobiology is to advance as a science.

The Choice of a Medium

The functions that a communication system can serve vary widely, depending on the biology of the species. One animal may help others to find their way about, to get to food and water, to avoid capture by predators, and to achieve effective reproduction. In more general terms, communication must maintain the particular societal structure of the species, preserving the required patterns of spacing within and between groups.

Consider the elementary requirements for a signal used to space out groups, whether troops of monkeys or tribes of mice. The first stage of an efficient exchange will involve signaling over a distance and requires that a respondent be able to determine the position in space from which the signal has come. The possibilities depend in part on the particular sensory modality, whether the signal is chemical, visual, or auditory, or even electrical. Given such a problem in communication, an animal is confronted with an evolutionary choice, within the limits set by the basic sensory and motor equipment with which it is endowed. For a mobile forest species such as birds or monkeys living in groups, requiring a signal to maintain the spacing from one group to another, auditory signals are ideal. They can be given day or night; they are less affected by obstacles than, say, visual signals. They are fairly easy to locate, and offer many possibilities for species identification, with frequency and temporal coding.

For communication at closer quarters, however, as within a monkey troop, the odds favor visual signaling as the best medium for many purposes, at least during the day. Within a crowd, an auditory signal is not so easy to locate, whereas it is in the very nature of visual stimuli to be easy to locate (Marler & Hamilton, 1966).

The inherent directionality of visual stimuli also opens up rich possibilities for spatial coding, hard to envision with auditory signals. Thus a monkey or a person signals visually with several independently varying configurations of the face and body, and even with somewhat independent elements within one area, such as the face. There is, however, the obvious restriction that, aside from the special case of animals which provide their own light source, visual signals have limited value at night.

In this situation, chemical signals come into their own, as well as in the multitude of simpler organisms that lack well-developed directional eyes. There are other advantages than the lack of dependence on ambient light. Chemical signals possess a durability that is absent from auditory signals and only rarely accomplished with such visual signals as nests, rubbing posts, trails, and the like, at least by animals. By contrast, our own species makes extensive use of durable visual signs, including, of course, writing. If an animal requires a durable signal, as often as not a chemical means is chosen, perhaps in part because the potential control of rates of fading out adds another valuable dimension to signal diversity. There are many examples of chemical secretions placed on objects in the environment or on some other animal that continue to transmit in the absence of the original marking individual. Another consideration here is the remarkably small number of molecules sufficing for detection of some olfactory signals, a classical case being the substance bondecal, by which the female silkworm moth attracts the male. It is calculated that a receptor cell on the male's antenna, where the sense of smell resides, requires only one molecule of bondecal for activation.

But here arises another problem. The male may be able to detect the presence of the female and yet be unable to locate her. This is a serious drawback with olfactory signals, for as long as the intervening medium, air or water, is still, the only clue available for location is the diffusion gradient. Although this may be steep up to a meter or so from the source so that location is possible, at any further distances the gradient becomes so gradual that it no longer provides orientation clues. The escape from this dilemma lies in making use of movement of the medium, and this is exploited by many animals using olfactory signals over a distance. A female moth will delay transmission of her sexual attractant until there is a breeze blowing of the right velocity, strong enough to carry the scent downwind but not so strong as to generate undue turbulence. In this circumstance, the male, detecting the presence of the female, can just move upwind. Thus enabled to get fairly close, he can find her by using the concentration gradient. A similar strategy is employed by stream-living animals, salamanders, for example.

Each sensory modality has both advantages and drawbacks for distance signaling. Any choice is to some extent a compromise. For a small number of organisms, all of them fish so far as I know, there is still another choice, electrical signaling. Like sonar, it is a system with a double role, broadcasting signals that are perceptible to other organisms and at the same time functioning as an object-detection system. At close range, or when the communicants are in contact, other sensory modalities become available, such as the senses of touch and taste with special properties of their own. Perhaps for the very reason that they require contact, they often assume rather special functions to do with promoting peaceful gatherings and amelioration of the chance of outbreaks of social violence.

Animal Semantics

Within our own language, we usually think of the relationship between most words and whatever they signify as an arbitrary one. This is true in two senses. From a strictly semantic viewpoint, a word bears no physical resemblance to the referent it symbolizes, other than in onomatopoeia. The word *food* in no way resembles anything we eat, nor is the word *drink* like water. The relationship is an arbitrary one. By the same token, there is no reason the meaning of the two words should not become switched in the course of cultural evolution. Thus, as a more general kind of arbitrariness, there is nothing intrinsic to the process by which we usually convey information about food to one another through our language that requires a word with any particular properties.

In the first, semantic sense, many animal signals are also arbitrary. The food call of chimpanzees, by which discovery of a choice meal is announced, together with readiness to share it, is a deep grunting sound that has no conceivable physical relationship to the food object, perhaps a cluster of ripe palm fruits. The vervet monkeys of Africa provide another example with their distinct alarm calls for different types of predators. The calls that announce the threat of (1) an eagle hunting overhead, (2) a leopard stalking below, or (3) a cobra passing through the territory are each different, and each evokes a different response—the first, precipitant flight from the treetops into cover; the second, movement from the ground and lower branches into the canopy; and the third, a gathering of animals at a safe distance from the snake to escort it through the territory, mobbing as it goes. These three sounds, characterized by zoologist Thomas Struhsaker (1967) as a "raup," a "bark" and a "chatter," respectively, have no physical resemblance to the classes of predator they symbolize.

In the second, more general sense that signals might be arbitrary, we find many exceptions among animal signals. Calls of birds and mammals often exhibit acoustical properties adapted to the particular function that is served, making them less suitable for other functions. Thus they are less freely interchangeable than words in our own language may be.

Some sounds must travel great distances to serve their function, while others satisfy it at close range, and their loudness varies accordingly. The sound used by male forest guenons in East African forests to space troops apart is much louder than the sounds used within each group for coordinating movements in the foliage while feeding. The transmission properties of different sound frequencies also vary according to the structure of the habitat, and there is evidence that birds use in their songs those sounds that travel farthest in a given environment (Chappuis, 1971). The medium-pitched pure tones of many woodland bird songs are probably adapted to the range that travels farthest under these conditions.

Perhaps the most remarkable case of such adjustment has been described in humpbacked whales. Behaviorist Roger Payne (Payne and McVay, 1971; Payne and Webb, 1971) believes that by using very low frequency sounds, barely audible to our ears, and placing themselves at an intermediate depth in the ocean, these whales may hear one another calling over distances to be measured in hundreds of miles, a phenomenon almost unbelievable until we reflect that this is what the navies of the world accomplish with their underwater sound-signaling systems.

Can we say then that the physical structure of animal signals is related to their function? In some cases, the answer is obviously yes. The importance of location of the source of a signal in many communicative situations has already been emphasized. It calls for numerous adaptations in signal structure. The alarm signals of some birds are designed to facilitate localization by companions, while others are structured to minimize the clues available for vertebrate localization—an adaptation to spread alarm without giving location clues to a potential predator.

Examples of another type of adaptation to signal dissemination are found in the olfactory signals of insects. E. O. Wilson and his colleagues have shown that the molecular properties of pheromones often match the functional requirements nicely, if one uses the emission rate in molecules per unit time and the behavioral threshold concentration as points of departure (Wilson, 1970). A low ratio of the former to the latter indicates a slowly emitted signal with a very small "active space," the space where the hormone molecules exceed the threshold level for a behavioral response. Such properties characterize the constituents of the pheromone used by fire ants in trail marking. Compounds used for this purpose would be unsuitable as alarm hormones, where larger active space and more rapid diffusion rates are required. Chaos would result, however, if the alarm system had the high ratio and huge active space that characterizes the sex attractants used by female moths. These function over distances much greater than is appropriate in an alarm situation.

Among visual signals, it is not hard to find adaptations to the spatial and directional requirements of the situation, as in the difference between displays broadcast in all directions and others sent to a particular "address," the displayer facing the intended recipient and fixing him with a binocular stare.

Discrete and Graded Repertoires

Ethologists have placed strong emphasis on the stereotypy of many animal communication signals, going so far as to label many of them "fixed action patterns." The stereotypy of some is indeed striking, as great as we expect to find in the structural products of growth and development. The variability of some duck displays, the claw-waving display of fiddler crabs, and the strutting display of the sage grouse is remarkably low (Hazlett, 1972; Wiley, 1973). By equivalent measures, some animal sounds are highly stereotyped, such as certain bird songs and the loud calls of some adult male monkeys. One of the most stable biological phenomena known is the pulsed signaling of electric fish.

I assume that some function requirements must be satisfied by this unusual restriction of normal biological variation. In certain cases, accurate identification of the signal at a distance, under noisy conditions, is probably aided by extreme stereotypy. But there may be other functions as well—the fixity of electrical signaling in fish may be more of an adaptation to the object-location function than to requirements for communication.

With the advent of more quantitative study, it is evident that extreme stereotypy is by no means the general rule. While some signals are almost fixed, others are exceedingly variable, with all grades between. Some duck displays are 20 times more variable than others, and there is an equivalent spectrum among bird songs. In contrast with the stereotyped monkey calls we have mentioned, the variability of other monkey calls is much greater.

Are we just witnessing variation in the effectiveness of developmental control, or is there some communicative significance to the differences in variability? Shifting view from variation in particular signals to the way in which entire signal repertoires are constructed, we encounter a similar problem. Analyzing recordings of the full array of sounds used by a species and then submitting them to a classification is sometimes a relatively easy process. Once all major categories have been sampled, the assignment of those analyzed subsequently is easy because the repertoire is arranged in a series of discrete categories, without intermediates.

The loud call and the "ka" call of the male blue monkey, for example, are superficially similar, but when analyzed every call can be placed without hesitation in one category or the other (Marler, 1973). There are no gradations between them. With other groups of sounds, the classification is more difficult. Identification of the blue monkey sounds described as growls and pulsed grunts is confused by the existence of intermediates. This type of organization is referred to as "graded" rather than as "discrete." The sound repertoires of some animals contain few if any discrete sound types. Of those studied so far, the extreme cases come from certain primates, notably the red colobus (Marler, 1970), macaques, and the chimpanzee. Here most or all of the vocal repertoire consists of a single graded system. The grading occurs independently in several acoustical dimensions, such as duration, frequency, and tonal structure, each varying continuously, making it very difficult to classify sounds according to typological categories.

What interpretation can be placed on this contrast between some species with a repertoire of discrete signals, others with a graded repertoire, the major types being connected by intermediates? The situation in primates may offer some clues, where graded repertoires are especially characteristic of species living in large, close-knit troops. Most are species prone to come to the ground and invade open habitats. They are not territorial, and most communication takes place within the troop, usually at close range. In this circumstance, communication is often achieved by combinations of visual and auditory signals, and there is a rich selection of gestures and facial expressions.

By contrast, more strictly arboreal monkeys tend to have a repertoire of mainly discrete sounds. They are territorial and often signal over distances between troops. Their use of visual signals is hindered by the foliage. Perhaps for efficient signaling in forest, often long-range, with noises of wind and other animals as a background, they rely more on stereotyped, relatively invariant signals, each distinguished with ease from others in the repertoire.

In the nonterritorial primates, often with large social groups, the emphasis shifts to communication within the troop, where the requirements in some respects are less stringent. If they are able to make use of the increased information content that could be carried by a graded repertoire— and we must not forget that this is an unproven assumption—then, with visual signals in support, the redundant, close-range signaling that they engage in may permit the exploitation of the rich potential of a graded repertoire. Further research will show whether this hypothesis is valid. One reason for hesitation is that some forest species, such as the red colobus, also have a graded call repertoire, although this may indeed prove to be associated with a greater emphasis on intratroop communication than in the other forest monkeys we have studied.

Specific Distinctiveness in Animal Signals

Every naturalist knows that behavior can be as revealing as external appearance in the diagnosis of difficult species. The original identification of some birds and insects was made on the basis of their song. However, the application of behavior to taxonomic problems is not easy. While species may differ in some respects, they are exceedingly similar in others. This is true of many aspects of their structure, their feeding behavior, and also their communication signals.

Why are some signals in the repertoire of a species so much more specifically distinct than others? We must remember that species do not live alone, but in communities that include many other kinds of organisms, also transmitting signals. For many purposes, it is an advantage for a species to possess, as it were, a private line for those functions most efficiently performed by restricting responses to members of the same species. This is the case with reproduction and often with aggression. We are most likely to find a high degree of species specificity among signals associated with these kinds of events.

A survey of bird vocalizations shows that the male song, typically serving these functions, is usually more specifically distinctive than other calls in the repertoire. The same is true of animals as diverse as crickets and monkeys. The territorial forest monkeys already mentioned maintain their intertroop spacing with male loud calls that are distinctively different from species to cohabiting species.

That specific distinctiveness is not a universal requirement for all calls is easily demonstrated by comparing signals with other functions. Sometimes when we find that specific distinctiveness is minimal, this fact becomes intelligible after inspection of the function served. Alarm calls are often similar in groups of species living together. In both birds and monkeys, interspecific communication by alarm signals is frequent. The similarities of the calls used can only facilitate this interchange, thus serving a definite function. This finding serves to remind us that we should never overlook the community in which a species lives if its communication system is to be understood.

Experimental Use of Synthetic Signals

Just as the scientific study of human language has not gone far beyond syntactic analysis, few zoological studies have progressed beyond the descriptive phase. Some investigations that point the way to more analytical approaches are worthy of note. Having established the functional role of a communication signal, a next step is to establish which particular components of the signal are necessary for a given response and which are redundant. The likelihood that a different set of components is significant in other contexts, with other recipients, must also be borne in mind. The ideal experimental approach is to generate copies of these signals artificially, to change their structure systematically in one direction or another, and to establish the limits of effectiveness in different situations.

There are places in the southeastern United States where one can hear as many as 20 species of tree crickets producing sound at the same time. Most conspicuous are the calling songs of males, serving to attract a female when both are ready for mating. Walker (1957) demonstrated this attractiveness in a cage with loudspeakers at either end. A female released in the center would move toward the loudspeaker broadcasting the recorded song of her species. Knowing from descriptive studies that the males of each species of tree cricket have a distinctive pulse rate in their song, he synthesized a train of pulses at the same frequency. The artificial song remained effective as long as the rate did not deviate from what is character-istic of the species at that temperature. The rate of singing movements varies with temperature, faithfully enough that some are known as "thermometer crickets." You might suppose that these temperature-induced variations would throw the female into confusion, but Walker (1957) showed that her responsiveness changes in nicely parallel fashion.

The repetition pattern of cricket song is relatively easy to synthesize. The same is true of another remarkable animal communication system based on the electric discharges of certain fish. Known for some years to function as an object-location system, they were recently shown to serve in social communication. Working in Guiana, Hopkins (1972) found ten species of electric fish living in the same river.

In one species, *Sternopygus macrurus,* he found the discharge pattern to be distinctly different from those of the other fish present, the pulse repetition frequency being unique. Exploring further, he found that male and female frequencies differ consistently, and, working during the rains when they breed, he described males embarking on courtship activity as the electric signals of an approaching female *Sternopygus* became detectable.

Hypothesizing that the frequency difference was basic, he generated synthetic songs in which the only remaining natural property was the frequency, carried by a sine wave. As long as this frequency fell within the normal female range, the males courted the electrodes. If the frequency was too low, approaching that of male *Sternopygus,* or too high, getting into the range of another form, *Eigenmannia,* then the courtship ceased. Thus, although the electric discharges have other distinctive properties, such as pulse shape, the frequency seems to be the key property in this situation.

Another animal sound signal that can be synthesized is the croaking of a bullfrog. Within a terrarium, male frogs studied by Capranica (1965) readily croaked in reply to recordings of their species, but failed to respond to sounds of 33 other frog species. Of its many distinctive attributes, Capranica chose to concentrate on its spectral structure and wave-form periodicity. Exhaustive analysis with synthetic calls demonstrated that two spectral peaks are required for maximum responsiveness, one around 200 Hz, the other around 1400 Hz, present in the normal adult bullfrog call and in no other species among those tried. Interestingly, addition of a third peak around 500 Hz, such as is likely to be present in calls of sub-adult male bullfrogs, can inhibit the response entirely. As another parameter, the optimal pulse-train frequency of around 100 Hz closely approximates that of natural calling of adult males.

Playback studies with natural and artificial birdsongs confirm that, with more complex social behavior, some new functions emerge. Again species recognition tends to rely on those features shared without much variation by songs of all species members. But there are often individual differences as well, conveyed by different properties of the song. Playback studies demonstrate that these are in fact used by birds themselves to tell close neighbors from strangers (Emlen 1972). There is a similar separation of the attributes of our own speech into those necessary for intelligibility and those that permit recognition of the sex, mood, and identity of the speaker.

The Uses of Animal Signals

How do animal signals come to have survival value to the members of a species sufficient to call forth this great variety of evolutionary adaptations? One way to assess the value of one animal's signal to another is to assume that it permits the "anticipation" or "prediction" of future events. To give a simple illustration, a bird which gives an alarm call on seeing a hawk permits other birds within earshot, rushing for cover, to behave as though they were "anticipating" or "predicting" arrival of the approaching predator. If the reaction evoked by the signal is associated on other occasions with a particular environmental situation—in this case, catching sight of a hunting predator—then we think of the signal as serving as a symbol for that situation. A similar interpretation can be applied to the "rough grunting" of chimpanzees that serves as a food call. Other chimpanzees within earshot approach hastily, anticipating a choice morsel, as though the call were truly a symbol for food.

However, if we study the reactions of animals to the signal repertoire of their species, they often seem to be based not so much on prediction of a particular environmental situation that must be dealt with, such as food or danger, as on a prediction of how the signaling animal is likely to react on being approached. If a male bird in full courtship approaches a female uttering the soliciting call, unique to the brief period of the annual cycle when she is sexually receptive, his actions are based not on some external circumstance about which she has been signaling but on her anticipated or predicted behavior.

Production of both the alarm call and the sexual call must be associated with particular physiological states of the signaling animal. The process of symbolization would be easier to understand if we knew how these physiological states come about. Clearly the soliciting female chaffinch is signaling about physiological events that presage copulation. This condition is not necessarily contingent on any immediate trigger from the environment that we could think of the call as symbolizing. The triggering is often endogenous rather than exogenous. There are other signals of which this is true, such as the begging call of a nestling bird, occurring without external provocation as it gets hungry. The singing of many male birds often starts without detectable triggering from the outside.

How fundamental is this distinction between signals that are externally and internally triggered that so complicates the identification of a semantic referent? One might be tempted to think of the role of internal physiology in the production of an alarm call as being minimal. But even here the physiological state at the time of confrontation with the predator cannot be ignored. A bird which is nervous and on edge is more likely to give alarm than one which is relaxed and sleepy. There can be no doubt that alarm signals have varying effects on the same respondent at different times as a result of prior learning.

One may go further and suggest that no reaction of an animal to a stimulus can be understood without taking the physiological state of the animal at that moment into account. It is true that reactions to some stimuli proceed in such a variety of physiological states that one is tempted to ignore the importance of internal events. Such are cases where the particular reaction has high biological priority, so that the necessary physiological machinery is primed and accessible for much of the time.

The proper way to think of all stimulus–response relationships is as *interactions* between the organism and its environment. The environment may provide a trigger responsible for the timing and perhaps orientation of the reaction. But the particular "morphology" of the reaction, its internal timing, often its intensity and even orientation, can be understood only by reference to the prior history of the individual, its genotype, and the particular pattern of environmental stimulation experienced up to the instant of the confrontation with this stimulus, all brought to a focus in the physiological state of the subject at the time of stimulation. I am, of course, assuming that the traces that persist of the network of actions and interactions comprising the history of an individual organism are physiological and not metaphysical in nature.

According to this view, physiological considerations are as important in understanding the origin of a signal that has an external trigger as of those with an internal trigger. Conversely, those signals that appear to be endogenously generated cannot be thought of as completely independent of the external world, other than in the sense that no immediate outside trigger is detectable. The sequence of events that has brought the signaler to this moment involves a myriad of environmental interactions, many doubtless explicitly required for the emergence of this particular action. The onset of the sexual calling of a female bird when she is ovulating depends on many environmental interactions, some with only a general bearing on ovulation, such as the requirements for normal growth, and others with a very specific bearing such as the increasing day length, social stimulation, and sensory feedback from nest-building activities.

Speaking of a reaction as being "internally" or "endogenously" triggered implies no more than that its timing and nature are functions of prior events in the history of the individual, with an influence conveyed to the present by physiological means.

Manifestations of Emotional State, or Something More?

A contrast is sometimes struck between human speech and animal signals to the effect that animal behavior is more susceptible to control by the kind of physiological states described in common parlance as "affective" or "emotional." This is not to say that speech cannot be emotional, only that the key differences in physiology that mediate the different meanings of words do not lie in such generalized states.

It is not always easy to understand what is implied by an "emotional" state. Recurring notions are that the states are generalized, affecting many patterns of behavior; that autonomic arousal is often involved; that often there is some connotation of emergency in the demeanor, tempo, and intensity of the animal signaler; that there is often strong "momentum" so that the pattern of behavior once begun tends to continue for a period of time, apparently resisting rapid change. Emotional states also tend to be thought of as involuntary and less susceptible to modification by learning or conscious effort; as a further point, the behavior is often placed somewhere on a dimension of pleasantness or unpleasantness.

Our speech is supposed to provide contrasts, in being voluntary, lacking any necessary tie to generalized physiological states or autonomic arousal, not necessarily being associated with behavioral emergencies, and involving physiological states whose nature can change very rapidly.

That there is a valid contrast here is unquestionable. In most of the circumstances in which animal signaling occurs, one can sense some prominent and demanding function to be served, often associated with a significant emergency for survival or procreation. To the extent that physiological states of "emotion" or "affect" can be distinguished from other substrates for behavior, they have surely evolved expressly to impose a certain order on the temporal organization of patterns of behavior, to avoid inefficient vacillation in the face of conflicting demands. We ourselves know all too well the pervasive influence they can have on behavior, especially on interactions of a social nature. But it seems intuitively reasonable to assert that much of our speech, if not our other signaling behaviors, can occur without these emotional undertones.

The vagueness of ideas about emotions makes firm resolution of this problem difficult. To take one example, we have considered Struhsaker's vervet monkeys using different alarm calls for different types of predators. The calls do not intergrade, and one is hardly inclined to ascribe the differences to varying levels of arousal. In fact, the animals tend to be highly aroused in each case.

To explain the vervet monkey's complex alarm-signaling behavior, several different physiological states must be postulated, more specific in nature than the cluster of emotional behaviors denoted as "fearful." Conforming with another common attribute of emotional behavior, however, the vervet alarm calls are each associated with a complex of other behaviors, and rarely occur in isolation from them. Insofar as monkeys are not known to engage in relaxed discourse about past events or those in the distant future, there will be few if any occasions when a signal will be disassociated from the signaler's other overt responses to a situation.

There is one circumstance in which such disassociation can often be detected, in animal play. Among the diagnostic criteria for play behavior are several characteristics that are reminiscent of distinctions between human speech and animal sounds. A separation of behavior from its normal emotional substrate is often mentioned, and there is correspondingly more freedom in switching from one pattern or social role to another than is customary in the adult, "emotional" version of the corresponding behavior. A signal given in play is sometimes separated from the other ongoing behaviors that are its normal accompaniment. The relaxed enjoyment we sometimes derive from discussion and peaceful argument might indeed be thought of as play much of the time rather than as functional in the sense of directly, immediately modifying the behavior of others. The subsong of birds, a vocal pattern that has playlike qualities, is somewhat reminiscent of the solitary babblings and later monologues of the child developing speech.

One may ask whether our speech is as free from emotional constraints as we are prone to think. Polygraphic lie detectors operate on the assumption that autonomic arousal is indeed a correlate of speech. Some psychoanalytic practices rest on a similar assumption. One does not need a skin galvanometer or an electrocardiograph to be sure that a great deal of speech uttered in actual communicative situations has strong emotional components. Furthermore, recent research on the physiology of human emotions seems to contradict the old notion of a few simple physiological dimensions.

Schachter and others are proposing two distinct components, present even in the most basic emotions (Schachter and Singer, 1962). One is concerned with the level of arousal, and incorporates many of the autonomic and hedonic functions imputed to emotion; the other, sometimes labeled as the "cognitive component," seems to specify the particular emotion that will be experienced. The latter are thus specific to the particular emotion, while the former may be shared by several. Given what seems to be very similar physiological machinery, it is likely that, to the extent it is a correct model of human emotions, this interpretation is relevant to animals as well. Thus the distinction between the generalized and specific physiological states is not always clear. Whatever distinction we are groping for between speech and animal signaling, my own conviction is that the underlying physiological processes will prove to be different in degree rather than kind. If only to provoke reappraisal, I am inclined to assert that no firm proof has yet been advanced of any fundamental difference between animals and man in this regard.

Learning and Signal Development

Modifiability through learning, for which our language has such rich potential, is sometimes thought to play no significant role in animal communications, and innateness is often coupled with the presumption of an emotional basis. This view would not of course deny animals remarkable learning capacities, only that they do not play a significant role in the development of signaling behavior.

We know this to be a mistaken view. Many songbirds learn their songs and probably some other vocalizations as a matter of course (Marler and Mundinger, 1971). If they are raised in social isolation, their songs will develop abnormally. Exposure to an adult model, often required at a particular phase of life, a critical period for vocal learning, will restore the pattern of development that normally occurs in nature. Remarkably enough, this learning has other characteristics reminiscent of speech development. In both child and bird, there are predispositions emerging during this critical period, with the effect of guiding learning in certain directions. Dialects result in each case. Hearing plays a part in both, allowing the young organism to hear parental sounds and playing another vital role in allowing it to hear its own voice. The possibility that vocal imitation is essentially self-reinforcing has been advanced to explain the course of both song development and speech. There are properties in common between the so-called babbling of infants and what is called "subsong" in birds. Nottebohm (1970) has discovered a remarkable parallel in the tendency for one side of the brain to assume dominant control of the sound-producing equipment of birds, an echo of the dominance of the left hemisphere in the control of our speech.

We are gathering glimpses here of what may prove to be a basic set of rules for the organization of vocal learning to which any species might be expected to conform if the design of its societies depends on a series of complex, learned traits. While the full exploitation of the advantages of learning requires freedom, too much latitude in the realm of social behavior would result in patterns of behavior so divergent that communication would be impeded and the structure of society disrupted. Therein, I believe, lies the survival value of the predispositions that a species brings to the task of vocal learning from its past history, interacting with the complex models presented to it by experienced adults, from which it must extract norms for its own social behavior. That there should be even a suspicion of basic similarities in physiological machinery and learning strategy is remarkable when the specific problems confronting a child and a young bird are so vastly different.

Apes with Language?

It may seem bizarre that we are comparing children with birds. Surely if we seek insights into the evolutionary history of man, the appropriate place to be looking would be in monkeys and apes, which have so much else in common with us. There is much in common, it is true, in their structure and some aspects of their behavior. But correspondence in vocalizations, even in an animal as close to man in other respects as the chimpanzee, is hard to find. Laboratory and field study seems to confirm that their pattern of vocal development is very different. Whereas children begin to show an almost irrepressible tendency toward vocal imitation, even at a very early age, no one yet has discovered a comparable tendency in any other mammal. In contrast with human children, other primate young are not known to "babble." However, as mentioned previously, avian subsong has properties in common with infant babbling, perhaps a recurrent stage in learned vocal development.

It is true that chimpanzees raised in a home like children have, after much time and effort on the part of both subject and experimenter, learned to utter three or four words. But the process of acquisition, requiring the laborious step-by-step assemblage of the necessary mouth movements, rewarded at each stage, had little in common with vocal imitation proper. Remarkable though chimpanzee Vicky's breathy and unvoiced renditions of "cup," "papa," and "mama" were, they closed no gap between ape and man, but reminded us of its breadth.

It was tempting then to infer that the inability to copy speech is somehow a manifestation of a chimpanzee's lesser intelligence. Others have analyzed the chimpanzee vocal tract and concluded that it would not be capable of producing the full range of speech sounds anyway, hence the failure to imitate. Both views are, I believe, mistaken. If an inappropriately structured vocal tract were the only obstacle, chimpanzees would attempt imitation, but the renditions would be imperfect: witness the abnormal but still intelligible speech of people suffering laryngectomy or a cleft palate. Instead, chimpanzees make no attempt at all. We must look to deficiencies in neural mechanisms that engender the *predisposition* for vocal learning for an explanation.

That an intelligence deficit is not responsible was established in a different way by two remarkable investigations, setting out to teach chimpanzees language-like communication systems that did not require the imitation of sounds. Allen and Beatrice Gardner, aware of the extent to which chimpanzees use their hands in natural communication, employed the hand sign language of deaf people, American Sign Language (Gardner and Gardner, 1971). With a variety of training techniques, including shaping, guidance, and observational learning as well as imitation, they were able to teach the young female chimpanzee Washoe to perform 85 signs, each equivalent to a word, in a 3-year period. Many nouns were included such as *flower, dog,* and *toothbrush,* adjectives such as *red* and *white,* prepositions such as *up* and *down,* verbs such as *help, hug* and *go.* Many were used in appropriate combinations such as the invitation for a walk, "You me go out hurry," or the request to "Please gimme sweet drink." The appropriateness of combinations of actions and objects, and other constructions, indicates a grammar not very different from that of children in their earliest two-word sentences.

The other chimpanzee, Sarah, whose accomplishments in the use of language will go down in history with those of Washoe as engendering something of a revolution in our understanding of animal accomplishment, was taught in a more formal way. Premack (1971) trained her to use colored plastic shapes instead of words, these serving as symbols for objects and actions. A blue plastic triangle served as the symbol for "apple." The one for "banana" was a red square, and so on, the relation between symbol and referent being noniconic, the shape lacking any physical resemblance to the object to which it referred. After training her to present the appropriate shape when she wanted a piece of fruit, other nouns and then verbs were introduced such as *give, wash,* and *insert,* each performed by the experimenter when Sarah presented the appropriate symbol.

Within her repertoire of about 130 words were not only many nouns, verbs, and adjectives but also more complex constructions such as *same* and *different,* questions, and the conditional *if-then.* A definite "grammatical" order was required of Sarah in arranging the symbols on a board. Premack's aim was as much to test the conceptual abilities of Sarah as to see whether she could use language, reasoning that ability in this regard is closely mirrored in our own language. The ways in which we perceive and think about the world around us are much entwined with the ways in which we talk about it.

Can one infer that Sarah thinks in the language of these plastic shapes? Premack says yes. One test, he feels, is the ability "to generate the meaning of words in the absence of their external representation." In an intriguing study, Premack asked Sarah to perform a feature analysis of an actual apple, using the plastic words to name its color, shape, presence or absence of a stalk, and so on. Asked to perform a similar analysis on the plastic word for "apple," the blue triangle, she answered by describing an apple once more and not the blue shape. This bears on a further point, Sarah's ability to consider something that is not there at the moment, an illustration of the critical language requirement of displacement in time.

The importance of appreciating the natural motives of a subject in trying to understand its use of language is well illustrated by errors Sarah made in the use of shapes for different fruits. Required to present the appropriate shape for a fruit before she could eat it, she chose the wrong word for the fruit before her surprisingly often. In a moment of inspiration, Premack wondered whether Sarah was asking for what she preferred rather than for what was before her. An independent series of tests on her fruit preferences provided the explanation. If she presented the word for banana when confronted with an apple, this was not an error but an attempt to get the experimenter to give her something else, suggesting that she truly understood the symbolic significance of the shapes.

The Design of Animal Societies

The accomplishments of Washoe and Sarah raise a curious dilemma. If chimpanzees can achieve competence with language when provided with an appropriate vehicle, why has not this been demonstrated in nature? One possibility is that our knowledge of processes of natural communication in animals is still in such infancy that we cannot say whether language-like processes are present or absent. We have surely only begun to skim the surface of many and varied patterns of social exchange that occur in wild animals.

Another possibility is that as studies proceed we shall find the social organization and ecology of animals so structured that they have little use for the special patterns of communication our language makes possible. In social interactions of most vertebrates, the competitive element is seldom far below the surface, even within a family. In wild chimpanzees, for example, aside from occasional cooperative group hunting for meat, there is little evidence of close careful coordination of the behavior of several individuals toward a common end. Indeed, the more striking examples of mammalian cooperation, still primordial by human standards, are probably not to be found in primates at all. One thinks of group hunting in the African lion, or porpoises supporting one of their group in difficulty. The acts of communication involved in these patterns of behavior are worth careful study.

As a final comment, we should be careful not to underestimate what can be achieved with the means we already know animals have available to them. Many vertebrates live in close-knit groups in which each member is well acquainted with the faults and foibles of other members. If signals thought of as primarily "emotional" are given by one member, respondents may gain much additional information from the knowledge that the individual signaling has particular idiosyncrasies, perhaps delighting in a particular food, especially fearful of a certain predator. Long familiarity with the responses of group members to a variety of environmental situations will serve to sharpen a respondent's ability to extract information from a signal about these differing situations as long as the identity of the signaling animal is known.

In simple form, this represents a process we carry to extremes when we gauge the appropriateness of one response or another by our judgment of the competence and idiosyncrasies of the person conversing with us. Emotional signals, as compared with those more symbolic in nature, probably permit more sensitive responsiveness to this kind of information, giving a dynamic register of the state of the person which, if we know him well, can be extraordinarily informative. There seems no reason to refrain from assuming that animals have a similar capacity.

From a biological viewpoint, symbolic communication is highly specialized. It works most efficiently with particular kinds of problems. For many of the uses to which animals can put their signals, largely social in nature, taking place within groups in which members are familiar with one another over a long history of acquaintanceship, affective signals can probably do the job better. Students of human *social* behavior may find that something similar is true of ourselves. As research shifts focus to the semantic functions of our language, rather than formal syntactic analysis of speech and the written word, we can hope for a better appreciation of the rich potential of affective signals in performing the great variety of functions that sustain a complex social organization.

What then are the prospects for further advances in the study of animal communication? Detailed predictions would be rash, but I will venture one general forecast. Perhaps the greatest gap in our understanding of animal communication derives from our ignorance about the structure of natural societies of living things and the forces that shape and sustain them. The maintenance of societies is a primary function of animal communication, and variations in societal design must eventually be attributable to variations in processes of social communication. Before we can begin to understand what is involved, careful quantitative studies are required, under natural conditions, to determine how animal societies are organized. As these much needed studies are accomplished and we achieve a fuller picture of the basic biological function required of animal signals, the stage will be set for a dramatic enlargement of our picture of how patterns of animal communication evolve. Field ethology, both time-consuming and intellectually demanding, deserves closer attention from talented young biologists. As a research theme, it is a worthy one, rife with challenging questions. Perhaps we will eventually be able to decide whether or not the societal whole is something more than the sum of its communicative parts.

References

Brower, L. P., 1970, Plant poisons in a terrestrial food chain and implications for mimicry theory, in: *Biochemical Coevolution* (K. L. Chambers, ed.), Oregon State University Press, Corvallis, Ore.

Capranica, R. R., 1965, *The Evoked Vocal Response of the Bullfrog*, M.I.T. Press, Cambridge, Mass.

Chappuis, C., 1971, Un exemple de l'influence du milieu sur les émissions vocales des oiseaux: l'Evolution des chants en foret equatoriale, *La Terre et la Vie*, **2–71**: 183–202.

Cherry, C., 1966, *On Human Communication*, 2nd ed., M.I.T. Press, Cambridge, Mass.

Dethier, V. G., 1970, Chemical interactions between plants and insects, in: *Chemical Ecology* (E. Sondheimer, and J. B. Simeone, eds.), Academic Press, New York.

Dodson, C. H., 1970, The role of chemical attractants in orchid pollination, in: *Biochemical Coevolution* (K. L. Chambers, ed.), Oregon State University Press, Corvallis, Ore.

Eisner, T., 1970, Chemical defense against predation in arthropods, in: *Chemical Ecology* (E. Sondheimer, and J. B. Simeone, eds.), Academic Press, New York.

Emlen, S. T., 1972, An experimental analysis of the parameters of bird song eliciting species recognition, *Behaviour* **41(1–2)**: 130–171.

Gardner, B. T., and Gardner, R. A., 1971, Two-way communication with an infant chimpanzee, in: *Behavior of Nonhuman Primates*, Vol. IV (A. Schrier and F. Stollnitz, eds.), Academic Press, New York.

Grant, K. A., and Grant, V., 1968, *Hummingbirds and Their Flowers*, Columbia University Press, New York.

Grant, V., and Grant, K. A., 1965, *Flower Pollination in the Phlox Family*, Columbia University Press, New York.

Hamilton, W. D., 1971, Selection of selfish and altruistic behavior in some extreme models, in: *Man and Beast: Comparative Social Behavior* (J. F. Eisenberg, and W. S. Dillon, eds.), Smithsonian Institution Press, Washington, D. C.

Hazlett, B. A., 1972, Ritualization in marine crustacea, in: *Behavior of Marine Animals*, Vol. 1 (H. E. Winn and B. L. Olla, eds.), Plenum Press, New York.

Hopkins, C. D., 1972, Sex differences in electric signalling in an electric fish, *Science* **176**: 1035–1037.

Lindauer, M., 1961, *Communication Among Social Bees*, Harvard University Press, Cambridge, Mass.

Marler, P., 1970, Vocalizations of East African monkeys. I. Red colobus, *Folia Primatol.* **13**: 81–91.

Marler, P., 1973, A comparison of vocalizations of red-tailed monkeys and blue monkeys: *Cercopithecus ascanius* and *C. mitis* in Uganda, *Z. Tierpsychol.* **33**: 223–247.

Marler, P., and Hamilton, W. J., 1966, *Mechanisms of Animal Behavior*, Wiley, New York.

Marler, P., and Mundinger, P., 1971, Vocal learning in birds, in: *Ontogeny of Vertebrate Behavior* (H. Moltz, ed.), Academic Press, New York.

Nottebohm, F., 1970, Ontogeny of bird song, *Science* **167**: 950–956.

Payne, R. S., and McVay, S., 1971, Songs of humpback whales, *Science* **173**: 585–597.

Payne R. S., and Webb, D., 1971, Orientation by means of long range acoustic signalling in baleen whales, *Ann. N.Y. Acad. Sci.* **188**: 110–142.

Premack, D., 1971, On the assessment of language competence in a chimpanzee, in: *Behavior of Nonhuman Primates*, Vol. IV (A. Schrier and F. Stollnitz, eds.), Academic Press, New York.

Schachter, S., and Singer, J. E., 1962, Cognitive social and physiological determinants of emotional state, *Psychol. Rev.* **69**: 379–399.

Struhsaker, T., 1967, Auditory communication among vervet monkeys (*Cercopithecus aethiops*), in: *Social Communication Among Primates* (S. A. Altmann, ed.), University of Chicago Press, Chicago.

Von Frisch, K., 1954, *The Dancing Bees*, Methuen, London.

Walker, T. J., 1957, Specificity in the response of female tree crickets (Orthoptera, Gryllidae, Oecanthinae) to calling songs of the males, *Ann. Entomol. Soc. Am.* **50**: 626–636.

Whittaker, R. H., 1970, The biochemical ecology of higher plants, in: *Chemical Ecology* (E. Sondheimer, and J. B. Simeone, eds.), Academic Press, New York.

Wiley, R. H., 1973, The strut display of male sage grouse: A "fixed" action pattern, *Behaviour* **47**: 129–152.

Williams, C. M., 1970, Hormonal interactions between plants and insects, in: *Chemical Ecology*, (E. Sondheimer, and J. B. Simeone, eds.), Academic Press, New York.

Wilson, E. O., 1970, Chemical communication within animal species, in: *Chemical Ecology*, (E. Sondheimer, and J. B. Simeone, eds.), Academic Press, New York.

CHAPTER 3

Application of the Concept of Levels of Organization to the Study of Animal Communication

William N. Tavolga

Department of Animal Behavior, American Museum of Natural History
and
Department of Biology, City College of the City University of New York
New York, New York

The influence of the behavior of one animal on the behavior of another of the same or a different species is a well-known, extensively studied phenomenon. Whether this phenomenon is called "communication," "interaction," "signaling," "language," or some other name is often a matter of definition. It is sometimes reminiscent of Alice's conversation with Humpty Dumpty:

> "When *I* use a word," Humpty Dumpty said . . . "it means just what I choose to mean—neither more or less."
> "The question is," said Humpty Dumpty, "which is to be the master—that's all.". . . "Impenetrability! That's what *I* say!"
> "Would you tell me please," said Alice, "what that means?"
> . . . "I meant by 'impenetrability' that we've had enough of that subject. . . ." (From *Through the Looking Glass*, by Lewis Carroll.)

In a recent collection of papers edited by Hinde (1972), practically every contributor had his own lexicon. Definitions of "communication" ranged from the most restricted ("goal-directed"—MacKay, 1972) to the broadest that would include virtually all aspects of behavior. We are indeed faced with a plethora of phenomena and a plethora of definitions. To quote Andrew (1972): "Animal communication is so complex and involves so many levels, that it is usually possible for a worker to find examples of whatever he expects to find."

For a scientist, it is only partially satisfying to describe a phenomenon. To discover underlying mechanisms and causes still leaves the intellectually curious unsated unless the relationship of the phenomenon is examined in the context of a larger pertinent body of knowledge. Thus the taxonomist becomes a systematist by integrating his new species into the broad concepts of evolutionary theory; the physicist seeks to understand the movement of subatomic units in terms of quantum or field theory. It is even more satisfying to be in a position to establish a theory, and the field of animal communication, it seems to me, still lacks the unifying conceptualization for which we seem to be striving. Each of us, I am sure, would like to be an Einstein or a Darwin.

Using a less loaded term, i.e., "interaction," we can see a gamut of kinds of interactions among animals. How can they be compared? How can the mechanism of sperm exchange between a pair of hermaphroditic earthworms be compared to the complex precopulatory activity in fruitflies? The initial contact between a pair of earthworms is probably based on simple tactile and chemical cues, although the resultant alignment of the two within their connubial mucous capsule is remarkably precise. Studies on the mating behavior of various species and strains of *Drosophila* have demonstrated not only highly species-typical activities (Spieth, 1952) but also the involvement of simple Mendelian inheritance in determining such differences (Ehrman, 1964).

A gamut of complexities can be observed in the courtship and pairing interactions in various groups of vertebrates, especially among fishes. These range from brief spawning encounters in schooling species to intricate and extensive signal exchanges in territorial and nest-building fishes. Most of this information was summarized and compiled in an encyclopedic work by Breder and Rosen (1966). A comparison of the two well-investigated orders of amphibians shows a substantial difference in mating interactions. In most Anura, the spawning amplexus is preceded by the emission of highly species-typical vocalizations by the males (Bogert, 1961). In many urodeles, however, the deposition of spermatophores by the male and their subsequent pickup by the female involve an interplay of tactile, chemical, and perhaps some visual cues (Organ and Organ, 1968). Song is only a part of the communication system in birds, yet volumes have been written on birdsongs alone. Here one finds that visual and acoustical modalities are preeminent, while tactile and chemical stimuli play a relatively minor role. Interactions among mammals can also range from the simplest tactual, olfactory stimuli, as in the orientation of newborn kittens to their mother (Rosenblatt, 1971), to the unique complexities of human speech.

Given all this accumulated and accumulating information, how can one deal with it on an overall, synthetic basis? One technique is taxonomic, to simply pigeonhole and classify according to some scheme of convenience. This may be useful for descriptive purposes, but it can hardly serve as a theoretical framework, since the classification would be necessarily arbitrary and devised for the observer's convenience. A classification according to modalities, for example, might include the trail-marking ants in the same group as dogs urinating at fire hydrants. A classification based on the function of the signals might form the basis for a theoretical framework, and indeed, several approaches along this line have been made.

In 1961, Hockett proposed a set of "design features" that characterized acoustical communication—in particular, human speech. For descriptive purposes, this scheme has proved quite useful, and the features are defined in operational terms. Some of the features, such as "broadcast," "directionality," "rapid fading," are defined according to the physical characteristics of acoustical signals. Some of these are defined in terms of the message sender, e.g., "complete feedback," "prevarication," "reflexiveness." Some are actually semantic properties, in the sense of the relation of the signals to external events or states. Finally, some of the features refer to the communication system itself. This is, therefore, a list of the properties of the communication system that can carry information, but these are the properties of human speech primarily, and the list is essentially descriptive, not explanatory.

Thorpe (1972) attempted to apply Hockett's list of properties to communication in crickets, bees, birds, primates, and dogs, by simply tabulating those properties present and those absent in the various forms. The fact that some species other than man may or may not possess some of these anthropomorphically defined properties of human speech is not helpful as a theoretical framework. Indeed, it can be misleading. Even if one can say that both human speech and the "dances" of honeybees possess "semanticity," this does not help our understanding of either phenomenon. Semanticity, as defined by Hockett, constitutes the association between the signal and some feature of the outside world. The assignation of the same word for two superficially similar phenomena is not only metaphoric, but it conceals the enormous biological differences between the two.

Sebeok (1965) also tried to provide a general model for animal communication—"zoosemiotics." This term was "coined to identify a very rapidly expanding discipline within the behavioral sciences, one which has crystallized at the intersection of semiotics, the science of signs, and ethology. . . ." As defined by Sebeok, this is truly a field that encompasses virtually all aspects of animal behavior, and its breadth is certainly demonstrated by the fact that the huge volume edited by Sebeok (1968) and entitled *Animal Communication* can serve as a textbook in animal behavior on its own.

Sebeok's model, like Hockett's "design features," is derived from human speech, specifically from Bühler's field theory of language. The model consists of an *addresser* who *encodes* a *message,* and an *addressee* who must be able to *decode* the message. The message is accompanied by *context* and *noise,* and is transmitted along a *channel.* Classification of communicatory events can be made according to any or all of the above, i.e., based on the channel, the encoding (effector) process, the decoding (receptor) mechanism, the code or message and its information content, or any one (or combination) of the parts of the model. Although this kind of a model does have a powerful heuristic value, it fails to accomplish one of its goals. As stated by Sebeok (1965): "Their [students of zoosemiotics] distant goal is the provision of an ordered body of data as a basis for the investigation of the phylogenetic origins of interacting communicative elements, including verbal." In spite of Sebeok's model, the problem of comparative study is still with us, and, indeed, exacerbated by the tendency to use the same descriptive terms for very different phenomena, e.g., the "dances" of honeybees and human verbalizations.

A somewhat simpler division of the field of communication study (*semiotic*—the theory of signs) was proposed by Cherry (1957), in which the discipline comprises three major aspects: *syntactics,* the physical properties of the signals or messages; *semantics,* their informational content; and *pragmatics,* the role of signals in behavior. The last aspect, particularly the problem of motivation, appeared to be the primary interest of Marler's (1961) approach, and was restricted to social behavior in higher vertebrates (*cf.* Chapter 2, this volume). Smith (1969), on the other hand, concerned himself primarily with the information content of the message (semantics), although some of his categories included assumptions about motivational states of the senders.

The mysterious quality of motivation is certainly the key to many studies of a particular form of communication, aggressive behavior. Lorenz (1966) defined aggression as "the fighting instinct in beast and man which is directed *against* members of the same species," and he accepted as a truism the Freudian notion of an innate aggressive drive. He observed this form of communication in a great variety of animals, such as coral reef fish, birds, wolves, and men. In Cherry's terms, he concerned himself with pragmatics, and included as aggressive encounters all kinds of animal interactions that appeared to him to be aggressive. By showing the wide distribution of such activities in the animal kingdom, particularly vertebrates, he thus established the truth of his own axiom. This kind of generalization is a logical weakness in the general models reviewed above. Labels for objects or phenomena, no matter how seemingly objective or operational, are all terms of convenience for our own peculiar form of communication. Korzybski (1948) pointed out, at great length, that the symbol (or word) is *not* the object. The fact that we can apply the term "red," for example, to a variety of pigments and lights does not mean they are the same in all properties. Thus the incidents of one coral reef fish biting at another, or one wolf snarling at another, or one man punching another are similar and aggressive only in a superficial and anthropomorphic sense. In point of fact, the differences in mechanisms, ontogeny, and even motivation far outweigh the similarities. A solid application of Morgan's Canon is needed here.

Virtually everyone who has written about animal communication has touched on the well-known discovery by von Frisch (1946, 1950) of the communicatory "dances" in bees. The unfortunate label of "language" has been widely applied to this phenomenon. Certainly, the recent studies by Wenner and his coworkers (summarized by Wenner, 1971, and in Chapter 6, this volume) have made it evident that the "dances" performed by returning forager bees have a broader stimulative effect than was first thought and one not necessarily involved in communicating the location of food sources. The visual modality is probably negligible, since the hive is normally dark, but tactile, olfactory, and acoustical cues all serve to arouse the other workers in the vicinity of the returned forager. Far from being specific, the "message" appears to be only generally arousing and multichanneled. Furthermore, there is substantial doubt that the directional information presumably contained in the "dances" is actually used by the new recruits. The same cues of odor, terrain, wind currents, etc., that originally guided the foragers to the food source can also operate on the recruits. From a series of well-controlled, elegant experiments, Wenner derived a more parsimonious explanation, i.e., that the bees follow an odor trail to the food source and that the primary response to the stimulus of returning, food-laden bees is to leave the hive and fly upwind.

This was fine opportunity by Wenner to demonstrate the importance of Morgan's Canon. Instead of confounding the situation by labeling the phenomenon a "language," and implying thereby a high level of organization, the interpretation can by simplified. In Wenner's words, a more appropriate question can be asked: "How do recruited bees find a food source?" Thus the application of Morgan's Canon not only prevents errors in interpretation of data but also assists in the formulation of pertinent questions.

As a result of Wenner's examination of the problem, the entire situation has, in a sense, become simplified. We can now begin to identify the particular set of conditions and stimuli, some of which may be redundant, that increase the probability that bees will find a food source. Although the notion of a bee "language" may lose some of its mysterious Disney-type appeal, the communicative system becomes more plausible, more parsimonious, and certainly more in accordance with what one could expect from an organism with a relatively simple, ganglionic central nervous system and a limited, stereotyped behavioral repertoire.

Many new questions now appear, and one that occurs to me concerns the ontogenetic origins of this behavior. Unfortunately, nothing has been done on bee behavior that parallels the intensive studies by Schneirla (1971) on army ants. Some inferences can be made, however, since both species are hymenopterans and have a narrowly limited developmental history within a rigidly controlled, species-typical environment.

To make an extreme contrast, the development of social interactions in monkeys is highly dependent on a large variety of social encounters beginning with early postnatal relationships with the mother and extending through peer play (Harlow, 1969). Social behavior in monkeys and bees is obviously different, and differences are evident at all stages of development, from the zygote with its species-typical nuclear-cytoplasmic organization and on. It was to emphasize such differences in levels of organization that Schneirla (1953) coined the terms *biosocial* and *psychosocial*. The developmental pattern leading toward social structure in insects, for example, is termed *biosocial*. The social interactions in mammals, particularly primates, are developed with the additional, dominating influences of psychological, behavioral factors, and are thus termed *psychosocial*.

The above is illustrative of the application of the concept of levels of organization to behavior, but the concept is more universal. "The concept of integrative levels of organization is a general description of the evolution of matter through successive and higher orders of complexity and integration. . . . Each level of organization possesses unique properties of structure and behavior which, though dependent on the properties of the constituent elements, appear only when these elements are combined in the new system" (Novikoff, 1945). The whole becomes greater than the sum of its parts by virtue of adding new, qualitatively different, properties derived from the organization. Novikoff (1945) and Schneirla (1949, 1953) both showed how this concept can help us avoid the pitfalls of teleology, anthropomorphism, and the nature-nurture dichotomy. The concept of levels is also consonant with the principles of organic evolution, in that through evolutionary changes organisms can attain new levels of organization. In terms of behavior, the capacities of animals with different nervous organizations are different in a qualitative, quantum sense.

There is available, therefore, a broad, biologically sound concept that has already been demonstrated as applicable to the study of behavior. One need not be an Einstein or a Darwin to use the concept of levels to assist in formulating a theoretical framework for the study of animal communication (Tavolga, 1970) (see Fig. 1).

One of the pitfalls of the idea of a hierarchy of levels is the implicit assumption of a *scala naturae*. Comparative psychology is particularly prone to this type of error, as was noted by Hodos and Campbell (1969).

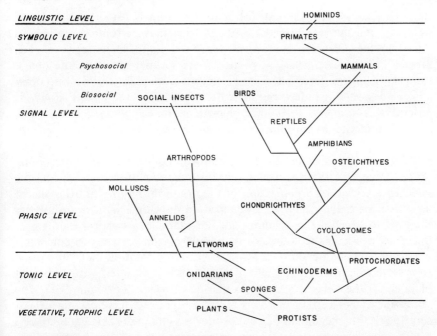

Fig. 1. A rough attempt to show graphically the relation between levels of organization in interactions and the positions of some major groups of organisms. Allocation of a group to a particular level is based on the highest level achieved by any of its members. Although the labels for the categories are arbitrary, the categories themselves are discrete, definable, and represent quantum differences in behavioral organization and capacities. Within the major groups listed, differences in levels also exist, and, of course, higher levels always subsume the capacities of the lower levels.

With virtually no paleontological data, various groups of contemporary organisms have been arranged in linear sequences as regards learning ability, for example, or other behavioral properties. It is well known (or should be) that any given species of fish does not represent *all* fish, nor is it ancestral to anything except some unpredictable future species of fish. The fact that birds, for example, may be on a lower level with regard to social organization than mammals does not imply in any way that birds are ancestral to mammals. At the same time, it is evident that a hierarchy of levels of organizations does exist, and various taxa of modern organisms have attained different levels via independent evolutionary pathways.

The Energy Source—the Emitter

Any organism that produces an energy change in its immediate environment is, by definition, an emitter of energy. The notion of change should be stressed, since a steady-state condition is usually not relevant to interactions among animals, although there may be some exceptions to this. I prefer the more operational term *emitter* to such words as "addresser" or "sender." It is possible, of course, that an inanimate object can also be an emitter of energy, and since it is sometimes difficult to draw a line, we should include such phenomena in any general scheme. For purposes of this chapter, I shall deal only with animate emitters.

Classification of emitters can be done in a variety of ways, some more artificial and arbitrary than others, e.g., according to the kind of energy emitted, the mechanism, or even motivational state. The criteria for classification I propose will be based on a combination of properties related to the level of organization of the organism and its emitting mechanism. In part, the degree of specialization of the mechanism determines the level to which it can be allocated. For example, acoustical energy produced by a fish in the course of its undulatory movement through water would be a phenomenon on a lower level of organization than the case of sounds produced by a specialized mechanism associated with the swim bladder, as the "elastic spring" in marine catfishes (Tavolga, 1962). The sex attractant of certain moths is a highly species-typical chemical (Wilson, 1968); the integument of trout produces a complex of exudates, among which are some amines to which lampreys respond (Kleerekoper, 1969). These are two examples of chemical emissions that represent different levels of complexity, specialization of the material involved, and the specialization of the emitting organs.

Allocation is also dependent on the phyletic standing of the species, with reference to the level of its nervous organization. The mechanisms that control and modulate the production of chemical, tactual, and visual signals among the members of a colony of social insects are dependent on a complex of interacting sensory, central nervous, and neurohumoral factors. By contrast, the interactions among annelid worms are on a simpler, less specialized, and, clearly, lower level of organization. Even without specific functional data on the emitting mechanisms, it is possible to allocate these phenomena on the basis of morphology and phylogeny. Assuming that the vast amount of information on evolution now available to us is correct, we can use it as the background skeleton for classification.

The Energy Receiver—the Responder

Any organism which is able, by virtue of its sensory equipment, to receive the energy change is potentially or actually a receiver. The most reliable way in which the receipt of the energy output can be determined is by some observable physiological or behavioral response, and therefore the receiver is not separable, in practice, from the responder. The response must be measurable as a correlated physiological or behavioral change. Specialization of the receiver may occur at two levels: by the refinement of the sensory receptors, and by the development of specific central nervous mechanisms. The ultrasonic receptors of certain moths exemplify the first of these specializations, in which considerable signal analysis and filtering take place in the receptor organ (Roeder and Treat, 1961). The eye of a frog has also been shown to act as a peripheral analyzer (Lettvin et al., 1961). The abilities of birds to discriminate among a variety of complex song patterns, however, indicates that the analysis occurs at the level of the central nervous system (Marler, 1960). Symbols and codes are the property of the highest of communicatory levels. Context, defined as including all internal and external stimuli that impinge on the receiver in addition to the energy output of the emitter, is of profound importance in determining the quality and strength of the response (Smith, 1965).

The mechanisms for detection of and response to stimuli are not the same as those involved in producing the stimuli. The evolutionary pathways of the two systems are different, since their requirements are different. The various kinds of energy receivers, however, can be categorized in terms of levels of organization in a manner parallel to the hierarchy of levels for emitters.

In actual interactions, it is important to recognize that the emitter and receiver do not necessarily operate on the same level. For example, the bright colors and distinctive shapes of flowers of insect-pollinated plants are the products of growth and differentiation on the vegetative level. The behavior of the insects which are attracted to these flowers is based on reception of specific signals, and, indeed, in one case the flower structure actually resembles the genital organs of a female wasp. The male attempts copulation with the flower and thereby accomplishes pollination. A predatory fish, such as a barracuda, responds to a rather specific concatenation of stimuli before attacking its prey, but the energy output of the prey is probably on the tonic level.

In predator–prey relationships, it is adaptive for the prey organism to produce stimuli that have the highest entropy level, i.e., stimuli closest to the noise level. Consequently, the likelihood is that the prey organism would be at the lowest possible level of organization in its energy emissions. The predator, however, must be able to discriminate the low signal level from the noise and, therefore, operate on a much higher, selective level.

In intraspecific interactions, as in reproductive and social behavior, the likelihood is greater that both emitter and receiver are on the same or a comparable level of organization. This must also be true in cases of echolocation, since the pulse output is controlled by the feedback of the echoes.

In responding to the energy impinging on it, the receiver organism must filter out what is relevant from what is not relevant at the moment. A large part of the filtering is accomplished by the sense organs, as, for example, in the case of the "bug detector" in the eye of the frog (Lettvin *et al.*, 1961). The sensitivity, range, and specificity of the receptor organs are the first step in separating signal from noise. Consequently, the specialization of sense organs results in a higher level of organization. The following levels are based on the increasing capacity of the central nervous mechanism for dealing with the inputs from various sensory systems, and, more significantly, including the effects of prior experience into the processing and eventual response. Included in the signal processing must be the effects of other stimuli, present and past, internal and external, that are not immediately or directly related to the signal in question; i.e., the context of the received information becomes part of the information.

In passing, I might point out that the concepts of "context" and "noise" are somewhat confusing and, often, difficult to separate. To a receiver organism, the total input on its sensory system is the sum of the "signal" (the specific energy output of the emitter organism), the "context" (other environmental energy that may modulate the response), and the "noise" (energy that is irrelevant to the response, or interfering with the reception). The judgment as to what is signal, context, and noise is based on the receiver organism and its response. Often, this judgment is made by the observer, who derives his conclusions on the basis of correlations, which may or may not be actual causal relationships. The situation is further confounded by the modulation of the response by an unknown number of internal factors, e.g., hormonal conditions, prior experiences, and even current state of the digestive system.

The approach here is an attempt at classification, but in dealing with the real world, lines of demarcation are often difficult to draw. This is certainly true of different levels of organization, which "while distinct, are not completely delimited from each other. No boundary in nature is fixed and no category airtight" (Novikoff, 1945). Furthermore, in such a classification, crucial information about the mechanisms, phylogeny, ontogeny, and function may be lacking. The inclusion of some phenomena in one or another category is frankly tentative and intended to be heuristic. This classification will attempt to follow the broad ramifications of phylogeny, rather than some arbitrary groupings, and, at the same time, to avoid the fallacious notions of a *scala naturae* (Hodos and Campbell, 1969). Implicit in the scheme is the notion that higher levels subsume lower levels in their functional capacities. Although the precise inclusion of one or another instance in a particular level may be arguable, since, in many instances, critical data may be lacking, the important idea is the recognition of qualitatively different levels of organization.

Vegetative, Trophic Level

Like an inanimate object, such as a rock or a body of water, an organism can be an energy emitter as a result of its physical presence alone. Unlike inanimate objects, living organisms grow and metabolize, but their physical form and growth pattern represent the lowest level of biological energy emission. Multicellular plants would be characteristic of this level, and interactions among plants, brought about by wind pollination, are essentially an expression of a cellular growth and differentiation process. Similarly, the specializations of form and color of insect-pollinated flowers are the result of species-typical growth patterns. The insects which respond to these floral patterns are, of course, behaving on a much higher level of organization. Perhaps a still lower level of energy emission may be subsumed here to include the more primitively organized unicellular algae and bacteria. Motility in itself does not necessarily indicate a higher level, since motile bacteria and both plant and animal gametes are no more specialized than any component cells of a tissue, as, for example, ciliated columnar cells, blood cells, osteoblasts, or fibroblasts.

Information transmission within a cell, as between DNA and RNA, the chemical basis of energy metabolism, high-energy phosphate transfer, and similar biochemical reactions, may be considered on a still lower level, but for purposes of this chapter, I shall not pursue this further.

Aside from plants, tissues, and unicellular organisms, some metazoa may be mainly vegetative in the process of energy emission, i.e., sponges, hydroid cnidarians, adult tunicates, and many other sessile forms. Embryonic and larval stages of some higher forms, particularly as plankters, are similarly organized. At some stage of development, of course, all organisms operate at this level, since it is a part of the entire concept that the higher levels subsume and include the lower.

The cell membrane is a specialized part of a cell that deals with the interaction of the cell with its environment. It is here that the received energy can be transduced into some other form: e.g., light energy on a retinal cell membrane becomes a chemical change; bending of the hair-like process of a neuromast or an organ of Corti cell is transformed into a microphonic or generator potential. Different portions of the same cell can even show different membrane specializations. A mechanical stimulus applied to the anterior end of a paramecium produces an increase in calcium ion permeability, while the same stimulus applied to the posterior end produces an increase in permeability to potassium ions. The data presented by Naitoh and Eckert (1969) showed how this difference in membrane response accounts for locomotor changes: i.e., when stimulated on the front end, the paramecium stops and reverses its ciliary beat; when it is stimulated on the hind end, the cilia speed up.

The response systems of protists would be considered to be on this level, even including the light-orienting locomotor behavior in plant flagellates. The taxis responses of *Euglena* or the colonial *Volvox* toward light are purely intracellular mechanisms, and, based on the level of organization of the cells, it would be parsimonious to include these phenomena on the cellular, vegetative level.

Cells, whether separate or as part of a tissue, respond to environmental changes by some alteration or adjustment of their metabolism: oxygen and carbon dioxide concentrations affect anaerobic and aerobic metabolic fluctuations; sunlight and nitrates affect photosynthetic activity of plant cells; appropriate nutrients affect growth and cell division; and so on and on. In this sense, all protoplasm is capable of responding to environmental changes, and, indeed, this is considered a basic property of living material: irritability. At this level, the response is a direct effect of the impinging energy, and, although adaptive, it is poorly adjustable. The organization, not mere aggregation, of cells into tissues grants new and more extensive properties for adaptive adjustment, and, perhaps for purposes other than those of the present chapter, it may be useful to subdivide this level.

Tonic, Organismic Level

In an organism, by virtue of its being an integrated whole, the level of integration of energy output is qualitatively different. All the processes that are involved in homeostasis, including not only cellular and tissue metabolism but also osmoregulatory, thermoregulatory activities and behavior, result in certain physiological and behavioral manifestations that emit energy into the environment and can affect the organism itself and other organisms. Such continuous processes that are basic to species-typical physiology and behavior have been defined as *tonic* (Schneirla, 1965). Thus the same term can be applied to energy output, on an organismic level.

Patterns of metabolic chemical emissions, including excretion, can be species typical, and basic patterns of locomotion are a result of particular kinds of nervous and muscular organizations. Energy emission at this level differs from the vegetative because the source is a functionally integrated organism.

For example, the behavioral repertoire of cnidarians, though limited, is made possible, to a large extent, by the presence of a connecting neuronal network. This network, although not centralized, serves to unify the tissues of organism into an integrated whole. Whether the myonemic network in some protozoans serves this function is not clear. Mere synchronization of cellular activity is still essentially on the vegetative, tissue level, as exemplified by the behavior of colonial protozoan forms or even colonial algae such as *Volvox*. However, neuroid conduction in sponges is now thought to be accompanied by the operation of neuron-like cells (Lentz, 1968), and the level of integration in Porifera may turn out to be higher than previously believed.

All animals are energy emitters on the tonic level at some stage of development, since one of the manifestations of living is the production of chemical by-products. Even normal locomotor patterns can produce energy in the photic and mechanical channels. Such outputs are the direct result of the organism's normal, tonic state. Herbivorous animals, near the bottom of the food pyramid, often serve as prey, and their energy output is primarily tonic, although species-typical and thus functioning as a signal to a predator. Trophallaxis and trail-marking in social insects are tonic, as long as the substances involved are normal metabolic products and not specialized chemicals, i.e., pheromones.

In applying the concept of entropy to biocommunication, Tembrock (1970) suggested that the information of a signal is determined by the unlikelihood with which it appears in a specific communication situation. Energy emissions on the tonic level, as defined here, could be species-typical, but they would be among the most likely to appear since they are associated with normal, ongoing processes of the organism. The entropy of tonic-level energy would therefore be relatively high, although lower than that of the vegetative level. The information content of this energy, however, would depend on the receiver and his selectivity.

Phasic, "Forced-Response" Level

Those processes during the development of an individual that occur as discontinuous, more or less regular stages or events have been defined as *phasic* by Schneirla (1959, 1965), and, by extension, where such processes emit energy they can serve as stimuli to other organisms and can be allocated to a separate level of organization. Although the energy output at this level may be broad spectrum and multichanneled, it is closely correlated not only with the species but also with its physiological and behavioral state of the moment.

For example, the behavior of forager bees would be on this level. The stimulation of the food on the foragers is temporarily arousing and results, on their return to the hive, in the emission of energy in the form of chemical exudates, regurgitated food, increase in locomotor behavior, and even sound production (Wenner, 1971). The interplay of visual, acoustical, and chemical stimuli in spawning fishes, e.g., *Bathygobius* (Tavolga, 1956), can also be allocated as phasic.

In Tembrock's (1970) terms, the phasic outputs would be on a lower entropy level and, consequently, more precisely species-typical. Additional differences between the phasic and tonic levels are that the phasic-level emissions are more limited in time of occurrence (i.e., they take place in relation to particular events or functions, as in some aspects of pairing and reproduction), the information content is more limited and thereby more precise, and the energy output is usually linked to specific structures and their integrated function.

Although phasic-level outputs can be recognized in most animals, they occur predominantly in flatworms, annelids, molluscs, and some lower vertebrates. The mating behavior of some polychaete worms (Evans, 1971) and among cephalopods and, possibly, gastropods can be characterized as phasic, and most arthropod behavior contains at least some aspects of this level. Among vertebrates, the phasic level predominates primarily among the more primitive fishes, although, of course, it is present to some degree in the higher forms.

Kineses and taxes, as described by Fraenkel and Gunn (1961), have been characterized as "forced movements" and "forced responses" in the sense that the direction of orientation is tightly controlled by the stimulus properties. The position of a stimulus source can change the velocity of locomotion (orthokinesis) or change the turning rate (klinokinesis). If the sense organs are bilaterally placed, the stimulus position can affect the orientation of the organism so that it turns toward or away from the source (taxis), and this appears to be mediated by the sensory system's effect on muscle tone on the appropriate side of the organism. The mechanism of compass orientations is not clear, but it is probably a modification of a taxis.

On this level, the response of an organism to stimuli from other organisms is primarily taxic, even though the level of specialization of the sense organs may be considerable. Most primitive bilateral animals, e.g., flatworms, annelids, and gastropods, respond at this level. At some time in their development, most animals exhibit taxes.

Among arthropods, the behavior of social insects is certainly highly stimulus bound, as demonstrated in Schneirla's (1971) studies on army ants. The mechanisms involved in schooling fish begin as simple optomotor orientations (Shaw, 1960, 1961), and it may be that their responses even as adults may be primarily taxic.

Signal, Message Level

Emitters on the signal level are characterized by specialized structures that produce their energy output along a single channel and, usually, within a narrow band of the spectrum of variation of that channel. The information content here is not only phasic, but may also be coded, in the sense that under a given situation the particular signal or combination of signals is closely linked to the emitter's condition. The complexity and specificity of signals are such that this level is primarily associated with intraspecific interactions, and, in this case, the receiver and the emitter must have a shared code.

It is at this level that one can begin to use that much-maligned term *pheromone*. Although, as described for social insects by Wilson (1965), the term refers to specific, specialized chemicals excreted under particular conditions, others have used the word for almost any chemical substance produced by any organism. According to this restricted definition of a pheromone, the food exchange (trophallaxis) that is such a basic aspect of social insect behavior cannot by itself be considered on the signal level, unless it can be demonstrated that the regurgitated food contains species-typical and unique chemical substances. In general, it is more parsimonious to assume this energy emission to be on a lower level of organization until it can be demonstrated that it can be allocated to a higher level.

Among other arthropods, the specialization of sonic organs in many insects, especially among the Cicadidae and Orthoptera (Alexander, 1960; Dumortier, 1963), the specificity of their acoustical outputs, and the close relationship of these to particular aspects of reproductive behavior all lead to the interpretation of these phenomena as signals. Equally, the waving behavior of male fiddler crabs can be termed a signal as defined here (Salmon, 1965).

Among lower vertebrates, it is possible that at least some fishes will be shown to emit such specific signals, particularly where sonic mechanisms are highly evolved and specialized, as in the toadfish (Winn, 1967). The mating calls of most anuran amphibians are produced by specialized structures, are quite specific in their acoustical characteristics, and are produced under special circumstances of season, temperature, and internal endocrine condition (Bogert, 1961; Blair, 1963). Among reptiles, the highly specific courtship behavior of many lizards can be considered a combination of signals (Carpenter, 1963; Blair, 1968).

The call notes of most birds are signals in the sense of being produced by a special structure and under more or less specific circumstances. Social communication among herring gulls (Tinbergen, 1959) is based on signals that are simple and involve narrow energy channels. The complex songs of many passerine species, however, are clearly on a higher level. The vocalizations of most mammals are signals in the sense of expressing an emotional state, as, for example, the bark of a dog, purr of a cat, and squeal of a porpoise. Many such vocalizations originate as phasic outputs, but as a result of conditioning they become associated with specific circumstances and thereby develop into signals. In the case of porpoise

sounds, despite much publicity to the contrary, it remains to be shown
that the high-pitched whistles and squeals of porpoises represent anything more than emotional outbursts, although there is evidence that these
sounds function in communication (Lang and Smith, 1965; Dreher and
Evans, 1964).

Busnel *et al.* (1962) described a form of communication based on
the use of whistles among some peoples of the Pyrenees, and these authors
compared this language to the whistle communication among dolphins.
In this comparison, it is easy to confuse two levels of interaction. The
human whistle language is based on symbolization and develops as part
of a culture, like the "talking" drums of Africa. It is comparable to the
symbolic gestures used for communication among skin divers. The symbols are derived from and convey in coded form messages that were originally in the normal spoken language. The standard Morse code is also
such a representation.

In dolphins, or any other infrahuman animal for that matter, the
communication signals are not a coded form of speech and are not
derived from a culture. If further data demonstrate the specificity of signals among these whistles, it is possible that this form of interaction may
be shown to be on the signal level, but it is clearly not a language.

This example well illustrates the danger of comparing behaviors on
the basis of superficial similarities and with no regard to ontogeny or to
level of organization.

Echolocation is a special case of an interaction on the signal level
in which the emitter and receiver are the same animal. Many insectivorous
bats and toothed whales possess elaborate mechanisms for the output of
sound pulses and the reception and analysis of their echoes (Busnel,
1967). In other species in which echolocation has been established, such
as shrews, oilbirds, and even man, the level of specialization for echolocation appears to be low. Tentatively, then, these echolocators should
be considered at the phasic level.

The mechanism of electrical location and prey detection described
for some species of fishes (Lissmann, 1963) is similar to echolocation in that
the animal uses its own energy output to gain information about the environment. Although the electric organs are highly specialized, the actual
output is broad-band and nonspecific. Thus, for the moment, it is doubt-
ful that these electrical pulses should be allocated to the signal level. An
instance of electrical communication in gymnotid fishes was recently discovered by Hopkins (1972), and the pulsed outputs of these fish show
changes in frequency, duration, and temporal patterning that would
clearly place them on the signal level.

Since signals, as defined here, are primarily associated with intraspecific interactions, it is clear that they are also associated with social behavior and the formation of the social bond. The development of the social bond, however, can be dependent on very different processes, and thus signal production may take place on more than one level of organization. For example, the development of social units, colonies, of hymenopterous insects is based on biosocial factors, as defined by Schneirla (1953), while in mammals the additional factors of reciprocal stimulation between mother and young place the social bond on the psychosocial level (Schneirla and Rosenblatt, 1961). To some extent, the development of specific song patterns among the higher passerine birds may be considered psychosocial, since the acquisition of the species-typical song is at least partially dependent on the kinds of sounds the young birds hears (Lanyon, 1961).

This level is characterized not only by highly specialized sensory systems, but by extremely specific responses as well. From among the many stimuli, specific signals are selected as appropriate for response at that particular time. The receptor acts as a primary filter to separate out the signal from the noise, but the central processing system must correlate this information with contextual data that include past experiences and present physiological states. At this level, then, the evocation of an adaptive response demands a high level of organization.

Among invertebrates, only some of the more advanced arthropods may possibly achieve this level of response, and it would appear to be extremely difficult to demonstrate. The responses of moths and other insects to long-range pheromones, although remarkable, can be explained on the basis of simple taxes or kineses (Farkas and Shorey, 1972).

Among vertebrates, signal reception and processing are most evident. In most demersal and territorial fishes, the interplay of interactions in territorial defense, courtship, and mating is dependent in many cases on the reception of highly specific signals, and the responses to these signals are such as to require considerable processing. The well-known zig-zag prespawning "dance" of sticklebacks is dependent not only on the immediate detection of particular color patterns or movements but also on the sequence of events and the interplay of signals. The processes of sex and species discrimination would be considered on this level.

In Anura, the responses to species-typical vocalizations and, in Caudata, the interchange of chemical and tactual stimuli during courtship must involve specialized signal processing. Also on this level one would include the responses of birds to their species-typical vocalizations and the interplay of social stimuli among mammals, particularly in the development of socialization between mother and nursing young. It is apparent that in tetrapods, at least, the predominant interactions are on the signal level for both emitter and receiver. It is at this level that one can begin to apply such concepts as design features, communication systems, information content of messages, and semantics.

Personally, I should prefer to limit the definition of communication to interactions on these levels, with the recognition that the emitter and receiver do not necessarily operate on the same level.

Symbolic, Goal-Directed Level

The numerous studies on social behavior in infrahuman primates, back as far as those of Yerkes and Yerkes (1929) and Köhler (1925), have shown not only that interactions among these animals are on the psychosocial level but also that primitive forms of symbolism can be observed. The "pointing" behavior and other gestures of a chimpanzee are clearly symbolic in an elementary fashion.

The large repertoire of facial expressions, vocalizations, and gestures of the anthropoids has been described by many authors, including Charles Darwin in his classic volume, *The Expressions of the Emotions in Man and Animals*. Studies on captive primates, especially chimpanzees, have demonstrated the specificity and complexity of these signals. Observations of wild colonies have substantiated the social basis for the development of communication. The complexity and variability of social communication in infrahuman primates have been emphasized in compilations by Altmann (1967) and Jay (1968). Studies on free-ranging anthropoids have described some of the complex interactions that begin in infancy and develop into plastic social organizations that have been likened to primordial cultures.

Although the development of social communication among infrahuman primates has been studied only indirectly and sporadically, communication appears to emerge rapidly as part of social development. In contrast, in songbirds and lower mammals, the development of a social bond is based on a concatenation of discrete signals and the gradual organization, through reciprocal stimulation, of complex patterns. For these reasons, and especially because of the primitive symbolism involved, the communication level in many infrahuman primates represents a distinct level.

MacKay (1972) proposed that the term "communication" be limited to cases of clear "goal-directed behavior." It is probably too restrictive a definition of this word, but it is certainly clear that it is applicable to the interactions among primates. Unfortunately, most of the studies on wild or semi-wild primate groups, such as those of Schaller (1965) and Goodall (1965), do not give enough developmental data to permit the allocation of primate signals to a particular level of organization. Thus it is probably more parsimonious to assume these to be signals in the sense of being narrowly specialized acoustical or visual energy outputs. The dramatic recent successes in teaching some elements of language to chimpanzees (Gardner and Gardner, 1969; Premack, 1971) have demonstrated the potentiality of obtaining a clearly symbolic performance from these animals. It is probable, further, that some specifically chimpanzee-forms of symbolism occur in the wild.

Does this mean that the chimpanzee possesses a language or communication system on a level with that of man? It is easy to forget that the chimpanzee is neither a small hairy human nor in any way ancestral to *Homo sapiens*. Curiously, mistakes of this sort occur, and there is need for a wider circulation and understanding of evolution by some psychologists, anthropologists, and primatologists (Hodos and Campbell, 1969). Witness, for example, the naivete of constructing a phylogenetic tree for "laughter" beginning with a "primitive mammal" and evolving in stages through *Cercopithecus, Macaca, Pan,* and finally *Homo* (van Hooff, 1972).

The chimpanzee, just as any other species of organism, is a uniquely evolved, adapted form, and its success in its particular niche is the result of its species-typical form, development, physiology, and behavior. Its level of social behavior, and communication as well, is clearly not equivalent to that of man. Human language, then, must represent a qualitatively separate level of organization.

In order for an emitter to operate on the symbolic level (as described earlier), it is necessary that the code be shared with the appropriate receiver. Consequently, all that was stated about the symbolic emitter level must also apply to the receiver, who is also an emitter. This level, then, would include only some of the primates, including man.

Linguistic Level

The term *language* has been used for several levels of communication, sometimes as distinct from and sometimes including "speech." For purposes of this thesis, I shall use language for that form of primarily vocal communication characteristic of man. Without reviewing the vast literature on linguistic theory, semiotics, and paralanguage (see, for example, Sebeok *et al.,* 1964; Lenneberg, 1964; Lyons, 1972), I should like to characterize this level of communication as one in which symbols are used in a teleological sense, in which abstract ideas are communicated, and in which not only present conditions but also past and future events are communicated. Yerkes and Yerkes (1935) pointed out that despite the complexity and primitive symbolism of intercommunication in many infrahuman primates the property of communication of ideas is still exclusive to human speech.

The development of human speech is unique. Carmichael (1964) reviewed the emergence of speech in the human infant and pointed out the difficulties in the study of prelinguistic utterances. The earliest sounds, including the so-called birthcry, appear to be nonspecific energy outputs. Subsequently, the psychosocial level is reached and surpassed with the use of specific sounds representing objects, classes of objects, physiological and mental states, and, finally, abstract ideas. The qualitative differences between human language and other forms of animal communication clearly set this level apart.

The basis for the fact that human language is unique lies in man's species-typical developmental pattern and the relation of this pattern to his social behavior. Man is an altricial organism, and, at birth, his stage of development is probably earlier than that of any other mammalian species. His period of total dependence on maternal care is longer than that of any other species. At birth, man is faced with an enormous number of new stimuli with which he must cope, but for which he is ill-prepared. A lengthy experience with his mother and other individuals is required for the proper development of his future "human" behavior. At the same time, this new world of the neonate is charged with highly variable stimuli, and the behavior developed is also, necessarily, variable. To a newborn infant human, the potentialities for a plastic behavioral development are enormous, since he begins with very few organized behavior patterns. Human communication, then, is typically variable, adjustable, and pliable, especially during early postnatal development. This is what makes us "human" and uniquely different from all other species.

This does not mean, however, that human communication does not or cannot contain aspects of lower levels of organization. There is much in human communication, especially in gestures, movements, and "paralanguage," that can probably be allocated to the signal, phasic, or even tonic level (as defined here).

In accordance with the definition of language, as used here, only man shows definite linguistic capabilities. I say this in spite of the remarkable advances in recent years in teaching chimpanzees some elements of human language, both vocal and gestural. It is still not clear whether the chimpanzee is actually being taught a language or is being trained to respond to a series of rather complex stimuli. These animals are certainly capable of solving rather intricate problems, and I question whether one can demonstrate that in the communication studies the animals are using true linguistic abilities.

In discussing the alternative to the nativistic approach to human linguistic development, Lyons (1972) stated: "there is no need to postulate any specifically linguistic 'knowledge' that is innate in the child and brought to bear upon the utterances he hears around him. It is assumed instead that the child gradually comes to an understanding of the formal principles underlying the construction of the utterances he hears by applying to his task abilities which, far from being specifically linguistic, are applicable in every aspect of his cognitive development." Human cognitive development is species-typical and based on a characteristically human development of socialization. There is no reason to assume that if a chimpanzee and a human infant both learn to make a sound or gesture indicating, say, hunger, the cognitive and learning processes are the same in both. Considering the separation of the two species by at least 10 million and probably 20 million years, it is extremely likely that the processes are quite different. To ignore such differences leads to the "naked ape" and "hairy human" kinds of fallacies.

Concluding Remarks

In his exposition of the theory of biphasic (approach-withdrawal) mechanisms in the ontogeny of behavior, Schneirla (1965) began by saying: "In the evolution of behavior, operations which appropriately increase or decrease distance between organisms and stimulus sources must have been crucial for the survival of all animal types."

The above statement, as well as the major part of Schneirla's exposition, applies to the evolution and development of communicatory mechanisms. At the vegetative and trophic levels, growth and metabolic phenomena predominate. At the tonic and cellular levels, approach–withdrawal movements dominate. At the phasic and organismic levels, taxes and kineses are present and interactions become more closely tied to specific behavior patterns, although the underlying approach–withdrawal mechanisms can often still be observed. The signal level includes the development of approach-fixation (i.e., imprinting) and the increasing role of recent experiential factors. New forms of social interactions appear on the symbolic and language levels.

A developmental study is of basic importance in this levels approach to communication. Since there are virtually no paleontological data from which to draw conclusions on the evolutionary relationship of various forms of interaction, it is necessary to rely on morphological data for making phyletic comparisons. Although ontogeny does not recapitulate phylogeny, as shown by de Beer (1958) and others, ontogenetic similarities may indicate relationships. In behavior, developmental analysis is an important tool in elucidating phyletic relationships.

In this connection, I might add that this necessity for developmental analysis is easily overlooked and masked by an urge to label and classify. In testing some of the ideas contained in this chapter on my colleagues and

students, I found that the most common questions concerned the classification of this or that behavior in one or another of the proposed categories. Although perfectly valid, such questions are often unanswerable
because there is a lack of information on the origin and development of
the particular interactions. Indeed, many of the examples cited here are
categorized without this information and are, therefore, only tentatively
allocated. It is not the purpose of this schema to serve as a rigid taxonomy
of interactions but, rather, to assist in the analysis of interactions and
point up the need for developmental data in such analyses.

The concept of levels is pervasive and heuristic. It is based not on
arbitrary definitions or lines, but on solid evolutionary principles. The
entire scheme of phylogeny is based on a hierarchy of levels of organization; therefore, it seems appropriate to utilize this concept in helping organize the mass of data in the field of animal communication. The concept
can be extended to other areas of behavior that have evoked semantic
controversy, as, for example, learning and orientation.

Orientation of flatworms away from light, birds navigating across
seas, and salmon swimming up to their home stream have been compared
often using similar criteria. Actually these represent orientations at
different levels of organization, and a hierarchy of levels can be constructed comparable to that developed here for communication: simple
approach–withdrawal movements, kineses and taxes, compass reactions,
integration of temporal and spatial cues, etc.

The modification of behavior by experience includes phenomena commonly called learning. However, the alleged conditioning experiments
with flatworms involve an obviously different level of integration and
nervous system organization than the operation of a rat in a Skinner box.
It might well be that an application of the levels concept, together with a
solid dose of Morgan's Canon, is the kind of strong medicine learning
theory needs.

What I have tried to present here is a different way of looking at a
problem. Instead of applying linguistic principles or information theory
to all animal interactions (anthropomorphic approach), or applying the
assumption of innate taxes or drives to human communication (zoomor-
phic approach), I suggest we look at each species as a unique product of
natural selection in its own right. Its species-typical morphology, developmental pattern, physiology, behavior, and, indeed, its environment are
all part of the adapted, integrated whole. Any cross-phyletic comparisons
must be made with the differences in evolutionary history in mind, as well
as the concomitant differences in level of organization.

"The concept of integrative levels indicates to research biologists the
crucial aspects of their problems, the solution of which puts the known
facts into proper perspective by revealing the decisive element, the element
imparting the uniqueness to the phenomena under study" (Novikoff, 1945).

Acknowledgments

Support for preparation of this chapter was derived, in part, from a grant (GB-6565) from the National Science Foundation, Psychobiology Program. I also want to thank Mrs. Brigitte Cappelli for her bibliographical and secretarial assistance.

References

Alexander, R. D., 1960, Sound Communication in Orthoptera and Cicadidae, in: *Animal Sounds and Communication* (W. E. Lanyon and W. N. Tavolga, eds.), pp. 38–92, American Institute of Biological Sciences, Washington, D.C., Publ. No. 7.

Altmann, S. A. (ed.), 1967, *Social Communication Among Primates,* University of Chicago Press, Chicago.

Andrew, R. J., 1972, The information potentially available in mammal displays, in: *Nonverbal Communication* (R. A. Hinde, ed.), pp. 179–206, Cambridge University Press, Cambridge.

Blair, W. F., 1963, Acoustic behaviour of amphibia, in: *Acoustic Behaviour of Animals* (R.-G. Busnel, ed.), pp. 694–708, Elsevier, Amsterdam.

Blair, W. F., 1968, Amphibians and reptiles, in: *Animal Communication* (T. A. Sebeok, ed.), pp. 289–310, Indiana University Press, Bloomington, Ind.

Bogert, C. M., 1961, The influence of sound on the behavior of amphibians and reptiles, in: *Animal Sounds and Communication* (W. E. Lanyon and W. N. Tavolga, eds.), pp. 137–320, American Institute of Biological Sciences, Washington, D.C., Publ. No. 7.

Breder, C. M., Jr., and Rosen, D. E. 1966, *Modes of Reproduction in Fishes,* Natural History Press, New York.

Busnel, R.-G. (ed.), 1967, *Animal Sonar Systems,* NATO Advanced Studies Institute, Paris.

Busnel, R.-G., Moles, A., and Gilbert, M., 1962, Un cas de langue sifflée utilisée dans les Pyrennées françaises, *Logos* **5:** 76–91.

Carmichael, L., 1964, The early growth of language capacity in the individual, in: *New Directions in the Study of Language* (E. H. Lenneberg, ed.), pp. 1–22, M.I.T. Press, Cambridge, Mass.

Carpenter, C. C., 1963, Patterns of behavior in three forms of the fringe-toed lizards (*Uma*— Iguanidae), *Copeia,* **1963:** 406–412.

Cherry, C. 1957. *On Human Communication.* Wiley, New York.

de Beer, G., 1958, *Embryos and Ancestors,* 3rd ed., Oxford University Press, Oxford.

Dreher, J. J., and Evans, W. E., 1964, Cetacean communication, in: *Marine Bioacoustics,* (W. N. Tavolga, ed.), pp. 373–393, Pergamon Press, Oxford.

Dumortier, B., 1963, Ethological and physiological study of sound emissions in Arthropoda, in: *Acoustic Behaviour of Animals* (R.-G. Busnel, ed.), pp. 583–654, Elsevier, Amsterdam.

Ehrman, L., 1964, Courtship and mating behavior as a reproductive isolating mechanism in *Drosophila, Am. Zoologist* **4:** 147–53.

Evans, S. M., 1971, Behavior in polychaetes, *Quart. Rev. Biol.* **46:** 379–405.

Farkas, S. R., and Shorey, H. H., 1972, Chemical trail-following by flying insects: A mechanism for orientation to a distant odor source, *Science* **178:** 67–68.

Fraenkel, G. S., and Gunn, D. L., 1961, *The Orientation of Animals,* Dover, New York.

Gardner, R. A., and Gardner, B. T., 1969, Teaching sign language to a chimpanzee, *Science* **165:** 664–672.

Goodall, J., 1965, Chimpanzees of the Gombe stream reserve, in: *Primate Behavior,* (I. DeVore, ed.), pp. 425–473, Holt, Rinehart and Winston, New York.

74 — William N. Tavolga

Harlow, H. F., 1969, Age-mate or peer affectional system, in: *Advances in the Study of Behavior,* vol. 2 (D. S. Lehrman, R. A. Hinde, and E. Shaw, eds.), pp. 333–383, Academic Press, New York.

Hinde, R. A. (ed.), 1972, *Non-verbal Communication,* Cambridge University Press, Cambridge.

Hockett, C. F., 1961, Logical considerations in the study of animal communication, in: *Animal Sounds and Communication* (W. E. Lanyon and W. N. Tavolga, eds.), pp. 392–430, American Institute of Biological Sciences, Washington, D.C., Publ. No. 7.

Hodos, W., and Campbell, C. B. G., 1969, *Scala naturae:* Why there is no theory in comparative psychology, *Psychol. Rev.* 76: 337–350.

Hopkins, C. D., 1972, Sex differences in electric signalling in an electric fish, *Science* 176: 1035–1037.

Jay, P. C. (ed.), 1968, *Primates: Studies in Adaptation and Variability,* Holt, Rinehart and Winston, New York.

Kleerekoper, H., 1969, *Olfaction in Fishes,* Indiana University Press, Bloomington, Ind.

Köhler, W., 1925, *The Mentality of Apes,* Harcourt, Brace, New York.

Korzybski, A., 1948, *Science and Sanity,* 3rd ed., International Non-Aristotelian Library, Lakeville, Conn.

Lang, T. G., and Smith, H. A. P., 1965, Communication between dolphins in separate tanks by way of an electronic acoustic link, *Science* 150: 1839–1844.

Lanyon, W. E., 1961, The ontogeny of vocalizations in birds, in: *Animal Sounds and Communication* (W. E. Lanyon and W. N. Tavolga, eds.), pp. 321–347, American Institute of Biological Sciences, Washington, D.C., Publ. No. 7.

Lenneberg, E. H. (ed.), 1964, *New Directions in the Study of Language,* M.I.T. Press, Cambridge, Mass.

Lentz, T. L., 1968, *Primitive Nervous Systems,* Yale University Press, New Haven.

Lettvin, J. Y., Maturana, H. R., Pitts, W. H., and McCullough, W. S., 1961, Two remarks on the visual system of the frog, in: *Sensory Communication* (W. A. Rosenblith, ed.), pp. 757–776, M.I.T. Press and Wiley, New York.

Lissmann, H. W., 1963, Electric location by fishes, *Sci. Am.* 208: 50–59.

Lorenz, K. Z., 1966, *On Aggression,* Harcourt, Brace & World, New York.

Lyons, J., 1972, Human language, in: *Non-verbal Communication* (R. A. Hinde, ed.), pp. 49–85, Cambridge University Press, Cambridge.

MacKay, D. M., 1972, Formal analysis of communicative processes, in: *Non-verbal Communication* (R. A. Hinde, ed.), pp. 3–25, Cambridge University Press, Cambridge.

Marler, P., 1960, Bird songs and mate selections, in: *Animal Sounds and Communication* (W. E. Lanyon and W. N. Tavolga, eds.), pp. 348–367, American Institute of Biological Sciences, Washington, D.C., Publ. No. 7.

Marler, P., 1961, The logical analysis of animal communication, *J. Theoret. Biol.* 1: 295–317.

Naitoh, Y., and Eckert, R., 1969, Ionic mechanisms controlling behavioral responses of *Paramecium* to mechanical stimulation, *Science* 164 : 963–965.

Novikoff, A. B., 1945, The concept of integrative levels and biology, *Science* 101: 209–215.

Organ, J. A., and Organ, D. J., 1968, Courtship behavior of the red salamander, *Pseudotriton ruber, Copeia* 1968: 217–223.

Premack, D., 1971, Language in chimpanzee? *Science* 172: 808–822.

Roeder, K. D., and Treat, A. E., 1961, The reception of bat cries by the tympanic organ of noctuid moths, in: *Sensory Communication* (W. A. Rosenblith, ed.), pp. 545–560, M.I.T. Press and Wiley, New York.

Rosenblatt, J. S., 1971, Suckling and home orientation in the kitten: A comparative developmental study, in: *The Biopsychology of Development* (E. Tobach, L. R. Aronson, and E. Shaw, eds.), pp. 345–410, Academic Press, New York.

Salmon, M., 1965, Waving display and sound production in the courtship behavior of *Uca pugilator*, with comparisons to *U. minax* and *U. pugnax*, *Zoologica* **50**: 123–149.

Schaller, G. B., 1965, The behavior of the mountain gorilla, in: *Primate Behavior* (I. DeVore, ed.), pp. 324–367, Holt, Rinehart and Winston, New York.

Schneirla, T. C., 1949, Levels in the psychological capacities of animals, in: *Philosophy for the Future* (R. W. Sellars, V. J. McGill, and M. Garber, eds.), pp. 243–286, Macmillan, New York.

Schneirla, T. C., 1953, The concept of levels in the study of social phenomena, in: *Groups in Harmony and Tension* (M. Sherif and C. Sherif, eds.), pp. 52–75, Harper, New York.

Schneirla, T. C., 1959, An evolutionary and developmental theory of biphasic processes underlying approach and withdrawal, in: *Nebraska Symposium on Motivation* (M. R. Jones, ed.), pp. 1–42, University of Nebraska Press, Lincoln, Neb.

Schneirla, T. C., 1965, Aspects of stimulation and organization in approach/withdrawal processes underlying vertebrate behavioral development, in: *Advances in the Study of Behavior*, vol. 1 (D. S. Lehrman, R. Hinde, and E. Shaw, eds.), pp. 1–74, Academic Press, New York.

Schneirla, T. C., 1971, in: *Army Ants: A Study in Social Organization* (H. R. Topoff, ed.), W. H. Freeman, San Francisco.

Schneirla, T. C., and Rosenblatt, J. S., 1961, Behavioral organization and genesis of the social bond in insects and mammals, *Am. J. Orthopsychiat.* **31**: 223–253.

Sebeok, T. A., 1965, Animal communication, *Science* **147**: 1006–1014.

Sebeok, T. A. (ed.), 1968, *Animal Communication*, Indiana University Press, Bloomington, Ind.

Sebeok, T. A., Hayes, A. S., and Bateson, M. C. (eds.), 1964, *Approaches to Semiotics*, Mouton & Co., The Hague.

Shaw, E., 1960, The development of schooling behavior in fishes, *Physiol. Zool.* **33**: 79–86.

Shaw, E., 1961, The development of schooling in fishes. II, *Physiol. Zool.* **34**: 263–272.

Smith, W. J., 1965, Message, meaning, and context in ethology, *Am. Naturalist* **99**: 405–409.

Smith, W. J., 1969, Messages of vertebrate communication, *Science* **165**: 145–150.

Spieth, H. T., 1952, Mating behavior within the genus *Drosophila* (Diptera), *Bull. Am. Mus. Nat. Hist.* **99**: 395–474.

Tavolga, W. N., 1956, Visual, chemical and sound stimuli as cues in the sex discriminatory behavior of the gobiid fish, *Bathygobius soporator*, *Zoologica* **41**: 49–64.

Tavolga, W. N., 1962, Mechanisms of sound production in the ariid catfishes, *Galeichthys* and *Bagre*, *Bull. Am. Mus. Nat. Hist.* **124**: 1–30.

Tavolga, W. N., 1970, Levels of interaction in animal communication, in: *Development and Evolution of Behavior* (L. R. Aronson, E. Tobach, D. S. Lehrman, and J. S. Rosenblatt, eds.), pp. 281–302, W. H. Freeman, New York.

Tembrock, G., 1970, Probleme der Biokommunikation, *Biol. Rdsch.* **8**: 129–141.

Tinbergen, N., 1959, Comparative studies of the behaviour of gulls, *Behaviour* **15**: 1–70.

Thorpe, W. H., 1972, The comparison of vocal communication in animals and man, in: *Non-verbal Communication* (R. A. Hinde, ed.), pp. 27–47, Cambridge University Press, Cambridge.

van Hooff, J. A. R. A. M., 1972, A comparative approach to the phylogeny of laughter and smiling, in: *Non-verbal Communication* (R. A. Hinde, ed.), pp. 209–241, Cambridge University Press, Cambridge.

von Frisch, K., 1946, Die Tänze der Bienen, *Österreich. Zool. Z.* **1**: 1–48.

von Frisch, K., 1950, *Bees, Their Vision, Chemical Senses and Language*, Ithaca, New York.

Wenner, A. M., 1971, *The Bee Language Controversy*, Educational Programs Improvement Corp., Boulder, Colo.

Wilson, E. O., 1965, Chemical communication in the social insects, *Science* **149**: 1064-1071.
Wilson, E. O., 1968, Chemical systems, in: *Animal Communication* (T. A. Sebeok, ed.), pp. 75-102, Indiana University Press, Bloomington, Ind.
Winn, H. E., 1967, Vocal facilitation and the biological significance of toadfish sounds, in: *Marine Bio-acoustics,* vol. 2 (W. N. Tavolga, ed.), pp. 283-304, Pergamon Press, Oxford.
Yerkes, R. M., and Yerkes, A. W., 1929, *The Great Apes: A Study of Anthropoid Life,* Yale University Press, New Haven.
Yerkes, R. M., and Yerkes, A. W., 1935, Social behavior in infrahuman primates, in: *Handbook of Social Psychology* (C. Murchison, ed.), pp. 973-1033, Clark University Press, Worcester, Mass.

CHAPTER 4

Social and Pharmacological Influences on the Nonverbal Communication of Monkeys and of Man

Robert E. Miller

Department of Psychiatry
University of Pittsburgh
Pittsburgh, Pennsylvania

Nonverbal behavior is a pervasive aspect of the daily lives of animals and man (Argyle, 1969; Bonner, 1955). Yet we are but rarely and fleetingly aware of others' subtle signs of eye contact, facial expression, or posture in a social transaction that convey the important messages of attention, interest, affection, annoyance, etc. Even less do we attend to the nonverbal cues that we transmit during an exchange unless there is some special reason to impress or deceive the other. In a sense, nonverbal behavior is like the atmosphere around us. We depend on air for life but, for the most part, use it unthinkingly. It is only when one encounters some difficulty in breathing, say at high altitudes or in respiratory illness, or when some odorous contaminant is mixed with air, that we begin to attend to the atmosphere in which we swim.

Similarly, we are immersed in a sea of nonverbal communication. Our every encounter and our every utterance are accompanied by expressive nuances that tell others something about our momentary mood and our more enduring personality characteristics (e.g., Argyle, 1972). Over the course of time and repeated exposures, we determine whether another individual is generally friendly, happy, confident, and likable, or tense, unhappy, and distant. Dozens of minute expressive cues are integrated into a global impression, and we make friends or enemies, pick lifelong mates, and enjoy successful careers or suffer failures, in part at least, on the basis of our skills in sending and receiving appropriate nonverbal signals. These skills are so much a part of us and have been acquired so informally during childhood that we pay little conscious attention to nonverbal signals until, as in the case of the air we breathe, something unusual or unpleasant occurs. A stranger stares at us in a bus and we are annoyed and uncomfortable. A passing acquaintance holds our hand too long in a handshake, and we try to disengage, feeling embarrassed and offended.

Despite the importance and pervasiveness of nonverbal behavior, we know surprisingly little about the details of the phenomena. Part of the difficulty in studying nonverbal communication in man is simply that it is so much a part of us and our lives that it is extraordinarily difficult to step back a pace or two and examine it. As Goffman (1967, 1971), has repeatedly pointed out, the members of a society thoroughly comprehend the rules of appropriate behavior, although they are largely unwritten and unspoken. They behave in accord with those rules without giving them a thought. The scientist is also learned in these same rules and has accepted them without question since childhood—they are part of the "givens" of his situation—and, therefore, he is just as surprised as the layman to discover, for example, that predictable momentary eye contacts regulate the verbal exchanges in a conversation.

Until the past couple of decades, nonverbal behavior did not receive adequate scientific attention. Earlier attempts to investigate these phenomena had not been very successful because of both methodical and conceptual problems. Despite the early impetus provided by leading scientists, notably Darwin (1872), and the recognition and description of expressive features by artists and writers for centuries, early scientific experiments indicated that man was not very discriminating of the facial expressive cues of others and that distinctions could be made only in very gross and broad categories (e.g., Woodworth, 1938). After a flurry of such experiments early in this century, the study of nonverbal communication was largely abandoned for a period of almost 25 years. Then, for a variety of reasons, including the manifest success of the ethologists in detailing the rich and elegant patterns of social communication of a wide variety of animal forms, there was a resurgence of scientific interest in the study of nonverbal phenomena. The use of recent technical advances such as television, high-speed photography, sound spectroscopy, and computer search techniques (e.g., Ekman *et al.,* 1969) has materially aided research in the field and in the laboratory. Even more importantly, however, clever investigators from a variety of different scientific disciplines have devised ingenious experimental approaches that have begun to tease out some of the significant factors associated with and instrumental to nonverbal communication.

In the past 20 years, there has been an accelerating literature in the nonverbal field, both in animals and in man. Each success adds impetus to the search for more detailed and refined data. Much of the effort to date has concentrated on the description of specific cues in face, posture, and vocal qualities that transmit information about the affective tone of the sender and are utilized by both sender and receiver to pace and modulate the interaction. This work on cues is, by its very exploratory nature, quite difficult, but it has provided us with some of the most interesting and provocative data on nonverbal behavior. Whether the descriptions be of the genital displays of the squirrel monkey (Ploog, 1967), or the eye contacts among interacting humans (Argyle and Dean, 1965; Exline and Winters, 1965), the cue-seeking studies have enabled us to focus on particularly significant aspects of behavior that serve as nonverbal signals to conspecifics in the social milieu. While great progress has been made in cue identification, it is likely that considerable effort will be required to complete an exhaustive search for communicatively relevant behaviors in animals and man, and it will be slow work at best.

It is possible, however, while acknowledging that we don't know all of the encyclopedia of cue behaviors, to conduct investigations concerning the impact of nonverbal facility on the short- and long-term social capabilities of experimental subjects. A number of experiments have, for example, attempted to relate various pathological social–emotional conditions with aberrations in nonverbal behavior (Grant, 1972). While it is not yet possible to draw cause–effect relationships between nonverbal expressiveness and psychopathological behavior, it is likely that deviations from normal expressive patterns of behavior are often the manifest symptoms of disorder that are perceived by others in the social environment. While the social group may accept a limited amount of deviant or exaggerated behavior from members in certain and specified circumstances, for instance, at an alcoholic New Year's Eve party, where excessive and inappropriate verbal and nonverbal productions can be attributed to a chemical toxicity, habitual behavior of this kind is not well tolerated by the social group and the deviant individual may be considered "queer" or "crazy" and avoided by his social peers.

We have been engaged for a number of years in the investigations of the transmission and reception of nonverbal cues among groups of rhesus monkeys. Through a series of approximations, we have developed a method, "cooperative conditioning," which permits the systematic and controlled study of selected samples of facial expressiveness. This technique does not, however, lend itself to the study of the total repertoire of nonverbal behaviors that are utilized in the natural environment of these animals. Fortunately, the encyclopedia of primate behaviors in the field is gradually being accumulated and reported by many skillful and resourceful ethologists (e.g., Altmann, 1967; DeVore, 1965; Morris, 1967; Rosenblum, 1971). Thus, while those of us who work intensively on small segments of expressive behaviors in the laboratory are able to study in detail and with considerable experimental rigor the variables, both behavioral and physiological, that are associated with nonverbal interactions, our colleagues in the field provide us with the essential framework within which we can interpret our quantitative results. These joint efforts in the field and laboratory have, in only a few short years, afforded some insight into the richness and flexibility of the interactions of the individual with his social group and with the challenges of environmental pressure.

Cooperative Conditioning in Animals

The cooperative-conditioning method is merely a simple extension of the principles of instrumental conditioning. The subjects are trained to perform a simple instrumental response, such as lever pressing, on receipt of a conditioned stimulus in order to obtain reinforcement. In the monkey, such conditioning is rapid, and the animal can be trained to a rigorous criterion of conditioning within a few experimental sessions. It is convenient to obtain concurrent physiological measures during the conditioning process, since the subject is typically restrained during the conditioning sessions. When subjects have acquired the instrumental response to a predetermined criterion, one of the trained subjects is selected as the "stimulus" animal and another is designated the "responder." The stimulus monkey is placed in an experimental chamber and is provided with the appropriate conditioning stimuli and reinforcement devices, but it does not have access to the manipulanda that are required to perform the instrumental conditioned response (CR) to the stimulus presentations. The responder is placed in another experimental chamber that is remote from the stimulus animal to preclude vocal or olfactory contact between subjects during the experimental tests. The responder is equipped with the manipulanda for the instrumental response and the appropriate reinforcement devices, but has no access to the conditioning stimuli that indicate when a response is required. A closed-circuit television camera is focused on the head and face of the stimulus animal, and the picture is displayed on a television monitor located in front of the responder. Thus if the stimulus animal responds to delivery of a conditioned stimulus (to which he cannot make an appropriate instrumental response) with a visible facial expression that can be detected and correctly interpreted by the responder, the responder can perform the response leading to reinforcement for the pair of subjects. The stimulus subject knows when to make a response but cannot make it himself; the responder can make the response but doesn't know when to make it, unless he can read the expressive behaviors of his partner.

Our early experiments with cooperative conditioning revealed that the rhesus monkey is extremely effective in sending and receiving nonverbal cues. Trained monkeys placed in the paired communication network performed with no significant loss in efficiency relative to their performance when performing individually, and they were able to make significant discriminations of the facial expression of their stimulus partners from their very first exposure to the social cues (Miller *et al.*, 1962, 1963). It was demonstrated that the animals performed at higher levels when aversive, rather than positive, reinforcement was employed. Moreover, subjects' heart-rate responses to social cues were of the same general shape and magnitude as those obtained when they were exposed to the actual conditioning stimuli (Miller, 1971; Miller *et al.*, 1966). A study using 16-mm color film instead of television enabled us to determine specific sequences in the film that consistently triggered instrumental responses, providing an opportunity to isolate some of the discrete expressive changes that mediated the communication between animals (Miller, 1967, 1971).

Since it was clear that normal monkeys were highly skilled in the utilization of expressive cues in the cooperative-conditioning situation, the question arose as to whether deficits in this very important ability might be detected in "abnormal" subjects. Dr. Harry F. Harlow and his colleagues at the University of Wisconsin have repeatedly demonstrated that social isolation for the first 6 months to a year of life produces profound and persistent disturbances in the social, sexual, and emotional responses of the monkey. Such animals are clearly not normal in terms of almost every dimension of socially interactive behavior (e.g., Mitchell, 1968), although they do not appear to be severely damaged in terms of motor and learning capabilities (Harlow *et al.*, 1969). We have recently been able to demonstrate, however, that adult isolates are aberrant in their ingestive behavior, being both hyperphasic and hyperdipsic (Miller *et al.*, 1971). It is not known at this time whether the differences in nutritional intake are indicative of basic metabolic or biochemical disorders or whether they are a function of the animal's learning experiences during the period of isolation.

Through Dr. Harlow's generosity, we were able to secure some adult monkeys which had been subjected to total social isolation during their first year of life (Rowland, 1964). These animals, along with control subjects which had been captured in the wild, were subjected to cooperative-conditioning experiments. The data revealed that while the isolates were competent in acquiring instrumental conditioned responses to visual conditioned stimuli, they were totally incapable of utilizing expressive cues from either the normal subjects or fellow isolates in a cooperative-avoidance situation. Further, they proved to be defective in their own expressive responses so that even ferally reared subjects had considerable difficulty in perceiving and responding appropriately to isolate stimulus monkeys during the paired tests (Miller *et al.,* 1967). These data suggested that, at least in part, the bizarre social behaviors observed in social isolates may be a reflection of their total inability to process nonverbal messages from other monkeys and their defectiveness in transmitting adequate and recognizable nonverbal cues to others (Mason, 1961).

Effects of Psychoactive Drugs on Nonverbal and Social Behavior

Along with my colleagues, Drs. John Levine and I. Arthur Mirsky, I very recently embarked on a new series of studies on the nonverbal and group social behavior of the rhesus monkey. The purpose of these experiments was (1) to investigate the relationships between nonverbal behavior in the cooperative-conditioning paradigm and interactions in free social situations and (2) to attempt to determine the effects of selected psychoactive drugs on both nonverbal and social behaviors (Miller *et al.,* 1973). It was hoped that specification of drug-induced distortions of nonverbal behavior and group social interaction would help to identify crucial features of nonverbal behavior among undrugged subjects.

Three drugs were selected for initial study, one from each of the classes stimulant, tranquilizer, and psychotomimetic. Since there was no good method for determining equivalency of the dosages of three drugs in terms of their psychoactive effects, it was decided arbitrarily to determine the minimal dosage of the most potent agent and then to use that same dosage of the other agents. It is clear that this approach is fraught with hazards, depending on the particular pharmaceuticals employed, but it did provide a starting point for the studies and, of course, allowed empirically determined dosage adjustments if necessary. Actually, we were extremely fortunate in our selection of drugs and were able to complete our experiment without manipulating dosages during the course of the study. Phencyclidine hydrochloride (Sernyl), which is utilized as a cataleptic agent in infrahuman primates, was picked as the psychotomimetic. This drug has been shown to produce profound disorientation and psychotic-like behaviors in human subjects (e.g., Luby *et al.,* 1959). On the basis of prior experience and some preliminary testing of the drug, an intramuscular dosage of 250 μg per kilogram body weight was chosen as the standard dose of Sernyl. This dosage does produce some locomotor ataxia within 15 min of administration, but the treated animal is still able to move around the cage and to respond to physical stimuli with appropriate orientations. This same dosage of 250 μg/kg was also used for the stimulant, amphetamine sulfate, and the tranquilizer, chlorpromazine. The route of administration for each of the drugs was an intramuscular injection in the hip, and the vehicle for all drugs was sterile physiological saline. It should be noted that neither amphetamine nor chlorpromazine in the very small dosages employed in this study had any very obvious effects on the animals as far as the human observers were able to notice. There was no effect on motor behavior or coordination, general activity levels were not noticeably altered, and the monkeys responded to environmental stimuli normally.

The experiment was conducted in two replications of three animals each. The subjects were adolescent male rhesus monkeys. The animals had been born and reared in the wild. They had been in our laboratory colony for some 9 months and had been subjects in a brief classical conditioning study that had been terminated 6 months prior to the beginning of the present experiments.

The first phase of the experiment consisted of cooperative-conditioning tests. The subjects were lightly anesthetized and placed in primate restraining chairs. The restraint devices, adjusted to permit the maximum amount of freedom of movement, were checked daily to insure that the monkeys were maintained as comfortably as possible. A plate at thorax level could be tightened during the experimental sessions to prevent the subject from removing or disturbing the heart-rate electrodes attached to the sternum and left side of the rib cage. The thoracic plate was retracted to permit free movement of the arms, hands, and trunk except during the actual testing periods.

The monkeys were first trained to perform an intrumental avoidance response. The subject was moved in his restraint chair into the conditioning chamber. This room was equipped with a wooden tunnel mounted on a table so that it was at eye-level height to the seated subject (Miller *et al.*, 1966). The proximal end of the tunnel was open and was equipped with two 7-watt fluorescent lamps to illuminate the subject's head and face. At the distal end of the tunnel was an end-lighted lucite plaque that served as the conditioned stimulus (CS) and a television camera. The lens of the camera was inserted through a light-tight seal and projected into the tunnel beyond the CS plaque to preclude the possibility that the conditioned stimulus would be apparent on camera. The stimulus plaque was lit by a lamp embedded in a light-tight enclosure so that only a slit of light directly over the edge of the lucite plaque escaped. Thus the stimulus plaque was dimly but evenly illuminated during trial presentations. During the initial conditioning sessions, a bar was mounted on the restraint chair to provide a means of escape or avoidance. Shock was delivered to the subject through the metal seat of the chair and a metal chain that was attached to the animal's ankle just prior to the testing session. The shock level was 4 ma. Heart-rate electrodes were attached at the beginning of the session using a commercial electrode paste and a rubber strap attachment.

On the first 2 days of training, the experimental subjects were taught by successive approximations to press the bar on receipt of a mild shock. No conditioning stimuli were presented during these shaping days but 20 shocks were delivered to the animal, and the experimenter, observing responses through closed-circuit television, reinforced the subject for hand movements toward the bar, touching the bar case, or touching of the bar handle. All of the monkeys learned to press the bar within a few trials.

On each of the succeeding conditioning sessions, the monkey was placed in the conditioning room and the necessary attachments of manipulanda and electrodes were made. The experimenter then returned to the control room, allowed 5 min for the monkey's heart rate to return toward resting level, and then took a 1-min sample of heart rate. A tape programmer was then activated to begin the conditioning trials. A trial consisted of illumination of the stimulus plaque for a period of 6 sec, followed by delivery of shock to the leg until the subject pressed the response bar. The CS and shock were both terminated by the instrumental response, and a bar press during the initial 6-sec stimulus period turned the CS off and avoided the delivery of the shock stimulus. Twenty trials were presented each session at random intervals of 1 1/2–4 min. At the end of 20 trials, the tape programmer was switched off, and 3 min later a final 1-min sample of heart rate was obtained to conclude the session. A conditioning session lasted a total of 50 min. The three animals in a conditioning squad were kept in a separate room from both the rest of the primate colony and the conditioning apparatus when they were not being tested.

Conditioning sessions were continued daily until the animals met the acquisition criterion, namely, that significant avoidance discriminations were made to the CS without high rates of bar-pressing responses during the intertrial intervals for a period of 6 consecutive days (Miller *et al.*, 1967, p. 234). It would be possible, both in acquisition and in subsequent cooperative-conditioning tests, for a subject to emit a high rate of bar pressing throughout the session without regard to stimulus conditions and thereby effectively avoid shock. To insure that such was not the case, the total of intertrial responses in a session was divided by the number of 6-sec periods when the CS was *not* present and the resulting SRs/6 sec was multiplied by 20 to obtain an estimate of CRs that would have occurred simply as a function of intertrial responding. This figure of chance or "false" CRs was compared with observed CRs to determine if, in fact, a stimulus discrimination had been made. On achievement of the criterion, the subject was placed in the second test room, the responder's room, and required to meet the criterion there for 3 consecutive days. The responder's room was equipped for these transfer sessions only with a CS identical to that of the stimulus tunnel. The CS was then removed from the responder's room for all subsequent communications tests.

Heart-rate responses were taken throughout conditioning and all cooperative-conditioning sessions. On each trial, heart rate was measured during the 6-sec period preceding onset of the CS and for the 12-sec period following CS onset. The actual data for analysis consisted of counts of beats per 2-sec interval, a measure that provides a reasonable estimate of the shape of the accelerative and decelerative changes in cardiac rate without the necessity for complicated on-line computation.

When each of the three animals of a squad had met the acquisition criterion and the criterion for transfer to the responder's room, cooperative-conditioning tests were begun. One of the trained animals was selected as the stimulus monkey, and the remaining two partners served as responders. The stimulus animal was placed in the stimulus room and the appropriate electrode attachments were made. The stimulus animal was not provided with a response bar. One of the partners was placed in the responder's room and the necessary instrumentation was attached. The responder was provided with a bar and with a television monitor displaying the head and face of the stimulus monkey. When both subjects were prepared, the doors to the conditioning chambers were closed, and the experimenters returned to the control room to administer the test trials. As in conditioning sessions, 20 trials were administered in a 50-min testing session. On each trial, a 6-sec CS was presented, and a 4.0-ma shock was administered to both subjects if an instrumental avoidance response was not performed. At the end of the session, the responder was removed and the third monkey of the squad was hooked up and placed in the responder's position. Thus the stimulus monkey served as stimulus to each of his partners for 20 trials per day over a 10-day period. Then another member of the squad served as stimulus for each of his partners for 10 days, and finally the remaining member of the squad had his turn as stimulus for each of the others for 10 days.

On completion of the series of cooperative-conditioning tests, the drug studies were begun. One of the subjects was given an intramuscular injection of 250 μg per kilogram body weight of one of the test substances. Fifteen minutes later, the treated animal was taken to the stimulus room and prepared with electrodes for the cooperative-conditioning test. A second subject, which was not drugged, served as the responder to the treated stimulus monkey. A standard 20-trial session was then administered to the pair of subjects. The treated animal was then moved to the responder's room, the third member of the squad, which was also undrugged, was placed in the stimulus position, and a second cooperative-conditioning session of 20 trials was given. At least 2 days were allowed to elapse between injections to the same individual, and the order of drug administrations was counterbalanced so that each material was equally often administered as the first, second, or third treatment. Each subject received each of the three drugs being tested.

The animals were then returned to colony living cages for a rest period.

Six weeks later, they were given a series of social dominance tests within the squads of three in the Wisconsin General Test Apparatus. The dominance determinations, which took about a month to complete, will not be reported in detail here.

Finally, intrasquad social behavior was measured with the three animals living in a large cage that was removed from the colony quarters to prevent interactions and disturbances from other monkeys in the colony. The monkeys were placed together in the cage, and daily observations of their social behaviors were obtained. The experimenters entered the test room and sat as quietly as possible in chairs located 8 ft from the front of the cage. The only light in the room during testing periods came from a fluorescent fixture attached to the top of the cage so that observers were relatively dimly illuminated. After the first 2 or 3 days, the monkeys did not appear to be distracted by the experimenters and directed almost no attention to them during the hour-long observation period. A categorization device operated with microswitches was used to record the frequency and duration of some of the major behaviors of interest, e.g., present, mount, groom, threat, attack, and to denote which of the animals was the originator of the behavior and which was the recipient. The second experimenter kept a running written account of the social interchanges within the squad and tallied categories of behavior during the session. The first 15 min of the observation period was recorded only in general terms, and the data were not used in analyses. During the second 15–min period, one of the animals was the target for recording with the clock-counter device, then in turn each of the remaining two animals was observed for 15-min periods. The observation of the individual animals was arranged in predetermined random order so that all individuals were watched equally often in each 15-min observation period.

A 9-day drug testing period was then initiated. One of the monkeys was removed briefly from the social cage, injected with 250 μg/kg of one of the test subtances, and then returned to the cage with his two undrugged partners. As in the baseline period, only general observations were made during the first 15 min after the treated animal was returned to the cage. Then individual subjects were observed for 15 min each in exactly the same way as before with the single restriction that the treated monkey was always the target for observation during the second testing interval; i.e., one of the untreated subjects was observed for 15 min, then the treated animal, and, finally, the second untreated subject. Each of the subjects was given each of the test substances with at least a 2-day period intervening between consecutive injections. The order of administration of the agents was again counterbalanced so that each of the materials was given first to some animals, second to others, and last to some.

Psychoactive Drugs and Nonverbal Communication

The results of this lengthy and complex experiment were quite revealing regarding both the communication process itself and the interrelationships between communication and the group social behaviors. In accord with our earlier experiments, the present subjects acquired the initial avoidance discrimination with ease and displayed the typical cardiac accelerations to stimulus presentation that have been shown elsewhere (Miller, 1967, 1971). The performance of the 12 pairs of subjects during the cooperative-conditioning phase of the study was noteworthy only in that one of the subjects was an unusually ineffective stimulus animal. With animal 236 in the stimulus position, one responder, 231, actually inhibited avoidance responses during the CS periods, making only 8% avoidances with a chance expected level of 61%. The second partner (237) also had considerable difficulty in responding to 236 as the stimulus, showing only 63% avoidance responses while the chance expected level was 52%, and only two of the ten sessions achieved statistically significant levels of discrimination. If the data from the pairing, 236 sending to 231, are dropped, the remaining 11 pairs of subjects performed avoidances on 78% of the trials, and in 71% of all individual sessions there was a statistically significant discrimination; i.e., the responders made CRs during the CS periods without performing numerous intertrial bar presses. An analysis of the differences between CRs and the number of CRs that would have been expected as a function of the intertrial response rates indicated that these 11 pairs of monkeys performed significant ($p < 0.001$) discriminations on the basis of the expressive changes in head and face of the stimulus subjects. Analyses of heart-rate responses revealed that stimulus onset was accompanied by a cardiac acceleration during the 6-sec stimulus period and the 6-sec poststimulus period. The cardiac response of stimulus animals was significantly greater than that obtained when the monkeys were responders ($p < 0.01$).

The effects of the administration of psychoactive drugs on nonverbal communication in the cooperative-conditioning situation are shown in Fig. 1. An equipment failure during one of the drug tests reduced the N to five pairings rather than six. The data are plotted as medians rather than means because of some extreme scores in the Sernyl condition for chance expected CRs. That is, one stimulus animal which had received Sernyl elicited high rates of intertrial responses from a normal viewer and, similarly, one responder treated with Sernyl pressed the avoidance bar continuously during the testing session. The data on CRs did not appear to violate the assumptions of normality and were subjected to an analysis of variance pro-

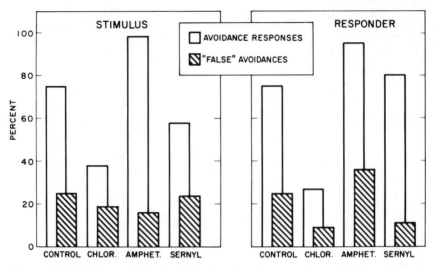

Fig. 1. Median percent avoidance behavior of monkeys in cooperative-avoidance conditioning as a function of drug treatments. "False" responses were calculated from intertrial responses and represent the number of CRs that would be expected by chance as a function of bar pressing in the absence of the CS.

cedure. There was a significant difference among treatments when the treated subject was the stimulus to undrugged partners ($p < 0.10$). The administration of chlorpromazine to a stimulus subject significantly impaired the performance of CRs by responders as compared with any of the other treatments ($p < 0.05$ in each case). A Friedman test was then applied to the data derived from the "clear signals," that is, the difference between the number of CRs and "false" responses, i.e., the number of CRs predicted on the basis of the responder's intertrial responses (Miller et al., 1962). The rate of intertrial responding during a session is probably determined by both spurious facial signals given by the stimulus animal and apprehension and "anxiety" of the responder. The difference between the number of observed CRs and chance expected CRs provides an estimate of the level of accurate communication between animals. The analysis of these data revealed that there was a significant effect on signal discriminability attributable to the treatments ($p < 0.05$), with amphetamine producing the sharpest and chlorpromazine the poorest discrimination.

An analysis of data obtained when the stimulus animal was untreated but the responder was drugged showed that there was an overall treatments effect ($p < 0.01$), and subsequent t tests indicated that the responders treated with chlorpromazine performed fewer CRs than with any of the other treatments ($p < 0.01$ in each case) and that the amphetamine-treated subjects produced more CRs than they did when given Sernyl ($p < 0.10$). The analysis of "clear" signals in treated responders did not achieve statistical significance.

Analyses were conducted on heart-rate data obtained from the three 2-sec periods preceding each trial and the three 2-sec periods commencing with onset of the CS. The 6 sec after stimulus were not included in the analysis, since in the event that communication was ineffective and avoidances were not performed, this period included the delivery of shock. Trend analyses conducted on the stimulus animals' heart rates (Fig. 2) revealed an overall treatments effect ($p < 0.01$), an overall change in heart-rate level as a function of time ($p < 0.01$), and a significant linear trend component in the treatments x time interaction ($p < 0.01$). Subsequent difference t tests of overall heart rates of stimulus animals in the four conditions indicated significantly higher levels in the chlorpromazine condition than in any of the other conditions ($p < 0.001$ in each case). A significant linear acceleration of heart rate over the six time periods was obtained in both the control ($p < 0.01$) and the amphetamine ($p < 0.01$) conditions. Neither chlorpromazine nor Sernyl produced a significant linear trend in heart rate.

Similar analyses on the heart-rate from drugged responders revealed

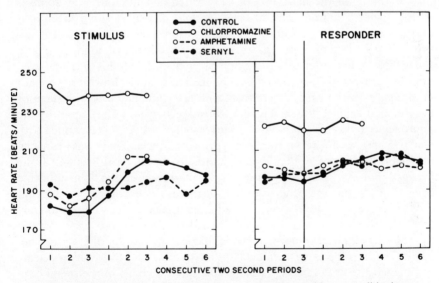

Fig. 2. Mean heart-rate response of monkeys in cooperative-avoidance conditioning as a function of drug treatments. Rates were obtained for three 2-sec periods preceding stimulus onset and for six 2-sec periods following stimulus onset. The vertical line in each of the panels represents onset of the CS. For conditions where communication was flawed and many shocks were delivered (e.g., chlorpromazine), the final 6 sec of cardiac rate is omitted in the figure.

overall effects due to treatments ($p < 0.05$), overall effects due to time periods ($p < 0.01$), and a linear trend component in the treatments x time interaction ($p < 0.01$). Again chlorpromazine-treated subjects had higher heart-rate levels than in each of the other conditions ($p < 0.001$ in each case), but none of the other treatments differed from each other. Control ($p < 0.001$), amphetamine ($p < 0.001$), and Sernyl ($p < 0.01$) conditions showed a significant linear trend in the heart rate from the prestimulus period to the stimulus period.

Psychoactive Drugs and Group Social Behavior

Although social behavior was observed and categorized during the initial 10-day period prior to the administration of the psychoactive agents, we have not included the data from the first 5 days in our analyses because the behaviors during this period are probably not representative in that the group structure was unsettled. The social observations from the second 5 days were quite stable and, accordingly, were used as the baseline against which drug effects were compared.

The injection of 250 μg per kilogram of body weight of Sernyl had a distinct effect on the behaviors of the treated and the untreated subjects in the social situation. The drugged animal displayed some locomotor ataxia within 15 min of injection and, in addition, made persistent approaches to his undrugged partners. The Sernyl-treated monkey would move directly toward a control animal, stare directly into his face, and even mouth the partner's head and face. The treated animals, however, were not at all aggressive toward the controls and never attempted to bite them or even defend against attack. The control subjects were visibly upset by the approaches and staring behavior of the treated monkey and responded with fear grimaces, escape responses, and aggressive attacks. There was less social interaction among all of the subjects in the squad, the controls as well as the drugged monkey, when any of the subjects had received the hallucinogenic drug (Fig. 3), but the proportions of aggressive behavior, especially that directed by controls toward the treated animal, increased by approximately 360% during sessions where one animal had received Sernyl.

The tranquilizer, chlorpromazine, did not manifestly affect gross behavior as far as the experimenters could determine, but the monkeys clearly detected the drug effects. The two untreated animals in the social cage interacted with each other during the testing sessions to the exclusion of the tranquilized monkey. Social exchanges between the two controls increased above baseline levels, while the treated animal was virtually ignored by his partners. The untreated subjects were not aggressive toward the animal with chlorpromazine but simply did not direct their social behaviors toward

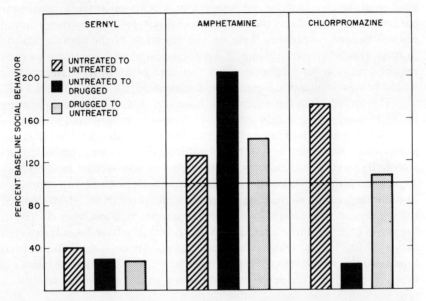

Fig. 3. The effects of drug treatments on group social interaction. The horizontal line represents average social behavior over the final five baseline periods. All categories of social interchange were added together for this figure so that the amount but not the quality of the exchanges can be compared. Behaviors are represented as a function of the initiator of the social interaction.

him. It was interesting to note that the tranquilized subject continued to maintain normal levels of initiated social interactions toward the controls, despite the fact that they did not reciprocate during the testing session.

The stimulant, amphetamine, had a particularly interesting effect on the group interactions. All social behavior was facilitated during the sessions where one of the animals had received 250 μg/kg of amphetamine. In particular, the treated animal appeared to be especially attractive to the untreated controls, and they increased behaviors directed toward the stimulated subject by some 200% (Fig. 3). When the treated subject had received amphetamine, the proportion of agonistic interactions within the groups diminished markedly to less than 10% of that observed during the baseline period.

Discussion

The present experiment was only the first in a series of studies that we have planned on the effects of psychoactive drugs on social communication and group interaction. We were probably very lucky in our choice of active agents and dosage levels, but results of this experiment have encouraged us to believe that further research may both enlighten us about the nature of the drug effects on complex social systems and, by distortion of normal behavior, shed new light on the essentials of the communication process. It is, of course, obvious that a great deal of additional work will be required on dose-level functions and there are many other materials that would be of considerable interest for investigation, e.g., alcohol and THC.

The present data have indicated, however, that social communication in the monkey is exquisitely sensitive to drugs commonly used by humans in both therapeutic and illicit situations. The results also revealed that in a group social situation the nontreated subjects detected and responded differentially to very subtle changes in the behavior of a treated monkey with augmented positive behavior in the case of amphetamine and with apprehension and aggression in the case of Sernyl. Chlorpromazine, which damped the expression and reception of affective communication, also elicited in the social group a marked decrease in the social attractiveness of the treated subject. Future investigations will, hopefully, provide additional information as to the relationships between facilitation or disruption of facial expressiveness in the cooperative-conditioning situation and the quality of ongoing social relationships within a group.

There have been several recent studies that have successfully employed the cooperative-conditioning method with humans. Both Lanzetta and Kleck (1970) and Buck et al. (1972) have reported a significant negative relationship between level of physiological response to stimulus onset and transmission of expressive cues. Jones (1935, 1960) distinguished between "externalizers," who manifest overt expressive changes with minimal physiological response, and "internalizers," who are covert in terms of expression but manifest large physiological changes in emotional situations. In addition, Lanzetta and Kleck (1970) have reported a significant negative correlation between the sending ability and the receiving ability of their subjects. Externalizers were effective transmitters of affect to others but relatively insensitive to the emitted cues from other individuals, while internalizers were poor senders but very sensitive responders to the expression of others.

We examined the data from the present monkey experiment and from a series of five previous squads of monkeys which had been subjected to cooperative-avoidance conditioning experiments. The data clearly revealed that some animals were especially good stimulus animals while others were very sensitive receivers of the expressions of others. Further, it was found that, as in humans, there is an inverse relationship between sending and receiving in the monkey (Table I). When one looks at the proportion of total sessions where a significant discrimination was made during the trial sequence, it may be seen that there is a marked difference between "good" and "poor" stimulus monkeys in the stimulus and responder roles. In each

Table I. Percent of Testing Sessions Statistically Significant for "Good," "Poor," and "Other" Stimulus Monkeys in Seven Squads of Animals Tested in Cooperative-Avoidance Conditioning[a]

	Percent significant sessions as stimulus	Percent significant sessions as responder
"Good" stimulus animals	78	27
"Poor" stimulus animals	26	75
"Other" stimulus animals	52	53

[a]A significant session required that the number of observed avoidance responses during trials significantly exceed the number of responses that would have occurred by chance as a function of intertrial bar-pressing responses (see Miller et al., 1962, pp. 344–345).

squad of animals, there was a third subject, called "other" in the analysis, which performed at about the same level as stimulus or responder. The "other" animal had an opportunity to respond to both the "good" and the "poor" member of his squad. The data from the present experiment revealed that the "other" animal very clearly discriminated between these two stimulus monkeys, achieving significant sessions on 90% of sessions to the "good" stimulus and 25% of the sessions to the "poor" stimulus. A χ^2 analysis of data from seven squads of animals confirmed ($p < 0.001$) that good stimulus animals were poor responders and poor stimulus animals were good responders. Thus there is an indication that man and monkey share the inverse relationship between expressiveness and the sensitivity to the expressions of others. An analysis of heart-rate data to determine if there was a similar correspondence between man and monkey regarding the phenomenon of "internalizer"–"externalizer" did not indicate that "good" senders responded less vigorously to the stimulus in terms of cardiac rate than did "poor" senders. Likewise, the monkeys did not differ significantly in heart-rate response when they were serving as responders. At least in terms of available data, there seems to be no support for the "internalizer"–"externalizer" distinction in monkeys.

Cooperative-Conditioning Experiments in Man

We have recently embarked on a series of studies on the variables associated with nonverbal expressiveness in man and the implications of communicative skills for successful interpersonal relationships. The co-operative-conditioning method has been modified for use with human subjects in order to provide a tool for the analysis of capabilities for sending and receiving of nonverbal cues in a standardized experimental situation. Lanzetta and Kleck (1970) have used cooperative-avoidance techniques with considerable success and have reported some important findings on the correlations between physiological responses and nonverbal variables. Gubar (1966) also employed a variation of the method in conjoint reward-avoidance study and was able to demonstrate that subjects who had been exposed to the conditioning situation themselves were able to respond appropriately to the facial expressions of others but that naive subjects were unable to discriminate reward from avoidance expressions of stimulus subjects during the 25-trial test phase. Unfortunately, no physiological responses were obtained in the Gubar studies.

A number of considerations arose when we decided to initiate our human studies. Since we wish to study relatively diverse groups of subjects, including children and patient populations, it was decided to attempt to work with reward situations rather than aversive reinforcements. The task itself was designed to be simple so that there would be no necessity for acquisition trials prior to the beginning of communications tests. And, finally, a plausible procedure was introduced for the stimulus subject so that he would be maximally involved in the task but would be unaware that he was serving as the stimulus subject for the other individuals in the experiment.

On the basis of these decisions, a slot-machine task was developed for use with monetary rewards. Stimulus subjects were placed in a comfortable chair facing the reward device. Heart-rate and PGR electrodes were attached to the subject and a three-bar response box was placed on the right arm of the chair. The subject was instructed to watch the "slot machine" and to attempt to discover how to obtain coins by pressing appropriate bars. A plastic sleeve contained 10 quarters and a second sleeve 10 pennies. Stimulus lights directly behind the sleeves were lit to indicate quarter or penny trials. A "correct" response dropped the appropriate coin into a "jackpot" chamber where successive rewards could build up to respectable amounts of money. A jackpot light was lit to indicate a "jackpot" trial and the subject was instructed that a correct response would release the accumulated coins into a chute where they would tumble into a transparent drawer and that, at the end of the session, they would be given to him. An incorrect response on a "jackpot" trial released the coins into an opaque, locked box where they would be lost to the subject. The instructions stated that a stimulus light would be illuminated for a period of 8 sec, that the subject could press any one of the three bars labeled A,B, or C at any time during the period when a light was on, and that the coin delivery, in the event that a correct response had been made, would occur simultaneously with the termination of the stimulus light.

Thus the stimulus subjects were confronted with a task that appeared to require problem-solving behavior in order to attain monetary rewards. The timing of the stimulus lights and the reward delivery was intended to elicit the active engagement of the subject for a period of at least 8 sec on each trial, and the use of the quarters, pennies, and jackpots was an attempt to manipulate the intensity of the subject's anticipatory behaviors.

In actual fact, of course, there was no problem-solving aspect to the task and the subject's bars were simply hooked to an event recorder. The scheduling of trials and reinforcements was controlled by the experimenters according to preselected programs. These schedules were designed to withhold more reinforcements during early trials than during the later trials, giving the subject the impression that he was learning correct bar-pressing sequences. The head and face of the stimulus subject were videotaped throughout the session through a concealed television camera with an audio channel on which the type of trial to be presented was noted by the experimenter and trial onset and duration were marked with a white noise. Physiological responses were taken 6 sec prior to the onset of a trial and for 12 sec starting with the stimulus onset.

Responders were shown the coin-delivery apparatus and were given a complete description of the task that had been presented to stimulus subjects. They were seated in a chair with the three-bar response device, which was now clearly labeled "quarter," "penny," and "jackpot." Their experimental room contained a coin-delivery device and a 20-inch television monitor. They were also instrumented for PGR and heart rate recording. The responders were instructed to attend to the videotaped faces of stimulus subjects presented on the monitor and to attempt, on the basis of facial expressive changes, to press the appropriate bar on any given trial. To provide additional information to the subject, the white noise that had accompanied each trial was delivered to the responder's room in synchrony with taped picture. Responders were given 6 sec following onset of the white noise to make a bar press. Only the first bar press was effective in producing reinforcements; any later responses to other bars were recorded on the event recorder but did not affect the reward, and any responses that occurred later than 6 sec after trial onset also had no effect on reinforcement. This latter contingency insured that the responder utilized only the anticipatory expressions of the stimulus subject and could not employ the expressions that occurred at 8 sec when the stimulus subject was reinforced.

The initial group of subjects tested in this experiment was composed of 13 junior medical students from a research seminar. Eight of the students were recruited as stimulus subjects, and all 13 of the students then served as responders. Each responder viewed, in a single session, a ten-trial segment of videotape of each of the eight stimulus subjects. Subjects were paid $2.50 per session for their participation in the experiment.

The eight subjects used as stimuli all believed they were engaged in problem-solving, so much so, in fact, that they argued vociferously that they had managed to find the solution to the task and were able to verbalize complex, rotating sequences of pressing bars A, B, and C. Thus the design of the trial sequences had been successful in leading the subject to believe that he had actually solved a problem. No stimulus subject had seen or even suspected that he was being videotaped, and all eight of them readily signed a release permitting the use of the tapes in further research.

Table II. Number of Correct Responses in Ten Trial Sequences of Each of Eight Videotaped Stimulus Subjects

Stimulus

Subject	1	2	3	4	5	6	7	8	Total
1	4	2	6*	7*	5	6*	2	6*	38
2	4	3	7*	3	7*	5	6*	5	40
3	6*	6*	6*	7*	7*	6*	7*	6*	51
4	6*	5	6*	5	5	6*	8*	4	45
5	3	5	3	2	7*	5	4	6*	35
6	1	7*	6*	4	4	7*	3	3	35
7	6*	3	4	0#	5	4	4	3	29
8	2	4	4	1	1	4	2	4	22
9	3	2	5	2	5	4	3	2	26
10	6*	4	4	1	5	8*	6*	3	37
11	5	4	3	2	6*	5	5	2	32
12	2	2	4	1	4	3	2	5	23
13	6*	3	5	2	4	5	3	3	31
Total	54	50	63	37	65	68	55	52	

Responder

*With three possible responses on each trial, six or more correct choices is significant beyond the 0.06 point.
#0 correct responses is significant beyond the 0.06 point, indicating below chance reception of nonverbal cues.

Much to our surprise, the responders performed exceedingly well in the nonverbal task. It was our initial feeling that medical students would be a relatively difficult group to use, in that they might be too suspicious, cynical, and sophisticated to fall for the relatively simple ploys used in the stimulus situation. With three possible responses (quarter, penny, or jackpot) on each trial, the binomial expansion with probabilities of $1/3$ for a correct choice and $2/3$ for an error, six or more correct choices in ten trials would be expected less than six times in a hundred by chance. The data from this experiment indicated that, of the 104 pairings tested, 30 achieved six or more correct responses (Table II). It can also be seen that there were large differences in the effectiveness of the eight stimulus subjects in terms of the ability with which responders were able to perform effectively. A difference t test between the performances of the 13 responders to the "best" and the "poorest" stimulus subjects was significant beyond the 0.001 level. Similarly, responders were markedly different from one another in terms of their ability to utilize cues from the videotaped expressions. Subject 3, for example, discriminated successfully on each of the eight stimulus subject tapes and was able to describe the kinds of cues that he utilized for each of the subjects. Subjects 8, 9, and 12, on the other hand, were poor responders and failed to perform at a significant level for any of the eight tapes that they viewed. Thus the cooperative-conditioning tests seem to discriminate well between individual subjects and to provide quantitative data that may lend itself to a variety of interesting experimental questions.

It should also be mentioned that an analysis of heart-rate data once again revealed that there was a significant negative relationship between expressiveness as a stimulus subject (as judged by the number of correct responses made by responders) and physiological response ($r = -0.71$). There was no significant relationship between physiological levels and performance as a responder. Also, on the basis of these preliminary data, there was no indication that the degree of familiarity or "friendship" among individual subjects was in any way related to their ability to utilize expressive cues; i.e., responders were no more accurate in their performance to videotapes of their close friends than they were to relative strangers.

Discussion

It should be clear that the human cooperative-conditioning experiment that I have described was designed only to make some preliminary tests of procedure and equipment. In fact, the data were much more interesting than we had anticipated, and the difficulties, which we had expected to encounter in testing a new procedure, were exceedingly minor.

It would appear that one could use this method to obtain reliable instrumental and physiological data on nonverbal processes in a number of experimental groups. We have proposed a number of questions that we believe the cooperative-conditioning method may help answer. Previous research has suggested that young adult women are more proficient transmitters and receivers of expressive cues than are young men (Buck et al., 1972). Men tend to be internalizers, and women are more apt to be externalizers. It has been proposed that the early socialization of the child may contribute to these adult differences (Jones, 1960; Lanzetta and Kleck, 1970), and the cooperative-conditioning method may prove useful in identification of age–sex differences in nonverbal fluency.

While there is now strong evidence for pancultural similarities in the facial expression of strong emotions (Ekman, 1971), there is also evidence that cultures differ in the display rules for nonverbal communication (Ekman, 1971; Eibl-Eibesfeldt, 1972; Scheflen, 1972), a question that would also lend itself to the present experimental model. Not only could one determine the accuracy of communication as a function of ethnic–racial congruence or disparity, but one could also investigate the potential ameliorative effects of integrating social experiences on the communicative systems.

There is a question concerning the learning of nonverbal capabilities as a function of interpersonal experience that would be most interesting to study. Do individuals engaged in close interpersonal relationships in their daily work learn to become more sensitive to the expressions of affect from others with whom they come in contact? Does the young psychiatric resident become more proficient at responding to nonverbal cues during his years of clinical experience? A related question, which is even more intriguing, is, Do individuals who are unusually skilled in the transmission and/or reception of nonverbal messages tend to elect and succeed in vocations that require such skills, e.g., sales, social work, psychiatry, while others who are less nonverbally fluent choose accounting, engineering, or pathology? Such questions are testable using the cooperative-conditioning method.

Finally, there is some evidence that flawed transmission and reception of interpersonal nonverbal capabilities are associated with certain of the psychopathological disorders (Grant, 1972; Vine, 1970) and in some psychosomatic diseases (Sapira et al., 1972). We intend to initiate further investigations of these disorders in the hope of characterizing the nature of the relationships between interpersonal perception and the pathological condition.

General Discussion and Summary

Despite the recent surge of interest in nonverbal communication, we still know very little about the details of the phenomena in man, almost nothing about how children learn to use expressive cues, and are virtually ignorant about the implications of nonverbal skills for the long-term success and happiness of the individual. It is abundantly clear, however, that many communicative expressions are exquisitely subtle (e.g., Ekman and Friesen, 1969), may in some cases be under autonomic rather than voluntary control (Hess, 1965), are, in general, not as consciously controlled and monitored as verbal behavior (Argyle, 1969), and deal largely with affective rather than symbolic or cognitive responses (Ekman *et al.,* 1972).

The present experiments were designed to investigate variables that affect nonverbal communications and to relate individual nonverbal fluency with social and physiological performances. Drugs that affect the transmission and/or reception of affective expressions between animals were also found to alter group social patterns. Undrugged subjects responded to treated animals in the social situation differentially depending on the agent that had been injected. The stimulant enhanced nonverbal communication and made the treated animal very socially attractive to his undrugged partners. Chlorpromazine, which dampened expressiveness, elicited rejection from social partners, and the hallucinogen almost completely wiped out social interaction between normals and drugged subjects. Most of us have, at one time or another, observed similar phenomena in man as, for example, the social aversion manifested toward a drunk on the street or on a public vehicle. It is our conviction that experiments of this sort may provide information about the pharmacological effects of drugs that affect the central nervous system, and, as well, shed some light on the nature of the nonverbal and social processes.

The second experiment that I have described may afford a simple, precise, and rapid method for the assessment of nonverbal skills in human subjects. It provides for physiological measures which accompany the social process so that correlations may be obtained between overt expressiveness and internal arousal responses. It is hoped that the application of the cooperative-conditioning paradigm to questions concerning human nonverbal communication will permit the investigation of some important and fundamental questions regarding the acquisition of such fluency and implications of interpersonal sensitivity for the individual in the social group.

Acknowledgments

The experimental investigations reported in this paper were supported by a research grant (MH-00487) from the National Institute of Mental Health, United States Public Health Service, and by the Commonwealth of Pennsylvania.
I would like to express my sincere appreciation to the several col-

leagues who have participated in various phases of this research program. Dr. I. A. Mirsky has supported and contributed to the investigations of nonverbal behavior since the inception of the program. Dr. John M. Levine, of the Department of Psychology, University of Pittsburgh, has been a valued colleague in the two experiments that are detailed in the paper.

References

Altmann, S. (ed.), 1967, *Social Communication Among Primates*, University of Chicago Press, Chicago.

Argyle, M., 1969, *Social Interaction*, Methuen, London.

Argyle, M., 1972, Non-verbal communication in human social interaction, in: *Non-verbal Communication* (R. A. Hinde, ed.), Cambridge University Press, Cambridge.

Argyle, M., and Dean, J., 1965, Eye-contact, distance, and affiliation, *Sociometry* **28**: 289–304.

Bonner, J. T., 1955, *Cells and Societies*, Princeton University Press, Princeton, N.J.

Buck, R. W., Savin, V. J., Miller, R.E., and Caul, W. F., 1972, Communication of affect through facial expressions in humans, *J. Pers. Soc. Psychol.* **23**: 362–371.

Darwin, D. R., 1872, *The Expression of the Emotions in Man and Animals*, John Murray, London.

DeVore, I. (ed.), 1965, *Primate Behavior*, Holt, Rinehart and Winston, New York.

Eibl-Eibesfeldt, I., 1972, Similarities and differences between cultures in expressive movements, in: *Non-verbal Communication* (R. A. Hinde, ed.), Cambridge University Press, Cambridge.

Ekman, P., 1971, Universals and cultural differences in facial expressions of emotion, in: *Nebraska Symposium on Motivation, 1971* (J. Cole, ed.), University of Nebraska Press, Lincoln, Neb.

Ekman, P., and Friesen, W. V., 1969, Nonverbal leakage and clues to deception, *Psychiatry* **32**: 88–105.

Ekman, P., Friesen, W. V., and Taussig, T., 1969, VID-R and SCAN: Tools and methods in the analysis of facial expression and body movement, in: *Content Analysis* (G. Gerbner, O. Holsti, K. Krippendorff, W. Paisley, and P. Stone, eds.), Wiley, New York.

Ekman, P., Friesen, W. V., and Ellsworth, P., 1972, *Emotion in the Human Face: Guidelines for Research and an Intergration of Findings*, Pergamon Press, New York.

Exline, R., and Winters, L. C., 1965, Affective relations and mutual gaze in dyads, in: *Affect, Cognition, and Personality* (S. Tomkins and C. Izard, eds.), Springer, New York.

Goffman, E., 1967, *Interaction Ritual*, Doubleday, New York.

Goffman, E., 1971, *Relations in Public*, Harper and Row, New York.

Grant, E. C., 1972, Non-verbal communication in the mentally ill, in: *Non-verbal Communication* (R. A. Hinde, ed.), Cambridge University Press, Cambridge.

Gubar, G., 1966, Recognition of human facial expressions judged live in a laboratory setting, *J. Pers. Soc. Psychol.* **4**: 108–111.

Harlow, H. F., Schlitz, K. A., and Harlow, M. K., 1969, Effects of social isolation on the learning performance of rhesus monkeys, in: *Proceedings of the Second International Congress of Primatology*, Vol. 1, *Behavior* (C. R. Carpenter, ed.), pp. 178–185, Karger, Basel.

Hess, E. H., 1965, Attitude and pupil size, *Sci. Am.* **212**: 46–55.

Jones, H. E., 1935, The galvanic skin reflex as related to overt emotional expression, *Am. J. Psychol.* **47**: 241–251.

Jones, H. E., 1960, The longitudinal method in the study of personality, in: *Personality Development in Children* (I. Iscoe and H. W. Stevenson, eds.), University of Texas Press, Austin.

Lanzetta, J. T., and Kleck, R. E., 1970, Encoding and decoding of nonverbal affect in humans, *J. Pers. Soc. Psychol.* **16:** 12–19.

Luby, E. D., Cohen, B. D., Rosenbaum, G., Gottlieb, J. S., and Kelley, R., 1959, Study of a new schizophrenomimetic drug—Sernyl, *Arch. Neurol. Psychiat.* **81:** 363–369.

Mason, W. A., 1961, The effects of social restriction on the behavior of rhesus monkeys. II. Tests of gregariousness, *J. Comp. Physiol. Psychol.* **54:** 287–290.

Miller, R. E., 1967, Experimental approaches to the autonomic and behavioral aspects of affective communication in rhesus monkeys, in: *Social Communication Among Primates* (S. Altmann, ed.), University of Chicago Press, Chicago.

Miller, R. E., 1971, Experimental studies of communication in the monkey, in: *Primate Behavior: Developments in Field and Laboratory Research,* Vol. 2 (L. Rosenblum, ed.), Academic Press, New York.

Miller, R. E., Banks, J. H., and Ogawa, N., 1962, Communication of affect in "cooperative conditioning" of rhesus monkeys, *J. Abnorm. Soc. Psychol.* **64:** 343–348.

Miller, R. E., Banks, J. H., and Ogawa, N., 1963, The role of facial expression in "cooperative-avoidance" conditioning in monkeys, *J. Abnorm. Soc. Psychol.* **67:** 24–30.

Miller, R. E., Banks, J., and Kuwahara, H., 1966, The communication of affects in monkeys: Cooperative reward conditioning, *J. Genet. Psychol.* **108:** 121–134.

Miller, R. E., Caul, W. F., and Mirsky, I. A., 1967, The communication of affects between feral and socially isolated monkeys., *J. Pers. Soc. Psychol.* **7:** 231–239.

Miller, R. E., Caul, W. F., and Mirsky, I. A., 1971, Patterns of eating and drinking in socially-isolated rhesus monkeys, *Physiol. Behav.* **7:** 127–134.

Miller, R. E., Levine, J. M., and Mirsky, I. A., 1973, The effects of psychoactive drugs on nonverbal communication and group social behavior of monkeys, *J. Pers. Soc. Psychol.* **28:** 396–405.

Mitchell, G. D., 1968, Persistent behavior pathology in rhesus monkeys following early social isolation, *Folia Primatol* **8:** 132–147.

Morris, D., 1967, *Primate Ethology,* Aldine, Chicago.

Rosenblum, L. A. (ed.), 1971, *Primate Behavior: Developments in Field and Laboratory Research,* Academic Press, New York.

Rowland, G. L., 1964, The effects of total social isolation upon learning and social behavior in rhesus monkeys, unpublished doctoral dissertation, University of Wisconsin.

Sapira, J. D., Scheib, E. T., Moriarty, R., and Shapiro, A. P., 1972, Differences in perception between hypersensitive and normotensive populations, *Psychosom. Med.* **33:** 239–250.

Scheflen, A. E., 1972, *Body Language and the Social Order,* Prentice-Hall, Englewood Cliffs, N.J.

Vine, I. 1970, Communication by facial-visual signals, in: *Social Behaviour in Birds and Mammals* (J. H. Crook, ed.), Academic Press, London.

Woodworth, R. S., 1938, *Experimental Psychology,* Holt, New York.

CHAPTER 5

Pheromonal Sex Attractants in the Norway Rat

W. J. Carr

Beaver College
Glenside, Pennsylvania

Beginning with the work of Calvin Stone (1922, 1923), considerable research effort has been directed toward an understanding of the role of olfaction in the regulation of social behavior among rodents. Recently, this effort gained impetus from the fascinating new concept of pheromonal communication. Pheromones are those substances emitted by animals that, via chemoreception, influence the behavior of conspecifics either directly by operating on neuroeffector mechanisms (releaser pheromones) or indirectly by triggering a chain of neurohumoral events (primer pheromones). In one or more species of Rodentia, releaser pheromones enable recipients to respond discriminatively to a number of attributes of the animal emitter, including location, species, strain, sex, level of development, state of sexual readiness, membership in one of several local groups, emotional state, and even its personal identity (Archer, 1968; Bronson, 1972; Calhoun, 1962; Wilson, 1968; Mykytowycz, 1970). Moreover, pheromones are known to influence a variety of social interactions, e.g., aggregation, mating, parent–young interactions, and the agonistic behavior associated with territoriality and dominance hierarchies (Barnett, 1964; Ropartz, 1968; Whitten, 1966). Presumably, pheromones involve communication because they allow recipient animals to predict the emitter's subsequent behavior and adjust accordingly (Haldane, 1955, p. 386; Smith, 1969). The literature on pheromonal communication in rodents is massive, and I'll not attempt to summarize all of it. Rather, I will concentrate on the pheromonal control of mating behavior. Recent general reviews are available (Wilson and Bossert, 1963; Gleason and Reynierse, 1969; Whitten and Bronson, 1970; Bronson, 1972; Cheal and Sprott, 1971; Eisenberg and Kleiman, 1972; Schultz and Tapp, 1973).

It is true that olfaction is not essential to mating behavior in rats.[1] Although they are less active than normal animals, male rats rendered anosmic continue to copulate (Stone, 1922, 1923; Beach, 1942; Heimer and Larsson, 1967; Bermant and Taylor, 1969). Further, anosmic female rats continue to cycle and exhibit lordosis (Rosen et al., 1940; Aron et al., 1970; Moss, 1971). However, in all of these studies, mating behavior was observed after placing the partners in close proximity. While these observations are important, they tell us little about the role played by olfaction in the intact animal living in a more natural environment (Beach, 1951, p. 396; Ewer, 1971).

Calhoun (1962, pp. 152–158) described the precopulatory phase of the mating pattern of wild rats living in a seminatural environment. Beginning the night before she becomes receptive, the female ranges farther than normally from her home burrow, dispersing her scent by rubbing the anogenital region on trees, rocks, and other objects along trails, and also on the ground outside of burrows. These scent posts are examined by males and may provide the basis for tracking the female to her home burrow. Therefore, it seems likely that odors from receptive females may be utilized by males for sexual rapprochement. More importantly, the observations suggest that rapprochement itself is an integral part of the mating pattern. Most laboratory studies on sexual behavior in rats short-circuit the rapprochement portion of the pattern by placing the potential sex partners in close proximity.

My aim is to summarize the research bearing on a relatively specific question: Among Norway rats (*Rattus norvegicus*), do odors from potential sex partners serve as sex attractants and, if so, under what conditions are they effective? Included among these conditions are the sex, gonadal state, and social history of the recipient animal. I will also discuss some of the research aimed at identifying the anatomical source(s) of pheromonal sex attractants in rats, as well as the neural substrate mediating their odor preference behavior. Along the way, I'll point to some of the major gaps in our knowledge and to flaws inherent in the techniques we use to study pheromonal sex attractants.

At the outset, let me define the term *pheromonal sex attractant* and then discuss the techniques used to study it. Strictly speaking, a pheromonal

---

[1] The copulatory pattern of the male and the female survives olfactory bulb ablation in most mammalian species tested, including mouse, guinea pig, rabbit, sheep, cat, and dog. Curiously, the copulatory pattern of the male golden hamster is completely eliminated by olfactory bulb ablation (Murphy and Schneider, 1970).

sex attractant is not what its name may imply—it is not the chemoreceptive stimulus that differentiates the males from the females of a given species. Rather, as I define the term, a pheromonal sex attractant is the chemoreceptive stimulus that differentiates the sexually active from the sexually inactive members of a given sex, which evokes an approach response on the part of conspecifics of the opposite sex. This "approach response" may take either of two forms. It may be direct, as in the case of gradient-oriented behavior, akin to a positive chemotaxis. Alternatively, the "approach response" may be indirect, as in the case of an increase in exploratory behavior, akin to locomotor arousal. As we shall see, pheromonal sex attractants may also influence the behavior of members of the same sex as the emitter. Sex attractants may even produce neurohumoral changes in the recipient animal, as in the case of primer pheromones, but I'll not discuss these primer effects (see Purvis and Haynes, 1972). Presumably, pheromonal sex attractants are adaptive because they allow for rapprochement of potential sex partners from a distance with a minimum of effort and danger. But these attractants may also play a role in other kinds of social interactions, including the agonistic behavior associated with territoriality and dominance hierarchies. Such phenomena suggest a nonreproductive function of sexuality (Telle, 1966; Wickler, 1972).

How does one demonstrate the existence of a pheromonal sex attractant? For example, how does one prove that male rats are responsive to such a sex attractant emitted by females? It seems to me that the ultimate proof depends on the outcome of a verification experiment having three essential features: First, the experiment must demonstrate that the males respond differentially to two test-objects (presented simultaneously or successively) which are equivalent in all respects except that one possesses the suspected attractant and the other does not. The differential response must be such that the males end up in closer proximity to the test object possessing the suspected sex attractant than to the one which does not. However, the word "attractant" implies an absolute as well as a relative preference, and the verification experiment must demonstrate both types of preference. For example, to qualify as a pheromonal sex attractant, the receptive female odor must not only be preferred over the nonreceptive female odor (a relative preference), but the receptive female odor must also be preferred over "no odor" (an absolute preference). (This will be discussed later.)

Second, to establish some material as a pheromonal sex attractant, the verification experiment must demonstrate that the external control of the males' differential response is mediated exclusively via chemoreception, although in real life other sense modalities may also be involved in sexual rapprochement. Third, the males' differential response must be similar both in its typology and in its ontogeny to the way males react to the odors from sexual partners in the natural environment. This last requirement excludes the use of standard discrimination-learning techniques commonly used in the laboratory as proof of the existence of a pheromonal sex attractant. The fact that males can be trained, via operant or classical procedures, to discriminate between the odors from receptive versus nonreceptive females does not prove that the receptive female odor operates as an attractant in nature. In short, I am saying that the dependent variable of the verification experiment should be at least a reasonable approximation to the species-characteristic response to the female sex attractant. This discussion of the essential requirements of the verification experiment may strike some as being overly precise, but much of the literature on pheromonal communication is marred by faulty research methods (Jacobson, 1965, Chapter 2).

Of course, an animal cannot possibly respond preferentially to one of two odors unless it can discriminate between them. However, Carr and Caul (1962) showed that both normal and castrated male rats can be trained to discriminate between the odors from receptive versus nonreceptive females if the males are made thirsty and then rewarded with water for responding discriminatively to the two odors in a Y-maze. Similarly, both receptive and nonreceptive females can be trained to discriminate between the odors from normal versus castrated males. Carr et al. (1962) showed that the olfactory threshold for receptive female urine is uninfluenced by castration of male rats, and Dissinger and Carr (unpublished data) showed that olfactory bulb ablated males cannot discriminate between the odors from receptive versus nonreceptive females. With these findings in hand, the way is open for an experimental analysis of the rat's reaction to pheromonal sex attractants with little fear that olfactory sensitivity, per se, is influenced by the animal's gonadal state at the time of preference testing.

The Responses of Male Rats to the Female Sex Attractant

To my knowledge, Jacques Le Magnen (1952) was the first to demonstrate that female rats emit an odor serving as a sex attractant to males. He allowed sexually naive males to run to either arm of a T-maze, one containing the receptive female odor and the other the nonreceptive female odor. Le Magnen found that adult males which are sexually naive prefer the odor of receptive females—about two-thirds of his males chose the arm from which that odor flowed. Moreover, he reported that prepubertal or castrated males show no preference for either odor unless they receive exogenous testosterone. Thus Le Magnen's findings indicate that the preference for the receptive female odor requires the male gonadal hormone but not previous sexual experience. This conclusion is supported by Pranzarone (1969) and by Hitt *et al.* (1970).

Using a T-maze identical to Le Magnen's, Nodine (1959) and Carr (unpublished data) each tried but failed to demonstrate that naive adult males prefer the receptive over the nonreceptive female odor. Since then, a number of workers using a variety of odor preference techniques have also failed to show such a preference in naive males (Keesey, 1962; Carr *et al.*, 1965; Stern, 1969; Lydell and Doty, 1972; Yee and Carr, unpublished data). However, all of these workers did report that sexually experienced males prefer the receptive over the nonreceptive female odor. This brings me to the first gap in our knowledge concerning sex attractants in rats. We still don't know for certain whether the males' preference for the receptive female odor does or does not require previous sexual experience. I shall return to this issue later.

My collaborators and I have since abandoned the T-maze as the site for odor preference testing in favor of the subject's more familiar home

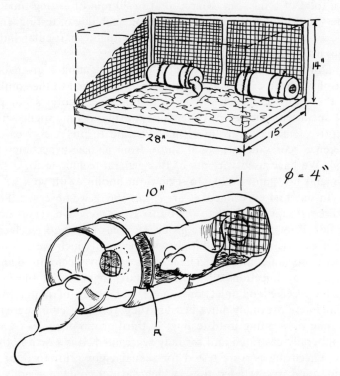

Fig. 1. The odor preference testing situation in *S*'s home cage and an enlarged view of the container housing the odorant animal. The odorant animal was not present in the container during testing.

cage, on the grounds that at least sexually experienced animals are most likely to exhibit preferences for sex attractants at the site where they received their sexual experience. Although our technique has changed slightly over the years, the general procedure is as follows: Just before testing, the four resident males are removed from their home cage and two disposable cardboard containers are installed as shown in Fig. 1. In our earliest study, one of these containers housed a receptive female and the other a nonreceptive female. The construction of the containers was such that the male subjects could smell the females housed inside, but not see or touch them. Later, we used empty containers that had previously housed receptive or nonreceptive females for 1 hr before testing, thus eliminating possible auditory cues. A small amount of clean sawdust remained in the containers to absorb bodily odors including urine and feces left by the females.

With the containers in place, one male at a time is returned to the home cage for a 5-min test, during which we record the number of seconds S spends investigating each container. This procedure is repeated daily for a total of 6 days, making a total of 30 min of testing time. New containers and different females are used on each day of testing. Incidentally, none of the males had ever cohabited with the particular individual females used during testing.

During a test, an S is said to be investigating a given odor if any part of S's head extends inside the atrium attached to the container housing the odor. For each animal, the difference score is computed (i.e., time spent with the receptive female odor minus time spent with the nonreceptive female). A group of males is said to prefer a given odor if the difference scores depart significantly from chance expectancy (Wilcoxon tests). We have used variants of this general technique for a score of experiments now, and I'd like to review our findings with you.

In our first experiment (Carr et al., 1965), we observed the responses of three groups of males to the odors from receptive versus nonreceptive females. Prior to testing, one group of males ($N = 29$) received extensive sexual experience by cohabiting with females which were sometimes receptive and sometimes not. The females were ovariectomized and rendered receptive by injections of estradiol and progesterone; the nonreceptive females received oil injections. A second group of males ($N = 24$) remained heterosexually naive because they were housed in segregation from the time of weaning until testing. A third group of males ($N = 23$) were prepuberally castrated and sexually segregated. It is worth noting that the experienced males were tested for sexual vigor prior to odor preference testing, and we excluded those which did not copulate readily. However, we did not screen the sexually naive males for sexual vigor. It is also worth noting that our sexually experienced males were what we call "polygamous" and possessed *savoir faire*. They were polygamous in the sense that they had earlier copulated with a number of different female partners and had *savoir faire* in the sense that they had the opportunity to learn that some females will readily accept sexual advances (i.e., those receiving ovarian hormones) and some will not. Some researchers (e.g., Pranzarone, 1969) use only "monogamous" males in the sense that they receive all of their experience with but one female; others (e.g., Stern, 1969) use males which have no *savoir faire* because they have access only to receptive females. These procedural differences might be responsible for the conflicting findings I will describe.

During the 30-min test as a whole, the sexually experienced males showed a reliable preference ($p < 0.05$) for the receptive over the nonreceptive female odor, but the sexually naive males and the prepubertal castrates showed no reliable preference for either feminine odor. These results indicate that the preference for the female sex attractant requires that the males be both sexually experienced and gonadally normal at the time of testing. Moreover, the experienced males spent significantly more time ($p < 0.05$) than the naive or castrated males investigating the nonreceptive as well as the receptive female odor. In other words, experienced males were more responsive to feminine odors, regardless of the female's sexual state.

Now it is possible that the sexually naive males or the prepubertal castrates actually exhibited a reliable preference for the female sex attractant during the early portion of the 30-min test but that the preference dissipated with increased testing time and disappeared completely at the end of 30 min. Such an effect, analogous to stimulus satiation, might well occur in animals with a weak preference at the outset. Therefore, we analyzed our data by cumulative 5-min periods. The sexually experienced males exhibited a reliable preference at each of the six 5-min periods, but the naive males and the castrated males exhibited no reliable preference at any of the six periods.

Several control tests had to be conducted before the results of the main experiment could be interpreted properly. In the first place, since the receptive and nonreceptive females were actually present during testing, the apparent preference for the sex attractant could have been due to auditory or vibratory cues. Therefore, we tested an additional group of seven experienced males with containers that were empty at the time of testing but had earlier housed receptive or nonreceptive females. These males showed a reliable preference ($p < 0.05$) for the receptive female odor. Incidentally, we now use the "empty container" technique routinely.

Second, it may be that naive or castrated males also prefer the receptive over the nonreceptive female odor, but only if the females are in their natural receptive or nonreceptive state—recall that our females were

ovariectomized and received exogenous ovarian hormones or oil. Therefore, we tested an additional group of 17 naive males, using as odorant
animals females which were naturally receptive or nonreceptive. These
naive males showed no reliable preference for either feminine odor during the 30-min test, nor did they at any of the 5-min intervals within the
30-min test. Therefore, under the present testing conditions, naive males
appear to be indifferent to the odors from receptive versus nonreceptive
females, whether their hormonal state is *au naturelle* or regulated by
exogenous ovarian hormones.

Finally, our main experiment provided no information about the response to the female sex attractant by sexually experienced males which
were castrated prior to odor preference testing. It is known that adult males
continue to copulate for some time after surgery (Beach and Holz-Tucker,
1949). Therefore, we tested two additional groups of sexually experienced
males; one group ($N = 19$) was castrated 2 months prior to odor preference testing, while the other group ($N = 17$) remained normal (Carr
et al., 1966). Further, we took the precaution of sex-testing all of these
males shortly after their period of cohabitation and prior to surgery, and
we excluded those males lacking in sexual vigor.

The results of this experiment showed that sexually experienced males
which are gonadally normal at the time of testing prefer the female sex
attractant ($p < 0.01$) but that equally experienced males which have been
castrated 2 months prior to testing exhibit no reliable preference for either
feminine odor. Moreover, intact males spend significantly more time
($p < 0.05$) investigating each type of feminine odor than do castrates,
suggesting that intact males are more responsive to feminine odors in
general.

Admittedly, it is a bit difficult to piece together the results of these
several experiments, but we are led to the following conclusion: Using
our odor preference techniques, only gonadally normal males which earlier
availed themselves of the opportunity to mate with females prefer the receptive over the nonreceptive female odor. Normal males which are sexually naive and castrated males show no reliable preference. Thus the male's
preference for the female sex attractant requires both prior sexual experience and circulating androgen at the time of testing. We also conclude
that males which are gonadally normal and sexually experienced are more
responsive than naive males or castrates to the odors from females, regardless of the female's ovarian condition. These conclusions are supported in
whole or in part by the findings of several other investigators, using a variety of odor preference techniques, including Keesey (1962), Stern (1969),
Pfaff and Pfaffmann (1969), and Lydell and Doty (1972).

Stern's (1969) experiment is especially important for present purposes. He not only confirmed our finding that naive-normal males are in-

different to the two feminine odors, but he also showed that this indifference is due to the males' sexual naivete and not to their lack of sexual vigor. He took the precaution of sex-testing his naive males shortly after odor preference testing and excluded from his odor preference data those males which failed to ejaculate during the *post hoc* sex test. Even the remaining vigorous males failed to show a preference for the receptive female odor. Later, Yee and Carr (unpublished data) repeated Stern's experiment with the same results. Stern (1969) also found that only a little sexual experience is necessary to render males reactive to the female sex attractant. Males afforded mounting experience but not intromission or ejaculation (using females with the vaginal orifices sewn closed) prefer the receptive female odor.

Unfortunately, for those who like unambiguous conclusions, we are faced with two sets of disparate findings concerning the gonadal and experiential determinants of the male rat's reaction to the female sex attractant. All agree that, under certain conditions, males prefer the receptive over the nonreceptive female odor, but we are not in agreement as to what these "certain conditions" are. One group of investigators believes that the female sex attractant is effective only in experienced-intact males, but the other group believes that the attractant is also effective in naive-intact males. Curiously, Pranzarone (1969) reported that the attractant is effective in naive-intact males but not in experienced-intact males. How are we to reconcile such disparate findings?

Although we have been unable to demonstrate it in my laboratory, I suspect that naive pubescent male rats which are sexually naive actually do exhibit a weak but reliable preference for the odors from receptive over nonreceptive females. I suspect this to be the case for three reasons: First, my colleagues and I (Carr *et al.*, 1970*b*) found such a preference in immature males (33–54 days old) injected with testosterone; untreated immature males were indifferent to the two feminine odors. Le Magnen (1952) reported similar findings.

My second reason for suspecting that the female sex attractant is effective in naive pubescent males stems from the work of Hitt *et al.* (1970). They showed that the preference for the receptive female odor is relatively weak and dissipates rapidly in naive-intact males. Weak and fleeting preferences are likely to be lost in the "noise" of admittedly crude odor preference techniques. Finally, an examination of the protocols of investigators studying sex attractants in rats indicates that, by and large, those who found significant preferences used younger males (aged 4–7 months) while those who failed used older males (7–15 months).

In view of this evidence, it seems rather likely that as young male rats reach sexual maturity they begin to exhibit a weak preference for the receptive female odor but that this preference dissipates unless it is augmented via learning associated with heterosexual mating. If such is the case, then the preference for the receptive over the nonreceptive female odor should increase as the males approach some critical point in sexual maturation and decrease sometime thereafter. In my judgment, testing this hypothesis is more important than trying to determine whether sexually naive males show the preference at all.

Some may believe this "critical period" hypothesis to be farfetched, but we already have evidence for a similar phenomenon in dogs, cats, and rats. Uzhdavani (reviewed in Kovach, 1971) reared puppies on a milk diet and varied the age at which they were first presented with the sight and smell of meat. The puppies did not approach or salivate to meat until they were about 20 days old, which is the age at which dogs normally begin shifting from suckling to solid food. However, puppies maintained on a milk diet until they were 8 months old gave weak responses or none at all to the sight and smell of meat.

Kovach and Kling (1967) provide a second illustration of the attenuation of a species-characteristic response to an olfactory stimulus if that stimulus is withheld beyond some critical period. They reared kittens from birth until 23 days post partum in social isolation and force-fed them so that they gained no sucking experience. When tested with a lactating female, the kittens could neither locate the nipple nor suck properly, but they sucked quite normally from a bottle. Kovach and King also showed that olfactory bulb ablated kittens can't suck from the mother's nipple but do suck normally from a bottle. Taken together, these findings suggest, that the isolated kittens lose a species-characteristic response to the olfactory stimulus (i.e., the nipple odor) that evokes sucking behavior in the neonatal kitten.

Finally, Leon and Moltz (1972) recently reported that lactating female rats begin to emit a pheromone at about 14 days post partum, which is coincident with the age at which pups become responsive to that pheromone. (The pheromone serves as an attractant to the pups.) At about 27 days post partum, the female ceases to emit the pheromone, which is about at the same time as the pups become unresponsive to it. Those of us who breed rats know that at about 14 days post partum the pups leave the nest for short jaunts into the world and by 27 days of age they are ready for weaning. Isn't it convenient that their mother begins to emit an attractant at about the time the pups need a signal on which to home, and that mother stops emitting and the pups stop responding to the signal when the litter is about to disperse?

With precedents like these, it seems clear that further research is needed to understand the effects of maturation on the male rat's response to the female sex attractant (Carr and Colyer, 1970). After we develop more sophisticated research methods, my colleagues and I plan to continue working on the problem.

The Responses of Female Rats to the Male Sex Attractant

In most species tested, only one of the two sexes emits a sex attractant (Le Magnen, 1952, pp. 300–303). Nevertheless, it would be interesting to learn whether male rats emit a sex attractant, defined as the odor differentiating normal from castrated adult males, that evokes an approach response on the part of females.

Le Magnen (1952) reported that females in unspecified ovarian states were indifferent both to the odors from normal versus castrated males and to the odors from males versus females. Apparently, he never tested females known to be receptive at the time of testing, but his findings lend no support to the existence of a sex attractant emitted by male rats. Other investigators have observed a difference between male and female rats in their responsiveness to sexual stimuli. Males run faster in a single alley to copulate with receptive females than do males running to nonreceptive females (Beach and Jordan, 1956), but receptive females run no faster to get to sexually active than to sexually inactive males (Beach, 1958, pp. 277–278; Bolles et al., 1968). Copulation appears to serve as a positive reinforcer for males, but not for females. Taken together, these findings would appear to support a "gentleman's explanation" of sexual rapprochement, at least in rats. Males are attracted to receptive females, but receptive females wait demurely on the pleasure of their mates.

However, our research (Carr et al., 1965) reveals quite a different perspective concerning the female rat's reaction to male odors. Using the same procedures already described, we tested four groups of adult females with the odors from normal versus castrated males. All of our females were ovariectomized at 1.5 months, and their mating condition was controlled by injections of ovarian hormones (estradiol and progesterone) or sesame oil. Prior to testing, one group of females ($N = 29$) received extensive heterosexual mating experience (polygamous, but without *savoir faire*) while the other group ($N = 30$) remained sexually naive. At the time of testing, approximately one-half the Ss in each group were receptive and one-half nonreceptive.

During the 30-min test as a whole, the experienced-nonreceptive females and the naive-receptive females showed a reliable preference ($p < 0.05$) for the normal male odor over that from castrates. But the experienced-receptive and naive-nonreceptive females showed no reliable preference for either masculine odor. Confusing, isn't it? Why should experienced-receptive females be indifferent to the normal male odor? The confusion quickly disappears when the data are analyzed by cumulative 5-min periods within the 30-min test. The experienced-receptive females showed a reliable preference ($p < 0.05$) for the normal male odor over that from castrates at the end of 5, 10, 15, and 20 min of testing, but not

thereafter. Presumably, these experienced-receptive females stopped pre-
ferring the normal male odor after 20 min of testing *not* because their
preference was weak but because their tendency to approach a male—any
male—was strong. On the other hand, the naive-nonreceptive females
showed no reliable preference for either masculine odor at any of the six
intervals throughout the 30-min test.

On the basis of the results just described we conclude that, regardless of their mating condition at the time of testing, sexually experienced
females prefer the male sex attractant, as do naive-receptive females. Only
the naive-nonreceptive females proved to be indifferent to the male sex attractant.

More recently, we showed that pregnant females are also indifferent
to the male sex attractant (Carr and Heft, unpublished data). Presumably,
the hormonal changes associated with pregnancy abolish the female's
responsiveness to the male's sex attractant. Next we plan to observe the responses of lactating females to the male sex attractant. The effects of pregnancy and lactation on the female's social behavior in general and on her
responses to pheromonal stimuli in particular deserve further study. In
this connection, Lissak (1962) reported that anestrous cats exhibit mating
behavior when stimulated by the odor of valeric acid or the vaginal smear
from an estrous cat. Similarly treated pregnant cats do not exhibit mating
behavior.

Two paradoxes stem from our findings on the responses of female
rats to the male sex attractant. First, why should experienced-nonreceptive
females be responsive to the attractant? After all, nonreceptive females will
repel any male which makes sexual advances. Could the effect be the
result of long-term ovariectomy? Apparently not—we tested a number of
intact experienced females and they also preferred the male sex attractant,
regardless of their ovarian condition at the time of testing (Carr, Loeb,
Dissinger, and Wylie, unpublished data). Perhaps prior sex experience
confers something akin to an "acquired need" on female rats. This hypothesis has yet to be tested.

A second paradox stems from our research on the responses of
female rats to the male sex attractant. How are we to reconcile our
finding that sexually experienced females and naive-receptive females
are responsive to the male sex attractant with reports by others (e.g.,
Beach, 1958; Bolles *et al.*, 1968) that copulatory behavior does not serve
as a positive reinforcer for females running in a single-alley? But note
that for the females in the single-alley studies, running was followed by
copulation, whereas in the present odor preference studies no copulation
occurred at the time of testing. It would seem, therefore, that females are
ambivalent (i.e., exhibit both approach and withdrawal behavior) in the
presence of sexually active males and that our odor preference test taps

only the approach component. Peirce and Nuttall (1961) have observed this ambivalence on the part of female rats. They showed that receptive females will work to get to an active male and then work to get away from him, following copulation.

One problem with the technique we use to study the female's reaction to the male sex attractant stems from our use, as odorant animals, of adult males which are gonadally normal or castrated. Since castrates rarely occur in nature, we may be dealing with an odor of little biological significance. I hesitate to use the odors from adult versus immature males, because they may differ in ways not related to circulating gonadal hormones. Perhaps it would be best to use immature males receiving either exogenous testosterone or placebo injections. Demonstrating that females prefer the odor of immature males receiving testosterone would lend validity to our technique.

Summary, Thus Far

At this point, it might be useful to summarize what we have learned about the responses of male and female rats to the odors from sexually active versus inactive members of the opposite sex. We know that sexually active male and female rats each emit a releaser pheromone of the sex attractant type that, under certain conditions, evokes an approach response on the part of potential sex partners. These "certain conditions" have to do with the combined effects of prior heterosexual experience and circulating gonadal hormones. Among male rats, the female sex attractant is clearly effective if the males have been heterosexually active and are gonadally normal. The female sex attractant may also be effective in sexually naive adult males, but it is weak and dissipates rapidly. The attractant is definitely ineffective in castrated males, regardless of their prior sexual history.

Among female rats, the male sex attractant is effective if the females are sexually experienced, regardless of their ovarian condition at the time of testing (except for pregnant and possibly lactating females). The male sex attractant is also effective in naive-receptive females, but not in naive-nonreceptive females. Taken together, these findings suggest that the females' responsiveness to the male sex attractant is not the result of straightforward discrimination learning taking place during mating sessions. Of course, other forms of modifiability (e.g., olfactory imprinting) may be involved in the ontogeny of the females' response to the male sex attractant.

Sex attractants may also modulate elements of the copulatory pattern in male and female rats. My colleagues and I observed a fair amount of male–male mounting behavior after male Ss had been odor preference tested. Pfaff and Pfaffmann (1969, p. 262) reported that a significantly greater proportion of males mounted male cagemates after tests involving the receptive female odor than those involving the nonreceptive female odor. Clemens et al. (1969) reported preliminary evidence indicating that the odor of adult males facilitates the lordosis reflex in females. It would be interesting to learn whether the castrate male odor also facilitates lordosis. Finally, Singer (1972) reported that prepuberally castrated male rats show an increase in anogenital exploration of receptive females when the males are injected with testosterone. Anogenital exploration almost invariably precedes mounting, and thus it may be considered as an integral part of the male's mating pattern. It would be interesting to learn whether testosterone also causes castrated males to show an increase in anogenital exploration of nonreceptive females.

A word is in order concerning the question: Just what kind of behavior is being measured in the odor preference testing situations I have described? Pfaff and Pfaffmann (1969, pp. 264–265) suggested that the male's response to the receptive female odor may be more exploratory than hedonic, implying to me that the response is more akin to arousal than to a gradient-oriented response. It is difficult to reconcile this view with the performance of males in a T-maze (Le Magnen, 1952); a preference in such a situation would seem to require a gradient-oriented response. In any event, exploratory behavior is not necessarily mutually exclusive with gradient-oriented behavior—both may be evoked by the receptive female odor. Perhaps sexually naive males are the ones most likely to exhibit the exploratory component. A number of workers observing male rats gaining their first sex experience noted what might be called hyperexcitability (Stone, 1922; Young, 1961; Larsson, 1956; Gerall et al., 1967).

The Responses of Rats to Odors from Individual Sex Partners

To this point, I have considered only the responses of rats to the odors from pairs of potential sex partners, both of which were strangers or novel to the subject being tested; that is, the subject had never been housed with the particular odorant animals prior to testing. Now I'd like to review some experiments on the responses of male rats to odors from two receptive females, one with which the male had just been copulating prior to the odor preference test, and the other a novel female. I will also consider the responses of females to the odors from two normal males, one her original sex partner and the other a novel male.

These experiments were prompted by recent interest in the so-called Coolidge effect—the greater tendency on the part of sexually satiated males to resume copulating with a novel female than with their original partner (Fisher, 1962). Although there is some debate as to the precise cause of the Coolidge effect, some believe that it is due in part to a reduction in the excitatory value of stimuli (possibly olfactory) arising from the original sex partner, relative to the stimuli arising from the novel female (Beach, 1965, p. 554; Fowler, 1965, pp. 74–75; Fowler and Whalen, 1961). If male rats prefer the odor from a novel sex partner over that from their original sex partner, such a finding would lend validity to the hypothesis. Moreover, the finding would establish that males can recognize females as individuals, via olfaction.

Carr *et al.* (1970*a*) observed the responses of three groups of male rats to the odors from the individual female with which each male had just been copulating versus the odor from a novel female. During the weeks prior to testing, one group of males ($N = 33$) received extensive polygamous sexual experience; i.e., they mated at different times with different females. A second group of males ($N = 31$) received the same amount of sex experience, but each with the same female; thus their experience was monogamous. A third group of males ($N = 34$) remained sexually naive (i.e., agamous) until the day of testing. Within each group, approximately one-half of the Ss were odor preference tested under highdrive (i.e., after copulating to one ejaculation) and the remaining Ss were tested after reaching sexual satiation. Odor preferences were measured during a single 10-min test.

The results of this experiment indicated that polygamous males show a reliable preference ($p < 0.05$) for the novel female odor over that from the original sex partner, whether the males copulated to one ejaculation or to satiation. However, the monogamous males showed no reliable preference for either feminine odor during the 10-min test. Presumably, the attractive property of the novel female odor is offset by the enhanced secondary reinforcing property of the odor from the females with which they had all their mating experience. Agamous males showed a reliable preference ($p < 0.01$) for the novel female odor only if the males copulated to satiation. These findings are congruent with the view that the Coolidge effect is mediated in part by olfactory cues from sex partners. The findings indicate not only that males are sometimes attracted to novel sex partners but also that males can discriminate between the odors from individual females.

Do females respond preferentially to the odors from original versus novel male sex partners? On two separate occasions, we tested polygamous females for their response to the two masculine odors and found no reliable preference for either odor. This finding lends support to Beach's (1965, p. 554) suspicion that female rats are less sensitive than males to the effects of stimulus satiation as regards their sexual relations.

The females' failure to respond preferentially is not the result of their inability to discriminate between the odors from individual males. Using a different technique, Krames (1972) showed that females can make such a discrimination. More recently, French *et al.* (1972) showed that female rats prefer certain males over others as sex partners, and French (personal communication) believes that the preference for particular males is mediated by olfaction. Finally, in a pilot study just completed, my colleagues and I found that monogamous female rats ($N = 8$) showed a reliable preference ($p < 0.02$) for the odor from their individual male consorts over that from novel males (Carr, Rodde, DeMesquita, and Maconi, unpublished data). Such a finding seems analogous to the term "thrall" used by psychiatrists to describe the special attachment exhibited by some human females for the male with whom they first had satisfactory sexual relations.

Recently, Krames and his associates extended significantly our understanding of the role played by olfaction in mediating the Coolidge effect (Krames, 1969, 1970, 1971; Krames and Shaw, 1973; Krames and Mastromatteo, 1973). Particularly relevant to the present discussion is the finding that if the copulatory sequence is interrupted prior to the first ejaculation, polygamous males prefer the odor from their original partner over that from a novel partner, suggesting a phenomenon akin to the Zeigarnik effect. Under the same conditions, polygamous females show no reliable preference for either masculine odor. If the copulatory sequence is interrupted while the males are copulating between the first and second ejaculations, neither the males nor the females respond differentially to the odors from original versus novel sex partners. Presumably, the males were caught at the point where they were shifting from a preference for their original female odor to a preference for the novel female odor.

The Sources of Pheromonal Sex Attractants in Rats

Little is known about the anatomical sources of the odors that differentiate receptive from nonreceptive females or those that differentiate normal from castrated males. Even less is known about chemical composition of the odorous materials themselves. The problem of identifying the anatomical sources is complicated by the likelihood that the systems are redundant, in the sense that more than one structure may be involved, and by the fact that the structures may produce more than one type of odorous material. Then, too, it is quite possible that of the many odorous materials that differentiate the sexually active from the inactive members of given sex, only one or a few may actually mediate the preference exhibited by members of the opposite sex. To my knowledge, only one pheromonal sex attractant has been identified within the mammalian group, and that in rhesus monkeys (Michael *et al.*, 1971; Curtis *et al.*, 1971).

Two research strategies are commonly used in an effort to identify the anatomical sources of pheromonal sex attractants in rats. The first involves a search for structures secreting materials to the external environment, especially those structures whose size or activity level is known to be dependent on circulating gonadal hormones. Interest now centers around the sebaceous glands (Montagna, 1956; Ebling, 1970), the preputial gland (Beaver, 1960; Ebling *et al.*, 1969; Krahenbuhl and Desaulles, 1969), the lacrimal gland (Hahn, 1969), and the urinary system (Carrera *et al.*, 1967).

The second strategy involves odor preference testing rats of one sex, using particular excreta from sexually active versus inactive members of the opposite sex. For example, Lydell and Doty (1972) reported that sex-experienced males prefer the odor of urine from receptive females over that from nonreceptive females. Such males do not, however, investigate normally voided urine more than urine drawn directly from the bladder. This finding not only eliminates the preputial gland and other accessory sex glands along the urogenital tract, but it also suggests that the female pheromonal sex attractant in rats is a filtrate of blood drawn by the kidneys into the urine. Lydell and Doty also found that aging the receptive female urine sharply decreases its attractive nature. More research using this interesting technique is certainly called for. For general reviews of mammalian scent-marking behavior, see Mykytowycz (1970) and Ralls (1971).

Electrophysiological Responses to Pheromonal Sex Attractants in Rats

Even though we still know very little about transducer processes in the olfactory epithelium, the use of pheromones and other biologically meaningful odors may provide a useful handle by which to sort out electrophysiological events in the olfactory pathways (e.g., Hara *et al.*, 1965; Pfaffmann, 1972; Salas *et al.*, 1970).

Pfaff and Pfaffmann (1969) compared behavioral and electrophysiological observations on the male rat's responses to the odors from the urine of receptive versus nonreceptive females, in an effort to identify the neural substrate mediating olfactory preferences. Their electrophysiological recordings were made from single units in the olfactory bulb and in the preoptic area of the hypothalamus. Mating behavior in rats is mediated by the preoptic area (Lisk, 1967), and Scott and Pfaffmann (1967) confirmed, electrophysiologically, previous anatomical evidence for a direct pathway from the bulb to the preoptic area.

Pfaff and Pfaffmann (1969) could find no single units in the bulb or in the preoptic area that responded to one type of urine but not to the other, nor could they find units that responded to urine odor but not to other (i.e., nonurine) odors. However, they did find units in both sites that were *differentially* responsive (i.e., judged to be more/less responsive to one type of urine than the other). Relative to the bulb, the preoptic area possesses a greater proportion of units exhibiting this differential responsiveness. Unfortunately, normal males did not differ significantly from castrates with respect to the number of preoptic units responding differentially to the two types of urine (Pfaff and Gregory, 1971). Therefore, the neural substrate mediating the male rat's preference for the receptive female odor has not yet been identified. Since the preoptic region is sexually dimorphic in certain anatomical respects (Raisman and Field, 1971), it would be interesting to learn whether receptive females differ from nonreceptive females in the proportion of preoptic units responding to the odors from normal versus castrated males. In any event, the findings of Pfaffmann and his colleagues demonstrated the potential usefulness of biologically meaningful odors as a means of studying electrophysiological events in the olfactory system.

The Responses of Immature Rats to Pheromonal Sex Attractants

Beginning at about the time of weaning, the adult copulatory patterns can be induced in immature male and female rats by injections of the sex-appropriate gonadal hormones (Young, 1961, pp. 1202–1204). Therefore, one might ask whether their precocial sexuality also renders them responsive to the adult sex attractants of the opposite sex, and whether this responsiveness is influenced by social conditions within the litter situation, i.e., cohabitation or sexual segregation. Olfactory stimuli arising from the litter situation are known to influence at least the male's sexual responsiveness later in life (Marr and Gardner, 1965; Marr and Lilliston, 1969). These questions seem especially important as regards male rats, in view of the "critical period" hypothesis I stated earlier, namely, that pubescent males are more likely to prefer the female sex attractant than older males, when both are sexually naive.

Therefore, Carr *et al.* (1970*b*) observed the responses of immature males ($N = 90$) to the odors from receptive versus nonreceptive adult females, and we observed the responses of immature females ($N = 70$) to the odors from normal versus castrated adult males. One-half of the immature males and one-half of the females were raised in single-sex litters (sexual segregation), while the remaining animals were raised in litters containing approximately equal numbers of male and female pups (sexual cohabitation).[2] Within each group of males, one-half of them received daily injections of testosterone, beginning 9 days before testing, using a dosage sufficient to induce mating behavior (Beach, 1942). The remaining males received placebo injections. Likewise, within each group of immature females, one-half received injections of estradiol and progesterone in dosages sufficient to induce lordosis; the remaining females received placebo injections. The odor preference tests were conducted when the subjects were 36–54 days old. The complete copulatory patterns in untreated male and female rats normally appear at about 65 days of age.

The results of this experiment indicated that, regardless of the social conditions within the litter situation (i.e., sexual segregation or cohabitation), those immature males receiving exogenous testosterone showed a reliable preference ($p < 0.05$) for the female sex attractant, while those males receiving the placebo injections showed no reliable preference for either feminine odor. On the other hand, immature females receiving estradiol and progesterone showed a reliable preference ($p < 0.01$) for the male sex attractant only if the females were raised in sexual segregation. Segregated females receiving placebo injections and females raised in cohabitation showed no reliable preference for either masculine odor. Wylie (1969) also reported that segregated-receptive immature females prefer the male sex attractant.

Clearly, the preference by immature male and female rats for the sex-appropriate attractant is hormonally dependent—only those which have been activated by the sex-appropriate gonadal hormones show a reliable preference for the odor from sexually active members of the opposite sex. We cannot explain why activated males raised in cohabitation prefer the female sex attractant while the activated females raised in cohabitation do not prefer the male sex attractant.

This is a convenient point to mention the work of other investigators on the effects of neonatal hormones on the responses of rats to pheromonal sex attractants. Neonatal hormones are said to have organizational properties, regulating the course of anatomical and behavioral differentiation (Young et al., 1965). Wylie (1968) reported that male rats castrated within 48 hr of birth and treated with testosterone at 35–40 days of age did not respond differentially to the odors from receptive versus nonreceptive females, but that sham-operated males treated with testosterone

---

[2] After the experiment was completed, we realized that males raised in single-sex litters actually cohabited with one female—their mothers. But females raised in single-sex litters were truly segregated sexually.

showed a reliable preference for the receptive female odor. Robertson
and Whalen (1970) reported that neonatally androgenized females also
prefer the receptive female odor. These findings support the view that
neonatal androgen serves to organize the neural substrate of one type of
odor preference.

The Responses of Rats to the Homotypical Sex Attractants

To this point, I have discussed only the responses of rats to the hetero-
typical sex attractant, that is, the attractant from members of the sex opposite to that of the responding animal. However, there are several
reasons why it might be important to learn about the responses of rats to
the homotypical sex attractant, here defined as the odor that differentiates sexually active from sexually inactive members of the same sex as
the responding animal. First, it seems important to determine whether the
responses of male and female rats to sex attractants are sex linked, that
is, whether males differ from females in their responsiveness to the male
or female sex attractant: keep in mind that both male and female rats
exhibit homosexual behavior—males sometimes lordose and females
mount. Second, even among rats there is good reason to believe that
"sexuality" extends beyond purely reproductive functions to influence
other types of social interactions, especially the agonistic behavior associated with territoriality and dominance hierarchies. Calhoun (1962)
confirmed an earlier report by Steiniger (1950) that clashes among group-
living rats usually involve two males, less often two females, and least often
one male and one female. Barnett (1963, p. 91) suggests that the odor
shared by females may inhibit attack by males. Brown (1973) showed that
the odor of urine from strange males evokes urine-marking behavior
in male rats. It would seem especially important for a symposium on communication and affect that we consider these nonreproductive functions
of the olfactory signals associated with sexuality.

For these reasons, Carr et al. (1970b) observed the responses of
116 adult males to the odors from normal versus castrated males, as well
as the responses of 91 adult females to the odors from receptive versus
nonreceptive females. To make this experiment comparable to those I
reported earlier, we used the same four experimental treatments; at the
time of odor preference testing, approximately one-half of our males and
females were sexually experienced and one-half were naive. Within each
of these groups, the males were either gonadally normal or castrated and
the females were either receptive or nonreceptive. Further, since the response to the homotypical sex attractant may vary with the age of the
responding animal, we also observed the responses of 100 immature fe-

males and 30 males. As before, these immature animals were raised in either sexual segregation or cohabitation. Within the two groups of females, one-half were injected with estradiol and progesterone and one-half received placebo injections. The male subjects received no exogenous hormones.

In the main, adult male and female rats are not particularly responsive to the homotypical sex attractants. None of the four groups of males we tested reacted differentially to the odors from normal versus castrated males. Further, of the four groups of adult females, only one reacted differentially to the odors from receptive versus nonreceptive females. Adult female Ss which are sexually naive and receptive at the time of testing show a reliable preference ($p<0.05$) for the nonreceptive female odor over that from receptive females.

The responses of immature males and females to the homotypical sex attractants are a bit more interesting. Untreated immature males raised in cohabitation or in segregation prefer the adult normal male odor over that from castrates ($p<0.05$). Wylie (1969) reported that immature cohabiting males treated with testosterone also prefer the normal male odor over that from castrates. Of the four groups of immature females we tested, only one reacted differentially to the female sex attractant. Immature females raised in segregation and receptive at the time of testing show a reliable preference ($p<0.05$) for the nonreceptive over the receptive female odor. This last point is consistent with our findings using adult females; our naive-receptive adult females had been raised in sexual segregation from the time of weaning and they also prefer the nonreceptive over the receptive female odor.

Four general conclusions can be drawn from the results of the experiments I described on the responses of rats to odors associated with sexually active versus inactive conspecifics:

1. *A pheromonal sex attractant is emitted by both male and female rats.* The odor that differentiates the receptive from the nonreceptive female serves as an attractant to normal males which have already mated. The attractant may also be effective in virgin males, but it is weak and dissipates rapidly. The attractant is ineffective in untreated immature males and in castrated adult males, regardless of their prior mating experience.

Moreover, the odor that differentiates the normal from the castrated adult male rat serves as an attractant in virgin adult females which are receptive at the time of testing, and in experienced females which are not pregnant. The attractant is ineffective in nonreceptive virgin females and in pregnant females.

2. *The responses of adult rats to pheromonal sex attractants are sex linked.* Male and female adults, subjected to the same experimental

treatments, exhibit quite different reactions to the homotypical and hetero-typical sex attractants. For example, at least one group of males (sexu-ally experienced and gonadally normal) prefer the receptive female odor over that from nonreceptive females, but females are either indifferent to the two feminine odors or actually prefer the nonreceptive female odor.[3] Likewise, under a variety of conditions, adult females prefer the odor from normal males over that from castrates, but adult males are indif-ferent to the two masculine odors. Young (1961, p. 1195) says that the sex-appropriate gonadal hormones strengthen homosexual as well as heterosexual behavior (i.e., testosterone causes males to lordose, and estradiol and progesterone cause females to mount), but the present re-sults indicate that this enhancement of homosexual behavior is not re-flected in their responsiveness to the homotypical sex odors. In this sense, the responses of adult rats to the pheromonal sex attractants are here said to be truly sex linked.

3. *Immature rats differ from adults in their responses to phero-monal sex attractants.* In both males and females, immature rats differ in some respects from adults in their response to pheromonal sex at-tractants. Among males, immature animals treated with testosterone show a clear-cut preference for the female pheromonal sex attractant, but the response of virgin adult males is equivocal—at best, they exhibit a weak and transitory preference. Moreover, untreated immature males are responsive to the male pheromonal sex attractant; that is, they prefer the odor from normal males over that from castrates, but adult males are indifferent to the two masculine odors. This phenomenon may be related to the nonreproductive functions of sexuality.

Among immature females, only those which are segregated and re-ceptive are responsive to the male pheromonal sex attractant. Nonrecep-tive females and cohabiting females are not responsive. Among mature females, responsiveness to the male sex attractant requires either prior sexual experience or circulating ovarian hormones at the time of testing. Immature females respond the same way as do adult females to the fe-male pheromonal sex attractant.

4. *Neonatal hormones serve to organize the neuromuscular sub-strate mediating the responses of rats to pheromonal sex attractants.* Neo-natally castrated males later (35–40 days old) treated with testosterone are not responsive to the female pheromonal sex attractant, but sham-operated males later treated with testosterone do respond preferentially.

[3] Hitt et al. (1970) also observed the responses of females to odors from receptive versus nonreceptive females. Further, they took the precaution of subdividing their female sub-jects into mounters versus nonmounters. Their findings are congruent with ours (Carr et al., 1970b) in some respects, but not in others. However, under no condition did they find males and females responding the same way to the female sex odors.

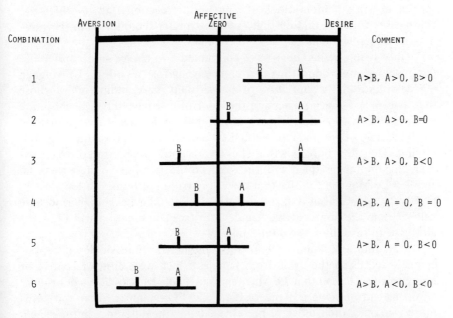

Fig. 2. Six possible combinations of single-odor reactions compatible with a preference for stimulus A over stimulus B in a two-odor testing situation. After Irwin (1961).

On the other hand, neonatally androgenized females are responsive to the female sex attractant, but nonandrogenized females are not. In the former case, the males appear to be demasculinized and in the latter case the females appear to be masculinized.

I might touch just briefly on one additional problem that stems from the use of two-odor preference tests as a means of establishing the existence of pheromonal sex attractants. We know that sexually experienced male rats which are gonadally normal prefer the odor from receptive females over that from nonreceptive females. However, this finding does not reveal the precise nature of the males' response to the individual feminine odors. When using a two-odor testing situation, one cannot be sure whether the males are attracted to, repelled by, or indifferent to either test odor.

However, Irwin (1961) has shown that when preferences are established in a two-choice situation with only a single odor present, it is possible to locate on Irwin's "affective continuum" the position of that odor, from strong positive valence (desire), through indifference or neutrality (affective zero), to strong negative valence (aversion).[4] Figure 2 shows

---

[4] Alternatively, a three-choice testing situation using two odors plus one "no odor" option would enable one to establish both a relative and an absolute preference simultaneously.

the six possible combinations of single-odor reactions, all of which are compatible with the finding that male rats prefer the odor from receptive over nonreceptive females.

Only a few researchers have conducted two-choice odor preference tests using a single odor, the other choice being for "no odor." Le Magnen (1952) found that about 90% of his sexually naive adult males chose that arm of a T-maze possessing the odor of a female and 10% chose the arm possessing "no odor." Interestingly, their preference was uninfluenced by the female's ovarian state—about 90% of the males chose the arm containing a female's odor whether she was receptive or nonreceptive. However, this finding, coupled with the results of his two-odor preference tests, enabled Le Magnen to infer that the odors from both types of females are positively valenced but that the receptive female odor has a higher positive valence than the nonreceptive female odor (see combination 1 in Fig. 2)—all this with sexually naive adult males.

Pfaff and Pfaffmann (1969) also conducted some single-odor preference tests, using the urine from females which were either receptive or nonreceptive. (Recall that Le Magnen used whole females as his odorants.) Also, instead of using a T-maze, Pfaff and Pfaffmann used an apparatus much like ours, their index of preference being the difference in time spent by the males investigating two containers, one housing the female odor and the other "no odor." They found that experienced-normal males showed a reliable preference for receptive female odor over "no odor," but were indifferent to the nonreceptive female odor versus "no odor." (see combination 2 in Fig. 2). On the other hand, prepubertally castrated males showed no reliable preference for either feminine odor when it was paired with "no odor." Lydell and Doty (1972) also reported that naive-normal males are indifferent to receptive female urine versus "no odor" (water) but that experienced-normal males prefer receptive female urine over "no odor." Taken together, these findings suggest that for experienced-normal males, receptive female urine is positively valenced but nonreceptive female urine is at Irwin's "affective zero" (i.e., neutral). However, for naive-normal or prepubertally castrated males, both types of female urine are at Irwin's "affective zero."

The apparent discrepancy between the findings of Le Magnen, on the one hand, and those of Pfaff and Pfaffmann and Lydell and Doty, on the other, is probably due to some combination of difference in methodology and the odorant employed. Le Magnen used a T-maze and the odor from the entire female's body, whereas the other investigators used a time-sharing method and the odor of the female's urine. Whatever the cause, I think the issue deserves further study in order to establish more precisely the nature of the male's response to feminine odors. This problem, coupled with the others I have posed, should be sufficient to keep several of us busy for some years to come.

Acknowledgments

Some of the research described in this paper was supported by Public Health Service Research Grant HD 00345 from the National Institute of Child Health and Human Development, and by Public Health Service Research Grant MH 24546 from the National Institute of Mental Health.

References

Archer, J. 1968, Effect of strange male odor on aggressive behavior in male mice. *J. Mammal.* **49**: 572–575.

Aron, C., Roos, J., and Asch, G., 1970, Effect of removal of the olfactory bulbs on mating behavior and ovulation in the rat, *Neuroendocrinology* **6**: 109–117.

Barnett, S. A., 1963, *The Rat: A Study in Behaviour,* Aldine, Chicago.

Barnett, S. A., 1964, Social stress, in: *Viewpoints in Biology* (J. D. Carthy and C. L. Duddington, eds.), pp. 170–218, Butterworths, London.

Beach, F. A., 1942, Analysis of the stimuli adequate to elicit mating behavior in the sexually inexperienced male rat, *J. Comp. Psychol.* **33**: 163–207.

Beach, F. A., 1951, Instinctive behavior: Reproductive activities, in: *Handbook of Experimental Psychology* (S. S. Stevens, ed., 1951), pp. 387–434, Wiley, New York.

Beach, F. A., 1958, Neural and chemical regulation in behavior, in: *Biological and Biochemical Bases of Behavior* (H. F. Harlow and C. N. Woolsey, eds.), pp. 263–284, University of Wisconsin Press, Madison, Wis.

Beach, F. A., 1965, Retrospect and prospect, in: *Sex and Behavior* (F. A. Beach, ed.), pp. 535–569, Wiley, New York.

Beach, F. A., and Holz-Tucker, A. M., 1949, Effects of different concentrations of androgen upon sexual behavior in castrated male rat, *J. Comp. Physiol. Psychol.* **42**: 433–453.

Beach, F. A., and Jordan, L., 1956, Sexual exhaustion and recovery in the male rat, *Quart. J. Exptl. Psychol.* **8**: 121–133.

Beaver, D., 1960, A re-evaluation of the rat preputial gland as a "Dicrine" organ from the standpoint of its morphology, histochemistry and physiology, *J. Exptl. Zool.* **143**: 153–173.

Bermant, G., and Taylor, L., 1969, Interactive effects of experience and olfactory bulb lesions in male rat copulation, *Physiol. Behav.* **4**: 12–17.

Bolles, R. C., Rapp, H. M., and White, C., 1968, Failure of sexual activity to reinforce female rats, *J. Comp. Physiol. Psychol.* **65**: 311–313.

Bronson, F. H., 1972, Rodent pheromones, *Biol. Reprod.* **4**: 344–365.

Brown, R. E., 1973, The fire hydrant effect: Stimuli eliciting urine marking in the rat (*Rattus norvegicus*), *Bull. Ecol. Soc. Am.* **54(1)**: 44.

Calhoun, J. B., 1962, *The Ecology and Sociology of the Norway Rat,* Public Health Service Publication No. 1008, U.S. Department of Health, Education and Welfare, Bethesda, Md.

Carr, W. J., and Caul, W. F., 1962, The effect of castration in rat upon the discrimination of sex odours, *Anim. Behav.* **10**: 20–27.

Carr, W. J., and Colyer, S. W., 1970, The effects of previous experience upon the response to sex attractants in rats, paper read at the Eastern Regional Conference on Reproductive Behavior, Delray Beach, Fla.

Carr, W. J., Solberg, B., and Pfaffmann, C., 1962, The olfactory threshold for estrous female urine in normal and castrated male rats, *J. Comp. Physiol. Psychol.* **55**: 415–417.

Carr, W. J., Loeb, L. S., and Dissinger, M. L., 1965, Responses of rats to sex odors, *J. Comp. Physiol. Psychol.* **59:** 370–377.

Carr, W. J., Loeb, L. S., and Wylie, N. R., 1966, Responses to feminine odors in normal and castrated male rats, *J. Comp. Physiol. Psychol.* **62:** 336–338.

Carr, W. J., Krames, L., and Costanzo, D. J., 1970a, Previous sexual experience and olfactory preference for novel versus original sex partners, *J. Comp. Physiol. Psychol.* **71:** 216–222.

Carr, W. J., Wylie, N. R., and Loeb, L. S., 1970b, Responses of adult and immature rats to sex odors, *J. Comp. Physiol. Psychol.* **72:** 51–59.

Carrera, G. F., Ponthier, R. L., and Rice, B. R., 1967, Absence of testosterone in urine of rats, *Nature* **216:** 1128.

Cheal, M. L., and Sprott, R. L., 1971, Social olfaction: A review of the role of olfaction in a variety of animal behaviors, *Psychol. Rep.* **29:** 195–243.

Clemens, L. G., Hiroi, M., and Gorski, R. A., 1969, Induction and facilitation of female mating behavior in rats treated neonatally with low doses of testosterone propionate, *Endocrinology* **84:** 1430–1438.

Curtis, R. F., Ballantine, J. A., Kerverne, E. B., Bonsall, R. W., and Michael, R. P., 1971, Identification of primate sexual pheromones and properties of synthetic attractants, *Nature (Lond.)* **232:** 396–398.

Ebling, F. J., 1970, Factors influencing the response of the sebaceous glands of the rat to androgen, *Brit. J. Dermatol.* **82:** 9–14.

Ebling, F. J., Ebling, E., and Skinner, J., 1969, The influence of the pituitary on the response of the sebaceous and preputial glands of the rat to progesterone, *J. Endocrinol.* **45:** 257–263.

Eisenberg, J. F., and Kleiman, D. G., 1972, Olfactory communication in mammals, *Ann. Rev. Ecol. Systemat.* **3:** 1–32.

Ewer, R. F., 1971, The biology and behaviour of a free-living population of black rats (*Rattus rattus*), *Anim. Behav. Monogr.* **4(3):** 127–174.

Fisher, A. E., 1962, Effects of stimulus variation on sexual satiation in the male rat, *J. Comp. Physiol. Psychol.* **55:** 614–620.

Fowler, H., 1965, *Curiosity and Exploratory Behavior,* Macmillan, New York.

Fowler, H., and Whalen, R. E., 1961, Variation in incentive stimulus and sexual behavior in the male rat, *J. Comp. Physiol. Psychol.* **54:** 68–71.

French, D., Fitzpatrick, D., and Law, O. T., 1972, Operant investigation of mating preference in female rats, *J. Comp. Physiol. Psychol.* **81:** 226–232.

Gerall, H. D., Ward, I. L., and Gerall, A. A., 1967, Disruption of the male rat's sexual behaviour induced by social isolation, *Anim. Behav.* **15:** 54–58.

Gleason, K. K., and Reynierse, J. H., 1969, The behavioral significance of pheromones in vertebrates, *Psychol. Bull.* **71:** 58–73.

Hahn, J. D., 1969, Effect of cyprotherone acetate on sexual dimorphism of the exorbital lacrimal gland in rats, *J. Endocrinol.* **45:** 421–424.

Haldane, J. B. S., 1955, Animal communication and the origin of human language, *Sci. Progr.* **43:** 385–401.

Hara, T. J., Ueda, K., and Gorbman, A., 1965, Electroencephalographic studies of homing salmon, *Science* **149:** 884–885.

Heimer, L., and Larsson, K., 1967, Mating behavior of male rats after olfactory bulb lesions, *Physiol. Behav.* **2:** 207–209.

Hitt, J. C., Phillips, I., and Asato, H., 1970, Hormonal determinants of preference for female sex-odors in rats, paper read at the annual meeting of the Psychonomic Society, San Antonio, Texas, November.

Irwin, F. W., 1961, On desire, aversion and affective zero, *Psychol. Rev.* **68:** 293–300.

Jacobson, M., 1965, *Insect Sex Attractants,* Interscience, New York.

Keesey, J. C., 1962, Olfactory preferences by heterosexually naive and experienced male rats for estrus and diestrus female urine, unpublished master's thesis, San Jose State College.

Kovach, J. P., 1971, Ethology in the Soviet Union, *Behaviour* **39**: 237–265.

Kovach, J. K., and Kling, A., 1967, Mechanisms of neonate sucking behaviour in the kitten, *Anim. Behav.* **15**: 91–101.

Krahenbuhl, C., and Desaulles, P. A., 1969, Interactions between a-MSH and sex steroids on the preputial glands of female rats, *Experientia* **25**: 1193.

Krames, L., 1969, The Coolidge effect in male and female rats, unpublished doctoral dissertation, Temple University.

Krames, L., 1970, Responses of female rats to the individual body odors of male rats, *Psychon. Sci.* **20**: 274–275.

Krames, L., 1971, Sexual responses of polygamous female and monogamous male rats to novel partners after sexual cessation, *J. Comp. Physiol. Psychol.* **77**: 294–301.

Krames, L., and Mastromatteo, L. A., 1973, Role of olfactory stimuli during copulation in male and female rats, *J. Comp. Physiol. Psychol.* **85**: 528–535.

Krames, L., and Shaw, B., 1973, Role of previous experience in the male rat's reaction to the odours from group and alien conspecifics, *J. Comp. Physiol. Psychol.* **82**: 444–447.

Krames, L., Carr, W. J., and Bergman, B., 1969, A pheromone associated with social dominance among male rats, *Psychon. Sci.* **16**: 11–12.

Larsson, K., 1956, *Conditioning and Sexual Behavior,* Almquist & Wiksell, Stockholm.

Le Magnen, J., 1952, Les phenomenes olfacto-sexuels ches le rat blanc, *Arch. Sci. Physiol.* **6**: 295–332.

Leon, M., and Moltz, H., 1972, The development of the pheromonal bond in the albino rat, *Physiol. Behav.* **8**: 683–686.

Lisk, R. D., 1967, Sexual behavior: Hormonal control, in: *Neuroendocrinology,* (L. Martini and W. F. Ganong, eds.), pp. 197–240, Academic Press, New York.

Lissak, K., Olfactory-induced sexual behaviour in female cats, in: *Proceedings of the International Union of Physiological Sciences,* **1**: 653–656.

Lydell, K., and Doty, R. L., 1972, Male rat odor preferences for female urine as a function of sexual experience, urine age, and urine source, *Hormones Behav.* **3**: 205–212.

Marr, J. N., and Gardner, E., 1965, Early olfactory experience and later social behavior in the rat: Preference, sexual responsiveness, and care of young, *J. Genet. Psychol.* **107**: 167–174.

Marr, J. N., and Lilliston, L. G., 1969, Social attachment in rats by odor and age, *Behaviour* **33**: 277–282.

Michael, R. P., Keverne, E. B., and Bonsall, R. W., 1971, Pheromones: Isolation of male sex attractants from a female primate, *Science* **172**: 964–966.

Montagna, W., 1956, *The Structure and Function of the Skin,* Academic Press, New York.

Moss, R. L., 1971, Modification of copulatory behavior in the female rat following olfactory bulb removal, *J. Comp. Physiol. Psychol.* **74**: 374–382.

Murphy, M. R., and Schneider, G. E., 1970, Olfactory bulb removal eliminates mating behavior in the male golden hamster, *Science* **167**: 302–303.

Mykytowycz, R., 1970, The role of skin glands in mammalian communication, in: *Communication by Chemical Signals* (J. W. Johnston, D. G. Moulton, and A. Turk, eds.), pp. 327–360, Appleton-Century-Crofts, New York.

Nodine, C., 1959, The effects of non-exposure to post-partum estrous odor at a critical period in infancy upon adult mating behavior in the rat, unpublished master's thesis, Bucknell University.

Peirce, J. T., and Nuttall, R. L., 1961, Self-paced sexual behavior in the female rat, *J. Comp. Physiol. Psychol.* **54**: 310–313.

Pfaff, D., and Gregory, E., 1971, Olfactory coding in the olfactory bulb and medial forebrain bundle of normal and castrated male rats, *J. Neurophysiol.* **34**: 208–216.

Pfaff. D., and Pfaffmann, C., 1969, Behavioral and electrophysiological responses of male rats to female rat urine odors, in: *Olfaction and Taste* (C. Pfaffmann, ed.), pp. 258–267, Rockefeller University Press, New York.

Pfaffmann, C., 1972, Recent advances in the study of olfaction, in: *Recent Contributions in Neurophysiology* (J. P. Cordeau and P. Gleer, eds.), pp. 185–203, EEG Supplement No. 31, Elsevier, Amsterdam.

Pranzarone, G. F., 1969, The male rat's preference for estrous odor as a function of differential exposure to females, paper presented at the meeting of the Southeastern Psychological Association, New Orleans, February.

Purvis, K., and Haynes, N. B., 1972, The effect of female rat proximity on the reproductive system of male rats, *Physiol. Behav.* **9:** 401–407.

Raisman, G., and Field, P. M., 1971, Sexual dimorphism in the preoptic area of the rat, *Science* **173:** 731–733.

Ralls, K., 1971, Mammalian scent marking, *Science* **171:** 443–449.

Robertson, R. T., and Whalen, R. E., 1970, Recent mating experience and olfactory preferences in androgenized female rats, *Psychon. Sci.* **21:** 266–267.

Ropartz, P., 1968, The relation between olfactory stimulation and aggressive behaviour in mice, *Anim. Behav.* **16:** 97–100.

Rosen, S., Shelesnyak, M. C., and Zacharias, L. R., 1940, Naso-genital relationship. II. Pseudopregnancy following extirpation of the sphenopalatine ganglion in the rat, *Endocrinology* **27:** 463–468.

Salas, M., Schapiro, S., and Guzman-Flores, C., 1970, Development of olfactory bulb discrimination between maternal and food odors, *Physiol. Behav.* **5:** 1261–1264.

Schultz, E. F., and Tapp, J. T., 1973, Olfactory control of behavior in rodents, *Psychol. Bull.* **79:** 21–44.

Scott, J. W., and Pfaffmann, C., 1967, Olfactory input to the hypothalamus: Electrophysiological evidence, *Science* **158:** 1592–1594.

Singer, J. J., 1972, Anogenital explorations and testosterone propionate–induced sexual arousal in rats, *Behav. Biol.* **7:** 743–747.

Smith, W. J., 1969, Messages of vertebrate communication, *Science* **165:** 145–150.

Steiniger, F., 1950, Beitrage zur Soziologia und sonstigen Biologie der Wanderratte, *Z. Tierpsychol.* **7:** 356–379.

Stern, J. J., 1969, Copulatory experience and sex odor preferences of male rats, *Proceedings of the 77th Annual Convention,* American Psychological Association: Washington, D.C., pp. 229–230.

Stone, C. P., 1922, The congenital sexual behavior of the young male albino rat, *J. Comp. Psychol.* **2:** 95–153.

Stone, C. P., 1923, Further study of the sensory functions in the activation of sexual behavior in the young male albino rat, *J. Comp. Psychol.* **3:** 469–473.

Telle, H. J., 1966, Beitrag zur Kenntnis der Verhaltensweise von Ratten, vergleichend dargestellt bei *Rattus norvegicus* und *Rattus rattus, Z. Angew. Zool.* **53:** 129–166. (Translated by V. N. Nekrassoff, Technical Translation Section, National Science Library, Ottawa, Canada, Translation No. 1608.)

Whitten, W. K., 1966, Pheromones and mammalian reproduction, *Advan. Reprod. Physiol.* **1:** 155–177.

Whitten, W. K., and Bronson, F. H., 1970, The role of pheromones in mammalian reproduction, in: *Communication by Chemical Signals* (J. W. Johnston, Jr., D. G. Moulton, and A. Turk, eds.), pp. 309–326, Appleton-Century-Crofts, New York.

Wickler, W., 1972, *The Sexual Code,* Doubleday: Garden City.

Wilson, E. O., 1968, Chemical systems, in: *Animal Communication* (T. A. Sebeok, ed.), pp. 75–102, Indiana University Press, Bloomington.

Wilson, E. O., and Bossert, W. H., 1963, Chemical communication in animals, *Rec. Progr. Hormone Res.* **19:** 673–716.

Wylie, N. R., 1968, Neonatal castration modifies responses to sex odors, *Proceedings of the 76th Annual Convention,* American Psychological Association, Washington, D.C. pp. 291–292.

Wylie, N. R., 1969, Effects of neonatal castration on responses of rats to sex odors, doctoral dissertation, Temple University. University Microfilms, No. 69–16817, Ann Arbor, Mich.

Young, W. C., 1961, The hormones and mating behavior, in: *Sex and Internal Secretions* (W. C. Young, ed.), pp. 1173–1239, William & Wilkins, Baltimore.

Young, W. C., Goy, R. W., and Phoenix, H., 1965, Hormones and sexual behavior, in: *Sex Research—New Developments* (J. Money, ed.), pp. 176–196, Holt, Rinehart and Winston, New York.

CHAPTER 6

Information Transfer in Honey Bees: A Population Approach

Adrian M. Wenner

Department of Biological Sciences
University of California, Santa Barbara
Santa Barbara, California

The question of a "language" among bees continues to hold the attention of scientists and laymen alike, but bees are not necessarily the focal point in this matter. Several factors complicate the issue. First, a question of more general interest is whether any nonhuman species has a "language" or communication system in any way equivalent to ours. A less obvious and perhaps more important question that continually surfaces is whether we can ever know if bees (or any other animals) have a language (Wenner, 1971). Professor Karl von Frisch (1946) emphasized both of these problems in his treatment of the possibility that bees might have a "language." In an introduction to his classic paper, he wrote:

> When dealing with the question of how the initiated bees find the food source indicated by the dancer, I said at a meeting of naturalists at Innsbruck (1924): "The problem gave rise to the most daring [of] hypotheses. Thus I thought of the possibility that the dancer might indicate the distance and direction in which the food had to be looked for by a secret sign. However false this assumption had been it did lead us further . . . ." This daring hypothesis was correct!

and (prophetically, perhaps):

> Nature's way often turns out to be completely different from any which can be seen at the time.

When my colleagues and I examined the bee language hypothesis more critically than it had ever been examined before, we found that von Frisch's interpretation of how recruited bees might find a food source did not

133

explain either all of the earlier data or experimental results we had just obtained. Over a period of time and aided by a series of accidents, we had obtained experimental results indicating that it was not necessary to postulate a "language" use to explain how recruited bees might find a food source exploited by successful bees. We found that an odor–population dependent hypothesis explained the circumstances quite well. However, when we wrote that our new evidence suggested that "Nature's way often turns out to be completely different from any which can be seen at the time," an intense polarization developed in the biological community.

More recently, we have come to appreciate more fully that the controversy that developed centers not so much on the credibility of the extensive amount of evidence available but more on the second of the above two questions—namely, the interpretation of those data. Wells and I wrote (1973):

> It is not what investigators observe (the data) but what they believe (infer) that is at the heart of the controversy.

The issue is now very complex and no easy matter for an outsider, but my colleagues and I are no longer alone in recognizing both that the controversy is healthy and that the issue hinges more on the nature of evidence and attitudes toward that evidence than on the data alone (e.g., Phillips, 1971; Altmann, 1972; McGill, 1973). Ultimately the resolution of this matter will depend on the manner in which the evidence is viewed, a topic dealt with fully elsewhere (Wenner, 1971; Wells and Wenner, 1973). Here I will only review some of the problems that have made testing the bee language hypothesis difficult.

Lure of the Exotic. Many animals have remarkable structures and/or behavioral patterns. The discovery of yet another remarkable event among animals will find a ready acceptance in a basically optimistic audience.

Anthropomorphism. One need observe bees for only a very short period of time before becoming impressed with the many human-like actions they have. An anthropomorphic interpretation may soon follow, even if subconsciously, but most are not as blatant or colorful as Unhoch's 1823 statement (von Frisch, 1967a, pp. 5–6):

> To many it will seem ridiculous if I mention that bees too, when the hive is otherwise in good condition, indulge in certain pleasures and jollity, and that at times they even set about a certain dance after their fashion.

Teleology. Lindauer (1971) expressed the appeal of this factor eloquently when he stated:

> One of the most fruitful guiding principles of biology has been that each morphological structure and behavioral act is associated with a special function.

But an interpretation that first comes to mind does not *necessarily* follow.

Although the above statement is accepted in principle by many biologists, Lindauer's next statement is a non sequitur:

> On this basis alone, it would seem highly unlikely that the information contained in the waggle dance of a honey bee is not transmitted to her nest mates.

Hypotheses Replace Questions. The question, "How do recruited bees find a food source?" disappeared with the general and unconscious acceptance of the bee language hypothesis as an established fact. Unfortunately, if the basic question is lost in this manner, an investigator may not recognize that experimental results obtained may actually contradict the predictions of the hypothesis under study. An apparently unconscious assumption by Gould *et al.* (1970) illustrates just how subtle this type of bias may be:

> Simply demonstrating that olfactory cues are sufficient in a particular situation does not mean that *the dance language* is not used under other conditions. [Emphasis mine.]

The act of replacing questions by hypotheses and then losing sight of the tentative nature of those hypotheses (i.e., treating them as fact) apparently stems from our human need for certainty, a topic also treated elsewhere (Wenner, 1971, 1973).

Focus on the Successful. If one starts with an implicit assumption that bees have a language (e.g., Gould *et al.,* 1970), he can readily gather experimental results to support that bias (Popper, 1957). In such a case, confirmations are easy to obtain because the early experiments were so remarkably repeatable and the logic so rational. On the other hand, this rationale suffices in the case of the bee language hypothesis *only* if one does not insert other necessary controls (Wenner, 1967; Johnson, 1967; Wenner *et al.,* 1969) and *only* if one focuses attention on those bees which are "successful." However, the vast majority of recruited bees do not perform as predicted by the language hypothesis.

In some cases, this focusing of attention on successful bees is more explicit. For example, Esch and Bastian wrote (1970):

> In two cases . . . we were able to see the newcomers approach the food site from a considerable distance. They came straight from the hive in a zig-zag flight which brought them down from a height of approximately 10 meters at the point where they were spotted to 1 or 2 meters near the food site. It was obvious from their behavior that they were *not* searching at random. One had the impression that they knew the location of the food site.

The "zig-zag flight" described above is a very typical behavior for insects flying upwind toward an odor source. If one considers the entire population of recruited bees, on the other hand, the relatively few bees which are "successful" must be viewed in another light (Wells and Wenner, 1973).

The above discussion has been a necessary diversion, as should be evident from the illustrative quotations used. Not only the quantity and quality of evidence must be considered. Relevant evidence can also be viewed in any of several ways, depending on ingrained and (oftentimes) subconscious goals. This is true, of course, for those of us who challenge the language hypothesis as well as for those who support it.

Let us return now to the basic question, "How do recruited bees find a food source exploited by successful bees?" and consider three possible explanations. In a random search pattern (which we have never proposed), a very small percentage of bees would be successful and would require much time in locating a food source. Alternatively, if searching recruits depend on the flight paths of foragers and interact with each other, then the percentage of successful searchers would be highly dependent on the magnitude of those flight paths, on odor concentration, and on wind patterns. Finally, if bees could use a "language" information (von Frisch, 1967a), then one could rightly expect that a high percentage of recruits would be successful and that most of them would require a very short time in flight.

The problem thus becomes reduced to one of degree.[1] Which of the three alternative explanations most accurately accounts for the search pattern of recruited bees? Which explanation can best accommodate *all* the available data? And which hypothesis best explains where recruited bees are flying as they travel between hive and food source?

In the remainder of this chapter, I will concentrate primarily on the second of the above three possible explanations: that recruited honey bees rely on the flight paths of regular foragers and also depend on the odors and wind patterns prevalent in the environment. First I will list anomalies uncovered during our study of the bee language hypothesis, anomalies that help us understand recruit behavior. Then I will develop a model that can explain the search dynamics of a population of recruited honeybees and that can be tested. Before proceeding further, however, some definitions are in order.

Foragers (experienced bees) are the bees which make repeated round trips to a known nectar source. These bees investigate such sources at frequent intervals when they are not yielding nectar and visit them regularly when they yield steadily (Johnson and Wenner, 1966). *Potential recruits* are the members of a recruit pool in the hive which contacts regular foragers. Some of them will leave a hive after such a contact and are called *recruits* (Johnson and Wenner, 1970). These recruits presumably search for the same odor combination that had been visited by the successful forager they

---

[1] There are, of course, those who argue that the truth may be somewhere in between. Although this may be a comfortable position, certainly science has never advanced rapidly under that rationale. It is more as McGill (1973) stated: "Science thrives on controversy."

contacted before leaving the hive (Waller, 1973). Finally, *successful recruits* are the searching bees which arrive at the *same* location in the field as that visited by the forager they contacted in the hive. The need for these distinctions will become more clear later.

Emergence of Anomalies

The bee language hypothesis is completely documented in a number of sources and will not be outlined here. For the most complete presentation, one should refer to the book by von Frisch (1967*a*). For a shorter summary, von Frisch's (1967*b*) challenge of one of our papers contains a relatively concise statement of that hypothesis.

When I first obtained results that clearly could not be reconciled with the classical hypothesis, my reaction was one of disbelief and near rejection of the data. Eventually there came the realization that other anomalies had existed earlier but had remained unrecognized by bee researchers and others. In subsequent years, the number of anomalies increased, particularly after we began our direct challenge of the language paradigm. Proponents of the language hypothesis, on the other hand, apparently still do not consider the results we and others have obtained as anomalies (e.g., Wilson, 1972; Morse, 1973).

Fortunately, an anomalous result with respect to one hypothesis provides insight into other possible explanations, and, when one has a sufficient number of anomalies, an alternative hypothesis may readily emerge. That is what happened in our case. Space does not permit a full treatment of each anomaly uncovered, nor is it necessary to review all the evidence. A detailed treatment of pertinent evidence is already in print. One needs only a guide to that evidence for a more detailed perusal. That guide follows.

Abbreviated Chronicle of Our Experimental Challenge

In this section, I will outline the appearance of anomalous results in our research, briefly describe the implications of each anomaly or pertinent bit of evidence, and provide a reference to the literature for those who wish to examine critically the arguments. In a following section, I will similarly outline the anomalies uncovered recently by other researchers.

Date	New Results	Implications
1958	Dancing bees produce sound (Wenner, 1959).	Do bees communicate information with sound signals?
1959	Dance sounds contain distance information (Wenner, 1962).	Did von Frisch measure meaningful elements? (His hypothesis was based on only circumstantial evidence.)

Date	New Results	Implications

"Although good evidence exists that information is sent (by means of the dance maneuver) . . . no direct evidence exists on how this information is received by other bees." (Wenner, 1962, p. 79.)

| 1959 | In von Frisch's step and fan experiments, successful recruited bees performed too well (Wenner, 1962). | An experimental design can dictate the nature of results (Wenner, 1971). |

"The interpretation of the results of the step-experiments of von Frisch and co-workers is questionable. . . ." (Wenner, 1962, p. 95.)

"The very design may have determined the results in all cases." (Werner, 1971, p. 47.)

(See Figs. 1 and 2.)

| 1960 | Unloaded bees average 7.5 m/sec during direct flight (Wenner, 1963). | The time for travel between hive and food source should be very short for searching recruits. |

(See Fig. 3.)

| 1963 | Esch (1963) obtained results opposite from mine on sugar concentration and dance information (unpublished). | Correlations are not necessarily reliable. |

| 1964 | The above (1963) correlation proved to be spurious and a consequence of temperature (Wenner et al., 1967). | A correlation, even if statistically significant, may not be biologically important. |

"The slight relationship obtained in a comparison of pulse-rate modulation and sugar concentration can be explained as a relationship between pulse rate and temperature." (Wenner et al., 1967, p. 343.)

". . . there is no direct evidence that a recruit bee uses any of the quantitative information contained in the dance elements which have been measured." (Wenner et al., 1967, p. 338.)

| 1964 | Bees can be conditioned rapidly (Wenner and Johnson, 1966). | The claim that the "language" is an instinctive signal system (von Frisch, 1962) comes into question. |

(See Fig. 4.)

"The results of these experiments contribute to the growing body of information which suggests that insects have a greater plasticity of behaviour than has been generally acknowledged. In the light of this information, we must also eventually consider the full role learning may play in insect communication." (Wenner and Johnson, 1966, p. 154. See also Wells, 1973.)

(See Fig. 5.)

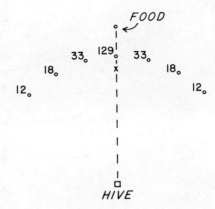

Fig. 1. In his classic fan experiment, von Frisch had a number of bees traveling between a hive and feeding place. He also had seven control sites between hive and food. The numbers beside each control site indicate how many recruits arrived at each site. The X represents the geographical center of all eight dishes. After Wenner (1971).

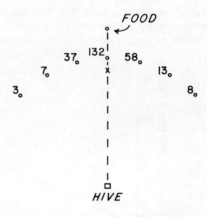

Fig. 2. If the same number of successful recruits as in Fig. 1 had arrived at the eight sites in a ratio related only to the distance of each dish from the center of all dishes, von Frisch would have gotten the same results. One need not conclude that successful recruits had used direction information provided by dancing bees. After Wenner (1971).

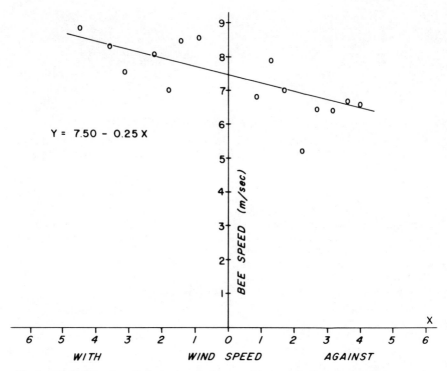

Fig. 3. Wind affects bees little as they fly between hive and feeding station. Values to the right of the ordinate are derived from bees which flew against the wind. Values to the left of this line represent bees flying with the wind. In a no-wind condition, an unloaded bee on a "beeline" would travel a 7.5 m/sec average speed. After Wenner (1963).

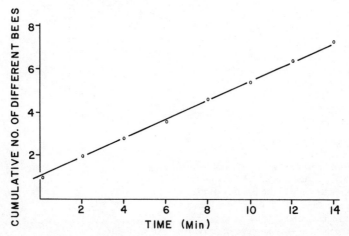

Fig. 4. Before a site begins yielding each day, foragers periodically inspect that site. From Johnson and Wenner (1966).

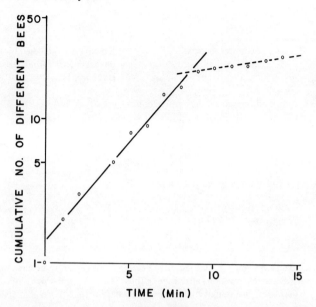

Fig. 5. Once a site begins yielding, foragers recruit other foragers (communication by means of conditioned response). Note the logarithmic scale on the ordinate for comparison with Fig. 4. From Johnson and Wenner (1966).

Date	New Results	Implications
1965	Experienced bees are recruited by capitalizing on previous conditioning (Johnson and Wenner, 1966).	Experienced bees can effectively "communicate" and recruit others by means of conditioned responses. The "language" would be useful at most for inexperienced recruits.

"Early build-up at a previously visited site by experienced foragers immediately after fresh provisioning at this site *closely resembles* the exponential increase one would expect from recruitment by dance communication." (Johnson and Wenner, 1966, p. 264.)

". . . although the dance may contain information concerning location of food sources, we lack clear evidence on the ability of bees to use this information." (Johnson and Wenner, 1966, p. 264.)

1965	Most potential recruits did not find the food source (Johnson and Wenner, 1970).	Recruits did not perform as well as predicted by the language hypothesis.

"Apparently, potential recruits commonly spend a considerable amount of time searching in the field before finally orienting to the food source. These observations are not consistent with the theory that recruits use distance and direction information instructions provided by dancing bees." (Johnson and Wenner, 1970, p. 15.)

Date	New Results	Implications
1966	We encounter the first resistance to challenge.	Even well-established biologists may have a need for final "answers" (Wenner, 1973).

"The natural and human tendency to encourage 'positive' findings and deemphasize 'negative' findings is most pervasive." (Wenner, 1973, p. 279.)

Date	New Results	Implications
1966	In a double-controlled experiment, recruits ignored direction and distance information and ended up preferentially in the center of an odor field (Johnson, 1967; Wenner, 1967; Johnson and Wenner, 1970).	One need not postulate *use* of dance information even for newly recruited (inexperienced) bees.

(See Figs. 6 and 7.)

"These results indicate ... that recruited bees apparently use [some cue other than quantitative dance information] after leaving their hive ... in the process of orienting to a particular food site visited by bees." (Wenner, 1967, p. 849.)

Date	New Results	Implications
1967	Without odor, recruits cannot find a food site (Wenner *et al.*, 1969).	Earlier experiments apparently were not adequately controlled with respect to odor cues.

(See Fig. 8.)

	New Results	Implications
	The longer foragers visit a site, the greater the percentage of successful recruits (Wenner *et al.*, 1969).	The number of successful recruits is directly correlated with the total number of forager visits.

(See Fig. 9.)

Date	New Results	Implications
1968	Given a choice between use of "language" information or use of odor, bees go to an odor source only (Wenner *et al.*, 1969).	The original experiments of von Frisch never had adequate controls against odor cues or aerial pathways of experienced bees (or both).

(See Figs. 10–12.)

"Recruits came to the site marked by the food odor but *not necessarily* to the sites presumably indicated in the hive by the dance maneuvers of returning foragers." (Wenner *et al.*, 1969, p. 86.) [Emphasis added.]

Date	New Results	Implications
1969	By altering odor in the food, one can control dance frequency in the hive, Nasonov gland use, and recruit success (Wells and Wenner, 1971).	The percentage of successful recruits can go down, even if dances and Nasonov gland use increase.

(See Figs. 13–15.)

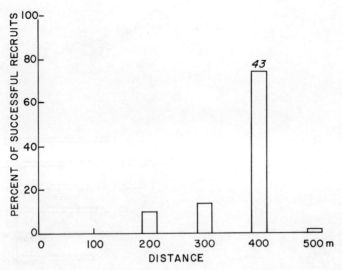

Fig. 6. A repeat of the von Frisch single control type of experiment with 43 bees from one hive yielded the same type of results he obtained. Foragers exploited the 400-m site and scented food was present at the other three control stations. Successful recruits came primarily to the experimental site. After Wenner (1967, Table 1).

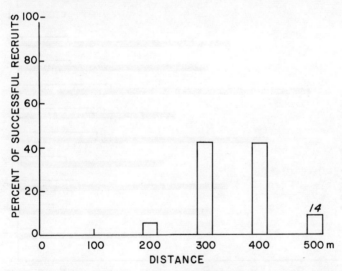

Fig. 7. When the experiment of Fig. 6 was repeated under similar conditions but with bee visitation at each control site (from a control hive) as well as at the experimental site, different results emerged. Successful recruits had arrived primarily at the two central sites and not at the 500-m experimental site. The number of arrivals at each of the sites was related to the distance of each site from the center of all. Recruits had apparently not used the distance information they could have obtained from dancing bees in their parent hive. After Wenner (1967, Table 1).

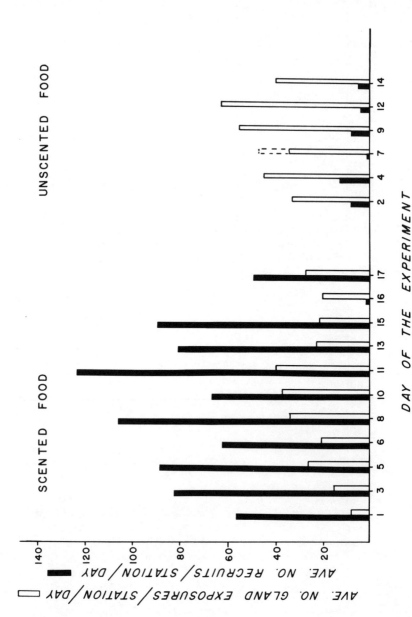

Fig. 8. Without odor in the food or at the locality, very few searching recruits can find a site exploited by foragers. In this case, scent was or was not provided on different days during a 17-day period. Recruits (black bars) succeeded when odor was present but did not do well when odor was absent from the food. This was true even though Nasonov exposure (white bars) was high when scent level was low. The broken white bar is an ex-

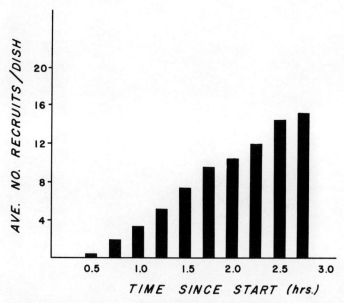

Fig. 9. Recruit success increases gradually each day, even with a constant number of foragers. From Wenner *et al.* (1969).

Date	New Results	Implications

"In spite of high levels of dancing in the hive and much Nasonov gland exposure at the feeding place, recruitment failed when we used unscented sucrose solutions." (Wells and Wenner, 1971, p. 208.)

"The results suggest a complex interrelationship between foragers and recruits both in the hive and in the field." (Wells and Wenner, 1971, p. 208.)

Date	New Results	Implications
1970	Recruits attending "disoriented" dances by foragers still preferentially ended up at the "correct" site, even though provided with no direction information (Wells and Wenner, 1973).	Environmental cues are entirely sufficient for recruit bee success.

"In the absence of compelling evidence to the contrary, it is conservative to suggest that olfaction alone is sufficient to account for recruitment of honey bees to a food source." (Wells and Wenner, 1973, p. 171.)

Date	New Results	Implications
1970	We fully recognized that the controversy no longer centers on the amount or adequacy of data but on interpretation.	We began research on other problems.

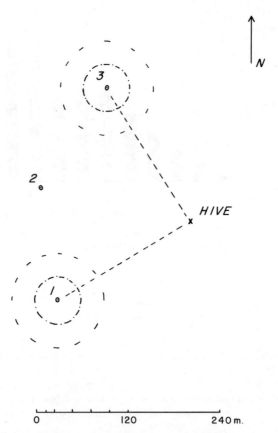

Fig. 10. Foragers were permitted to collect food at sites 1 and 3 but never at 2. They could thus provide location information for the outer sites but not the middle. The circles denote the predicted area of language effectiveness. For results, see Figs. 11 and 12. From Wenner *et al.* (1969).

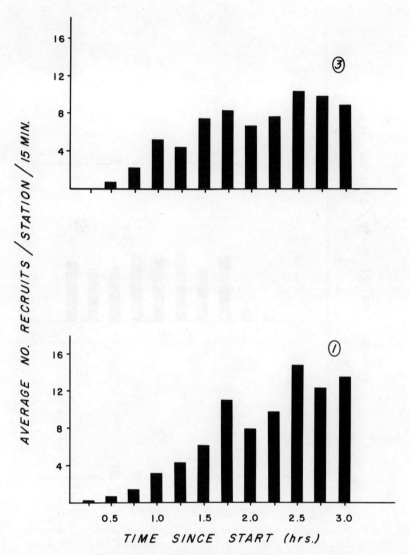

Fig. 11. Recruitment was as expected when odor was provided at sites 1 and 3. From Wenner *et al.* (1969).

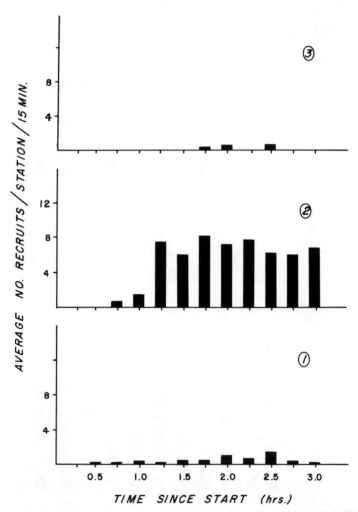

Fig. 12. When foragers were able to provide location information in their hive but collected unscented food at sites 1 and 3, recruits could not find those sites. Instead, recruits succeeded in finding scented site 2, about which they had obtained no quantitative dance information. From Wenner *et al.* (1969).

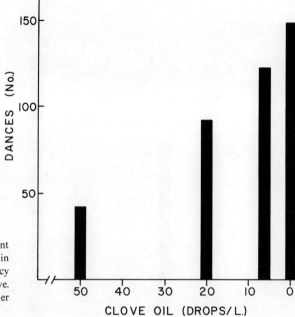

Fig. 13. Lowering the scent level in the food results in an increase in the frequency of dancing in the hive. After Wells and Wenner (1971).

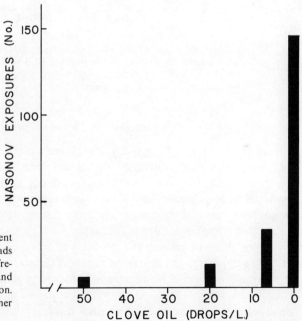

Fig. 14. Lowering the scent level in the food also leads to an increase in the frequency of Nasonov gland exposure at the station. After Wells and Wenner (1971).

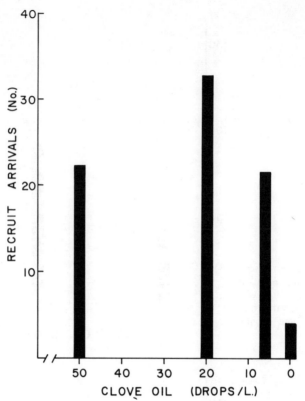

Fig. 15. Despite an increase in frequency of dancing and Nasonov gland exposure (Figs. 13 and 14), lowering scent in the food leads to a marked decrease in the success of recruits. After Wells and Wenner (1971).

Pertinent Data Gathered by Others

After a relatively long delay, proponents of the language hypothesis (i.e., those who have concluded earlier that bees have a language) began new experimentation. Most of the papers detailing their results have been discussed at length elsewhere (Wells and Wenner, 1973), but it is well to review here some of the anomalies these researchers have uncovered and cover some evidence not discussed earlier.

In an effort to resolve the question of whether odor or language use was more important for searching recruits, Goncalves (1969) conducted an interesting experiment. He had a single forager walking to a food source in an enclosed system. On its return to the comb and hivemates, the successful bee danced and presumably provided direction information to potential recruits. These recruits, not having access to the same food site as that visited by the successful bee, left the hive in search of the same type of food.

In the field, Goncalves had provided equidistant test stations in eight compass directions from the hive. The distances between hive and food, according to the experiment, varied from 4 to 40 m.

Contrary to the expectations provided by the von Frisch language hypothesis, recruits ended up at stations in all directions from the hive (Fig. 16). In accordance with the assumption that bees have a language, Goncalves calculated that odor was 65% responsible for recruit success and that language "use" was responsible for the remaining 35% success.

Unfortunately, the wind always blew from the hive toward the site "indicated" by the dancing bee. The experiment thus had a bias incorporated into its design and did not clearly distinguish between a possible "language use" and a reliance on odor cues. More recently, Friesen (1973,

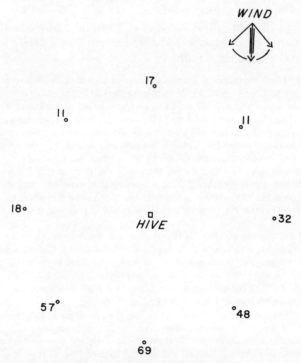

Fig. 16. In a closed system, Goncalves (1969) had a single bee dancing and presumably indicating a single direction. The sum total of his results indicates that recruits succeeded in finding stations in all compass directions from the hive. Wind always blew in the same general direction as that indicated in the dance. Compare these results with those obtained by von Frisch (e.g., Fig. 1 of this chapter). After Goncalves (1969, Fig. 2).

Figs. 12 and 13) gathered data indicating that a station a short distance downwind from a hive may have a greater recruitment rate than a station the same distance upwind from a hive.

All things considered, Goncalves' results can well be viewed another way. In a relatively rigorous test of the language hypothesis, he clearly obtained results not in accord with the expectations provided by that hypothesis (von Frisch, 1948, p. 10):

> We see that the majority of searching bees fanning out, moved within an angle deviating not more than 15° each to the left and to the right from the direction leading towards the feeding place.[2]

Other attempts at resolving the controversy have been far more supportive of the language hypothesis than was that of Goncalves. Wells and I have summarized and criticized these attempts elsewhere (Wells and Wenner, 1973). In this chapter, I will include only a little of our summary of their published accounts, particularly as it relates to the question, "How do recruited bees find a food source?"

Esch and Bastian (1970) conducted a careful study and reported on the performance of 70 experienced bees recruited by a single forager. We summarized their finding as follows:

> In each of their experiments, a group of bees was trained to feed at a scent-marked site near the hive, and ten of the foragers were marked and confined temporarily in a cage. The feeder was next moved to a new location 200 m from the hive and the number of regular foragers reduced to one marked bee. The ten marked former foragers were then released and observed, to discover whether they would be re-recruited to the scent-marked feeder at the new location, as they should be on the hypothesis of linguistic communication by dance attendance.
>
> Fourteen of seventy experimental bees did attend dances and subsequently found the new feeder location. Nineteen additional marked bees attended dances and flew from the hive without arriving at the feeder. The remaining thirty-seven marked experimental bees had no contact with the dancer and did not fly to the new location of the feeder.
>
> Ten of the fourteen successfully re-recruited bees required between one and nine exploratory flights with intermediate contacts with the dancer. Only four succeeded on the first flight, two of them within 1 min of flight time. Many of the nineteen unsuccessful dance attenders also made several flights from the hive; they attended between five and thirty-one dances (mean, 17.5) and made between one and nine exploratory flights (mean, 3.4), without finding the feeder.
>
> For the fourteen successfully re-recruited bees the mean time in flight between first attending the dancer and locating the feeder was 8.5 min compared with less than 0.5 min for experienced foragers (Wenner, 1963). Esch and Bastian did not report the durations of flights by unsuccessful dance attenders. Nor do they eliminate the alternative possibility, that re-recruited foragers were flying about, using wind and odour, while seeking the scent to which they had been trained.

---

[2] Part of the difficulty in evaluating the pertinent evidence in the bee language controversy has arisen from poor editorship. As stated, this quotation has the appearance of being a set of results rather than the interpretation it is.

Gould *et al.* (1970) did a more comprehensive study than Esch and Bastian, but got very much the same set of results. We summarized their findings as follows:

In their series 1 experiment, marked bees were trained to two feeding stations 120 m distant from and in opposite directions from the hive, and many workers in the hive were given individual marks. During experiments, of 277 potential recruits observed to attend dances, 240 failed to arrive at any station, and only thirty-seven were subsequently captured at the feeding stations. Of these, a third arrived at a station in a direction opposite and 240 m distant from that "indicated" in the dance manoeuvre. This result contradicts the prediction of the language hypothesis that all thirty-seven of the successful recruits should have arrived at the "correct" station.

These investigators also found that successful recruits spend a considerable amount of time in flight before reaching the food source. The direct line flight time between hive and a feeding station located at 120 m is less than 25 s (Wenner, 1963), and recruited bees generally fly from the hive within a minute and a half after leaving a dancing bee (50% leave within 30 s) (Johnson and Wenner, 1970). The data in Table 4 of Gould *et al.* (1970) reveal that the twenty-five bees which did arrive at the "correct" station flew an average of more than thirty times longer than would be necessary to "fly rapidly and with certainty" to the food source. The twelve bees which ended up at the station in the opposite direction averaged only thirty-six times as long as necessary for a direct flight.

Mautz's experiments (1971) had a different emphasis than those of either Esch and Bastian or Gould, Henerey, and MacLeod, but he obtained results that did not contradict the data obtained by the others. We wrote:

Mautz (1971) also was concerned with the behaviour of individually marked workers which came in contact with a forager dancing in the hive. In his experiments, 32% of marked workers that attended dances found the feeder, and the amount of time the potential recruits attended the dancer was positively correlated with success at finding the food. In addition, the average flight time for successful recruits was more than ten times that expected of experienced foragers and the mean flight time of bees which flew out but failed to find the feeder was twice that of the successful recruits.

To date, Lindauder (1971) is the only investigator who has repeated any of our experiments, but he did so only in part. We reported:

The first type of experiment undertaken by Lindauer resembled those of Gould *et al.* (1970) in design, and yielded similar data. Forager bees were trained from a hive to two feeding sites, and were then fed high molarity sugar at one and low molarity sugar at the other. Virtually all dancing was by bees visiting the high molarity sugar site, and most successful recruits landed there.

In his second experiment, Lindauer put out three stations in a geometry similar to that used in our experiments (Wenner, Wells, and Johnson, 1969) and trained bees to stations 1 and 3 but not to 2. Then, with scented sucrose at all three stations (a variation from our design), he collected recruits. Although the stations were deliberately asymmetrical (no foragers at station 2), approximately one-fourth of all captured recruits arrived at station 2.

Our account of the contributions of these several workers compares their results with the predictions of the language hypothesis and the odor-dependent hypothesis proposed by us earlier (Wenner *et al.*, 1969). Wells and I (1973) concluded:

> Thus all the authors we have discussed (Lindauer, Mautz, Esch and Bastian, Gould *et al.*, explicitly or implicitly assumed that the feeding stations they established in the field were in no way distinctive to bees and that the environment can be made symmetrical with respect to odours and other factors. They also assumed that, in order to find the food, a recruit must have prior quantitative information about its location. These assumptions lead the authors to interpret arrival of new workers at sites visited by dancing foragers as definitive evidence of linguistic communication. As pointed out earlier they have focused their attention on successful recruits. Experiments based on these assumptions invariably lead to affirmation of the consequence of the hypothesis (If bees have a language, recruits will reach the food. Some recruits find the food. Therefore, bees have a language). This reasoning is deductively invalid.

Odor Detectors as Vector Selectors of Nectar Collectors[3]

Relevant Evidence from Preceding Studies

The polarization and preoccupation inherent in the controversy over a "language" among honey bees have had some unfortunate side-effects, the most notable of which has been the neglect or rejection by some investigators of valid and significant results. However, the behavior of animals provides us with our only window into their world, and it is imperative that experimental results be viewed in as many ways as possible—not just with respect to how the data might relate to the controversy. Much of the evidence gathered by both proponents and challengers of the language hypothesis for example, bears directly on another question, "What is the flight path of searching recruits?" Even a partial answer to that question could be useful in agriculture as well as in our basic understanding of how flying animals orient.

A study of the evidence summarized in the previous section reveals several points that can be easily confirmed and that pertain to the particular question. For the sake of brevity, these points may be listed as follows:

1. Recruits preferentially orient toward the center of an odor field.
2. Recruit success rate is dependent on odor concentration but not on Nasonov gland secretions at the food source or dance frequency in the hive.
3. With no odor cues, recruits cannot find a food site.

---

[3] Title by Larry Jon Friesen.

4. Recruits attending disoriented dances can still find the "correct" site in the field.
5. Even with odor in the food or at the food location, most recruits do not find the site visited by foragers.
6. Most recruits require several flights out from the hive before they locate the food source visited by foragers.
7. Most recruits are in the air considerably longer than necessary for a direct flight.
8. Recruits apparently interact in the field and perhaps in the hive.
9. Recruit success is dependent more on the cumulative number of forager trips than on the given number of foragers involved.
10. Recruits do not begin arriving in quantity until about $\frac{1}{2}$ hr after foragers begin making regular trips.
11. Recruit success increases with time in a regular manner.
12. Recruits always arrive at a food source from downwind.

Apparently, only one person has formally directed his attention to the overall implications of the above points. Rather than focusing on the controversy itself, Friesen (1973) studied the behavior of searching recruits. He asked the general question, "What determines the flight paths and success of newly recruited bees?" For a full treatment of his work, one should refer to his paper. Here I will only summarize the results of his extensive experimentation.

The Number of Foragers and Recruit Success

When working with a single hive and with bees trained to visit a single site, Friesen found that a reduction in the number of foragers to one-half normal led to a reduction in the number of successful recruits to less than one-quarter normal. Since this was clearly an unexpected result according to any extant explanation of recruit behavior, he hypothesized that searching recruits somehow relied more heavily on the density of foragers in the field (at the dish and/or on their flight lines) than on frequency of dancing in the hive.

In an ingenious test of that premilinary hypothesis, Friesen used two hives 600 m apart in a field, each with its own color of bees. One of the hives had foragers flying downwind to a feeding site intermediate between the two hives, and foragers from the other hive flew upwind while on their way out to that same site (Fig. 17). He first ran the experiment for 3 days to obtain a base line for recruitment rate (average number of recruits per round trip per forager) for each of the two hives. He then repeated the experiment for 6 days with one-half the number of foragers from the downwind hive. His results were striking (see Table I):

Three important facts emerged. At the distance involved (300 m),

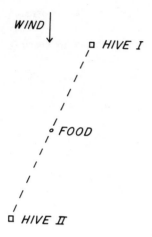

WIND

□ HIVE I

° FOOD

□ HIVE II

Fig. 17. Foragers from two hives exploited a food source between them. Recruits which could search for the upwind site were much more successful than recruits searching for the downwind site (see Table I).

Table I. Summary of Friesen's Results with Foraging Bees[a]

	Hive I	Hive II
Ten Foragers from each hive	0.46	1.33
Ten foragers from hive I, five from hive II	0.29	1.30

After Friesen (1973, Table II).
[a] Changing the number of foragers from one hive (hive II of Fig. 17) altered the recruit success rate for searching bees from another hive (hive I). Recruits which could travel upwind from hive II did not have an alteration of recruit success rate, even though the number of foragers was halved.

recruitment rate for an upwind site was considerably better than recruitment rate for bees from the other hive searching for that same location. Of even more interest, though, is the fact that a change in the number of foragers from one hive altered the recruitment rate of another hive. Friesen also found that search times of recruits from both hives increased when the number of foragers decreased.

With the three above results in mind, he concluded (p. 111):

the data suggest that the disproportionate recruit success with different numbers of foragers visiting a feeding site may be attributed to the density of these foragers in the field.

Odor Dependence of Searching Recruits

Early in his studies, Friesen recognized that extremely small amounts of odor could aid recruits in their search. At a time of year when forage was scarce for colonies, he found that even the odor of paper toweling could cling to the bodies of foragers and apparently later serve as a locality cue for searching recruits.

As a consequence of the above recognition of subtle odor cues, Friesen later strove for ever better control against odor artifacts. In time, he found he could have nearly complete cessation of recruitment by removing odor from the food, provided he worked in a relatively odor-free habitat (Fig. 18).

Friesen then explored the full implication of all of the above findings: If recruits can orient toward even very subtle odor cues, and if recruit success is correlated with forager density in the field, then recruits may well be aided in their search by the odors inadvertently carried on the

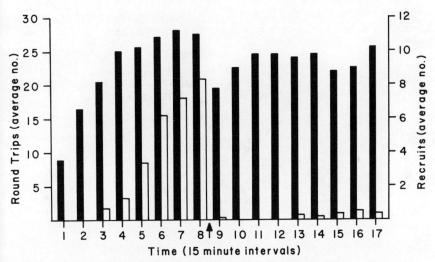

Fig. 18. When scent was removed from a feeding station (arrow), far fewer recruits were successful (white bars). The number of forager trips (black bars) remained relatively constant, and it should be noted that the frequency of dancing would have probably increased at the time of scent removal (see Fig. 13). Note how the results in Fig. 15 correspond with the results shown here. From Friesen (1973).

bodies of regular foragers. That is, characteristic odor molecules would drift downwind from the well-traveled flight paths and recruits could exploit that circumstance.

He next studied that possibility.

Forager Flight Paths and Searching Recruits

These experiments were quite complete and extensive, so I will review only some of the findings. Friesen used one 360-m feeding station at a time, either at a crosswind site or at a downwind site. He tested recruitment rate at one or the other station by scenting the food and capturing all recruits on arrival. The results were unambiguous. As can be seen in Figs. 19 and 20, recruits more readily located a crosswind food source than a downwind food source, despite the fact that recruits searching for a downwind site would presumably have the "advantage" of a tail wind.

As a partial test of where the recruit bees might be as they searched, Friesen ran a two-step experiment. In the first half of a 4-hr. period, foragers exploited scented food sources at one of the two 360-m sites. In the second half of that period, scent was removed from those regular stations (but food remained) and scented monitoring stations were set up, one at a time, at various localities in the field. By this means, the environment was sampled in order to locate the recruits as they searched.

The results were quite clear. When foragers visited an unscented crosswind station that had formerly been scented, recruits more commonly arrived at scented monitoring sites located upwind than they did at sites

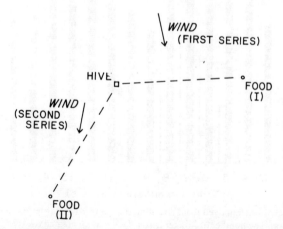

Fig. 19. When bees from one hive were trained out to either a crosswind station or a downwind station, recruits were more successful at finding the crosswind station (see Fig. 20).

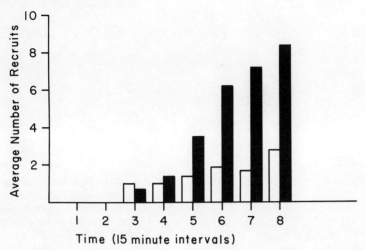

Fig. 20. The black bars represent the number of recruit arrivals per unit time at a crosswind site. The white bars show the increase in success at a downwind site. From Friesen (1973).

located downwind from the flight line of those foragers. The fact that a significant portion of the searching recruits did arrive at monitoring stations downwind from the flight line indicates that their search pattern carried them down there at least some of the time.

However, when the food was downwind from the hive, searching recruits were collected at monitoring stations only when they were near the flight line. And again recruitment rate was much lower at the downwind site than at the crosswind site. The entire set of results described is consistent with what one would expect if recruits somehow exploited odors drifting downwind from forager flight lines.

By keeping track of the arrival time of early recruits, Friesen learned that recruits found a station intermediate between hive and feeding place sooner than they found the feeding place itself and sooner than they found stations close to the hive. He concluded from all of the above (p. 121):

> An hypothesis consistent with the data from the previous experiments suggests that a population of searching bees accumulates within an area under the influence of bee and bee-carried odors. A monitoring station placed in this population of searching bees will receive recruits in numbers and times dependent on the odor of the station and the density of bees searching in that area for the same odor.

Wind, Distance, and Recruit Success

In all his earlier experiments, Friesen had worked only during times of low wind speeds (less than 5 m/sec). Yet if odor dependence is the key

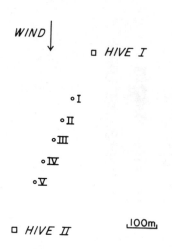

Fig. 21. Foragers from two hives visited one station at a time at varying distances either upwind or downwind from their hive. The results of recruit success are shown in Figs. 22 and 23. After Friesen (1973).

to recruit success, as indicated in those experiments, then the direction and distance of a site from the hive, with respect to wind direction, would affect the pattern of recruitment. So also would wind speed. The above implication is evident in the crosswind–downwind recruitment comparison (i.e., Fig. 19).

As an additional measure of these wind relationships, he used the two-hive system shown in Fig. 17. This time, however, he selected five potential sites for stations 75 m apart on a line between the two hives. As in the earlier case, each hive served as a control against the other. An equal number of foragers from each hive visited each station as it was run singly. Recruits from one hive thus had to find a site by somehow traveling downwind and recruits from the other hive had the presumed "disadvantage" of a head wind (Fig. 21).

The recruitment patterns for the two hives differed markedly. The distance between hive and food mattered little for those successful recruits which found an upwind station (Fig. 22). But that same circumstance was not true at all for recruits searching for a downwind station. With increasing distance, recruit success fell off markedly (Fig. 23). One more interesting comparison emerges from the above two figures. The two closest stations to the upwind hive (I and II at 150 m and 225 m, respectively) had a relatively good success rate for bees from that hive. That is, food stations only a short distance downwind may not be in a bad location recruitment-wise, compared to stations placed only a short distance upwind. This point needs further study, however, since no true control was run for that particular comparison.

Friesen then examined the influence of wind speed. He found that recruits from the upwind hive came into a station in greatest numbers just after each slight temporary increase in wind speed. Recruits from a

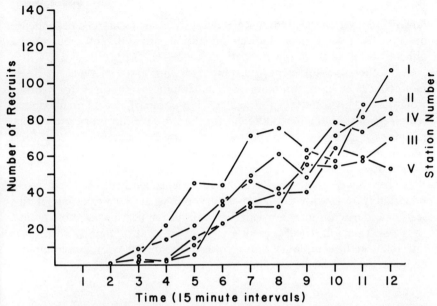

Fig. 22. The relative success of recruits which arrived at stations at different distances upwind from their hive. The fact that the stations were 75 m apart did not matter much in the recruitment rate. From Friesen (1973).

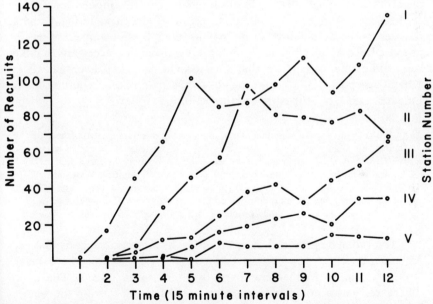

Fig. 23. The distance factor was very important for the success of recruits if the stations were downwind from the hive. The farther downwind the station, the fewer the recruits. From Friesen (1973).

downwind hive, on the other hand, did not show such a marked dependence on changes in wind speed. Downwind stations are apparently much more difficult to locate than upwind stations.

Another measurement substantiated this last inference. Friesen indirectly calculated minimum and maximum search times for recruits from the two hives for the intermediate, 300-m, site. The data on maximum search times were the most different for the two hives. In four experiments, the average maximum time spent searching by any successful recruit for a station upwind from that hive was only 8.8 min, while that figure for a station downwind from the hive was 24.3 min.

The above set of results gathered independently by Friesen agrees remarkably well with the 11 summary points at the beginning of this section and extends our knowledge beyond the implications of those points. In the next section, I will present a model that can explain how these facts interrelate in the complex system of forager–recruit behavior, i.e., communication at the population level in a social system.

Food Getting—a Study in Communication

Individual and Population Approaches

A traditional treatment of honey bee communication is that of viewing the problem of recruitment to food sources as a one-to-one communication act between a forager and a potential recruit. Under this paradigm, and as researchers became more aware of the complications inherent in the proposed use of a "language" among bees, it became necessary to credit bees with greater capabilities than ever recognized earlier. Eventually, with general acceptance of a "language" as fact, striking claims could be made. Lindauer (1961, p. 110) expressed this attitude as follows:

> Probably no means of communication and no act of orientation exists in the entire animal kingdom that requires for success such a constellation of varied sensory performances as the "language" of the bees. And it is not only the correlation in the central nervous system, translating impressions from the optical sense into the gravitational sense, or translating a rhythmic tactile sensation into the measurement of flight energy and therefore into the estimation of distance, that amazes us; it is also the precision of the purely physiological performance of the sensory organs.

The rationale provided in this chapter, by contrast, suggests that bees are not necessarily superbeings but may find odor sources by a means strikingly similar to that employed by other flying insects. The major difference, and a complicating factor it is, is the social advantage bees have. Now, largely as a consequence of Friesen's work on the behavior of searching recruits, the population (social) aspects of recruitment have become more clear. Bees apparently have a communication at the population level as well as at the individual level.

In this last part of the chapter, I will present a model for the communication process of honey bee recruitment to food sources. I now see this process as a three-stage sequence, including forager–forager and forager–recruit interactions at the individual level and a multiple interaction between recruits and foragers once recruits have left the hive. These three stages will be dealt with in turn, even though they do overlap in time in a real situation.

I. Forager Build-Up: Communication at the Individual Level. At the start of each day, foragers begin leaving the hive on inspection trips. They visit those sources at which they had had success on the previous day. If unsuccessful, they return to the hive and make similar trips out periodically.

Once successful (when blossoms begin secreting nectar), loaded foragers carry food and odor back into the hive, but they do not dance on these first few returns. Recruitment occurs nevertheless. Any other foragers conditioned to the same odor source which happen to contact a successful forager immediately leave the hive in response to that stimulus. With hundreds or thousands of bees involved, the net result is a logarithmic build-up of involved foragers, a communication by means of conditioned response. This is the behavior von Frisch noticed and described earlier (1946, p. 13):

> It follows further that a communication can be transmitted from the returning bee to other bees by touch alone, without the necessity for any dance.

It is also the behavior described by Ribbands at a later date (1954):

> the mere presence of the training scent in the hive, in the absence of either food-sharing or dancing, can encourage crop-attached bees to go to their crop.

Experienced bees can become involved in nectar collecting very rapidly by this means. Since each forager travels directly to the location it had exploited on the previous day, virtually all foragers can be recruited simultaneously in all directions from the hive within a $\frac{1}{2}$–1 hr period. A more comprehensive treatment of this communication act is detailed elsewhere (Wenner and Johnson, 1966; Johnson and Wenner, 1966; Johnson, 1967).

Aerial Pathways. Once involved, each forager travels its own "beeline," but the thousands of foragers visiting similar types of food collectively form aerial pathways. The hive and the various exploited sources may thus be viewed as a web, with the hive at its center and aerial pathways forming the strands of that web.

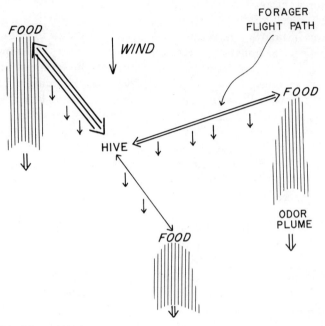

Fig. 24. Odors drifting downwind from the hive, from food sources, and perhaps from flight lines of foragers all can provide environmental cues for searching recruits.

One can easily locate these aerial pathways around a hive by lying on his back and counting the number of bees seen flying out from the hive directly overhead. If this tallying is done at a constant distance (50–100 m) and in varying directions from the hive, one can also determine the relative dimensions of each "strand." That dimension is, of course, related to the net worth of the food sources being exploited.

Although the pathways themselves are fixed in space, odor molecules necessarily drift downwind from the flying bees, from the hive, and from the food sources. Altogether, the system may appear as shown in Fig. 24.

II. Recruitment of Inexperienced Bees: Individual Communication in the Hive. After foragers begin unloading in the hive, potential recruits become stimulated. These recruits then apparently stimulate foragers to dance[4] and obtain a composite odor signal (e.g., food and locality) from that dancing bee. Without such an interaction, recruitment apparently does not occur, but there still is no good evidence as to what exactly

---

[4] The teleological implication has always been that foragers dance *in order to* recruit others, but evidence is lacking for that assumption.

transpires during that contact. It is evident, however, that the less odor on the forager, the greater the likelihood that it will dance (see Wells and Wenner, 1971, for a more complete treatment).

Before or after contact with a dancing bee, the potential recruit contacts a third bee (See also Núñez, 1970; p. 533). The recruit apparently obtains a drop of liquid (honey or nectar) from this third bee and then either stimulates another forager to dance or leaves the hive within a minute (the role of this third bee needs further study).

Those bees which leave become searching recruits.

III. Searching Recruits: Communication at the Population Level. Friesen's 1973 paper provides the basis for this part of the model. Some percentage of the potential recruits leave the hive and search. This search can be described quite simply—on receipt of a proper combination of odors (food odor, bee odor, location odor), these recruits fly upwind a short distance.

Just how an upwind flight pattern can get recruits to a downwind station requires some speculation (see Fig. 25). I propose that recruits, just after they leave their hive, fly downwind an average of 100–300 m

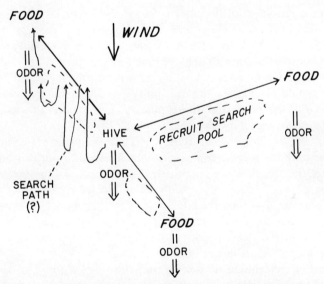

Fig. 25. A proposed model is based on the configuration shown in Fig. 24. Since recruits require more time for searching than necessary for a direct flight from hive to food source, they must accumulate in the field. The path of a searching recruit might well be a repetitious looping as it gets odor stimuli from various foragers traversing the flight line.

and then fly just outside the odor plume that drifts downwind from their hive. (Unfortunately, this speculation is a bit difficult to test, since a monitoring station placed in this area would have its effect masked by the odors coming from the hive.) This downwind flight would vary in distance according to wind speed.

Once a recruit has escaped the influence of hive odor, it could fly upwind on receipt of the proper combination of odors drifting downwind from one of the aerial pathways or from the food source itself. If reinforced shortly by the perception of other odor molecules, it would continue upwind. If not reinforced within a short time, it would again fly downwind until it received "familiar" molecules.

Searching takes time. This means that searching recruits necessarily accumulate in the field. It further follows that the recruit pool that would develop downwind from the flight line would provide for repeated contacts among searching bees as well as between searchers and foragers. It may be that such contacts stimulate use of the Nasonov glands by both foragers and searching recruits. Though the Nasonov secretion apparently does not attract recruits, it may serve as a cohesive force in the recruit pool.

Visual cues may also be important in this population interaction. Searching recruits often follow other bees into the station and appear to interact with each other visually when downwind from the food source.

Once a recruit pool becomes large enough, searching bees would be steadily siphoned off at either end. By flying upwind, recruits at the near end would be led back to the hive. At the remote end, recruits would find the food source and immediately become foragers themselves. In a natural system (where recruits are not killed on arrival), the increased number of foragers would strengthen the "visibility" of the aerial pathways, more recruits could be successful more quickly, and so on. Efficiency would increase with increased involvement.

Implications. Suppose searching recruits do form a nebulous mass in midair and downwind from each flight line and are drawn out of that pool once they reach either end. Several considerations emerge:

First of all, a study of virtually all published experiments and their results indicates that they are consistent with that model. This generalization applies especially well to the original experiments run by von Frisch (1946). Distinctive locality odors and flight lines have always been real potential sources of artifact in experimentation.

The low percentage of success and the large amount of time spent searching fit the model quite well. So also can one expect that an increase in the number of foragers would lead to a disproportionate increase in the number of recruit arrivals.

The difficulty in training bees to visit a food source in the spring of the year becomes perfectly understandable. The heavily traveled aerial pathways between hive and spring flowers would provide too much odor competition for a very weak odor cue drifting downwind from the relatively few foragers possible at an artificial station.

The relative success of recruits as they search for upwind, downwind, and crosswind stations becomes understandable. A searching bee in a downwind recruit pool is not as likely to end up in the odor plume of a downwind food source as its counterpart in an upwind recruit pool.

There must also be some distance downwind where recruitment is no longer feasible. This would, of course, be some function of odor concentration, forager number, and wind speed. The effective upwind distance for food exploitation would be considerably greater and would depend somewhat on wind stability.

The model is open to test. If, for example, foragers are visiting a crosswind station, one can introduce a new station either upwind or downwind from that site. According to the model, an upwind station should alter the former recruitment pattern more than would a new downwind station. A further testing in this manner would lead to a clarification of some parameters of the model.

Finally, practical field tests should now be run. Efficient pollination of field crops and avoidance of spray poisoning damage may both be enhanced if the model holds up to test. In areas with predictable winds, it should even be possible to place crops more efficiently so that pollination and spray poisoning can coexist.

Acknowledgments

I thank Dr. Larry J. Friesen for the use of original drawings and I am grateful to both he and Dr. Patrick H. Wells for their help in critically reading the manuscript. I am also indebted to Margaret Day for help in typing. The Office of Naval Research, the National Science Foundation, and the University of California have all provided financial assistance for the projects described herein. More specific acknowledgments of the help from those agencies can be found in the individual papers cited.

References

Altmann, S. A., 1972, Without a word (book review), *Nature* **240**: 361–362.
Esch, H., 1963, Über die Auswirkung der Futterplatzqualität auf die Schallerzeugung im Werbetanz der Honigbiene (*Apis mellifica*), *Zool. Anzieger. Suppl.* **26**: 302–309.
Esch, H., and Bastian, J. A., 1970, How do newly recruited honey bees approach a food site? *Z. Vergl. Physiol.* **68**: 175–181.

Friesen, L. J., 1973, The search dynamics of recruited bees, *Apis mellifera ligustica* Spinola, *Biol. Bull.* **144:** 107–131.

Goncalves, L. S., 1969, A study of orientation information given by one trained bee by dancing, *J. Apic. Res.* **8:** 113–132.

Gould, J. L., Henerey, M., and MacLeod, M. C., 1970, Communication of direction by the honeybee, *Science* **169:** 544–554.

Johnson, D. L., 1967, Honey bees: Do they use the direction information contained in their dance maneuver? *Science* **155:** 844–847.

Johnson, D. L., and Wenner, A. M., 1966, A relationship between conditioning and communication in honey bees, *Anim. Behav.* **14:** 261–265.

Johnson, D. L., and Wenner, A. M., 1970, Recruitment efficiency in honeybees: Studies on the role of olfaction, *J. Apic. Res.* **9:** 13–18.

Lindauer, M., 1961, *Communication Among Social Bees,* 143 pp., Harvard University Press, Cambridge, Mass.

Lindauer, M., 1971, The functional significance of the honeybee waggle dance, *Amer. Naturalist* **105:** 89–96.

Mautz, D., 1971, Der Kommunikationeffekt der Schwänzeltänze bei *Apis mellifica carnica* (Pollm.), *Z. Vergl. Physiol.* **72:** 197–220.

McGill, T. E., 1973, *Readings in Animal Behavior,* p. 277, Holt, Rinehart and Winston, New York.

Morse, R. A., 1973, Questions about the dance language of the honeybee, *Gleanings in Bee Culture* **101:** 151.

Núñez, J. A. 1970. The relationship between sugar flow and foraging and recruiting behaviour of honey bees (*Apis mellifera* L.), *Anim. Behav.* **18:** 527–538.

Phillips, E. A., 1971, *Basic Ideas in Biology,* pp. 504–514, Macmillan, New York.

Popper, K., 1957, Philosophy of science: A personal report, in: *British Philosophy in the Mid-Century: A Cambridge Symposium* (C. A. Mace, ed.), pp. 155–191, Macmillan, New York.

Ribbands, C. R. 1954. Communication between honey bees. I. The response of crop-attached bees to the scent of their crop. *Proc. Roy. Ent. Soc. London (A)* **29:** 141–144.

von Frisch, K., 1946, The dances of the honeybee, *Bull. Anim. Behav.* **5:** 1–32.

von Frisch, K., 1948, Solved and unsolved problems of bee language, *Bull. Anim. Behav.* **9:** 2–25.

von Frisch, K., 1962, Dialects in the language of bees, *Sci. Am.* **207:** 78–87.

von Frisch, K., 1967a, *The Dance Language and Orientation of Bees,* 566 pp., Harvard University Press, Cambridge, Mass.

von Frisch, K., 1967b, Honeybees: Do they use direction and distance information provided by their dancers? *Science* **158:** (1076–1077).

Waller, G. D., 1973, The effect of citral and geraniol conditioning on the searching activity of honeybee recruits, *J. Apic. Res.* **12:** 55–59.

Wells, P. H. 1973. Honey bees, in: *Invertebrate Learning. Vol. 2. Arthropods and Gastropod Mollusks* (W. C. Corning, J. A. Dyal, and A. O. D. Willows, eds.), pp. 173–185, Plenum Press, New York.

Wells, P. H., and Wenner A. M. 1971, The influence of food scent on behavior of foraging honey bees, *Physiol. Zool.* **44:** 191–209.

Wells, P. H., and Wenner, A. M., 1973, Do honey bees have a language? *Nature* **241:** 171–175.

Wenner, A. M., 1959, The relationship of sound production during the waggle dance of the honey bee to the distance of the food source, *Bull. Entomol. Soc. Am.* **5:** 142.

Wenner, A. M., 1962, Sound production during the waggle dance of the honey bee, *Anim. Behav.* **10:** 79–95.

Wenner, A. M., 1963, The flight speed of honey bees: A quantitative approach, *J. Apic. Res.* **2:** 25–32.

Wenner, A. M., 1967, Honey bees: Do they use the distance information contained in their dance maneuver? *Science* **155**: 847–849.

Wenner, A. M., 1971, *The Bee Language Controversy: An Experience in Science,* 110 pp., Educational Programs Improvement Corporation, P. O. Box 3406, Boulder, Col.

Wenner, A. M., 1973, Adam and Eve in science, *Am. Bio. Teacher* **35**: 278–279.

Wenner, A. M., and Johnson, D. L., 1966, Simple conditioning in honey bees, *Anim. Behav.* **14**: 149–155.

Wenner, A. M., Wells, P. H., and Rohlf, F. J., 1967, An analysis of the waggle dance and recruitment in honey bees, *Physiol. Zool.* **40**: 317–344.

Wenner, A. M., Wells, P. H., and Johnson, D. L., 1969, Honey bee recruitment to food sources: Olfaction or language? *Science* **164**: 84–86.

Wilson, E. O., 1972, Letter, *Sci. Am.* **227**: 6.

CHAPTER 7

Communication in Mother–Infant Interaction

Howard A. Moss

Child Research Branch
National Institute of Mental Health
Bethesda, Maryland

Observations of mother–infant dyads yield a host of impressions, both to the eyes of the naive, casual observer and to the scrutiny of the trained student of interpersonal interactions. Familiar reactions of a mother relating to her infant range from viewing the mother as warm and sensitive, the infant as wide-eyed and alert, and the dyad as exhibiting rapport to the other extreme, at which the mother is regarded as rejecting and obtuse, the infant as unresponsive and difficult, and the dyad as uncommunicative and disconnected. Observations of this sort are often stated with a deep sense of conviction and immutable certainty. The generally held agreement as to what the state of affairs is between a mother and infant, based on certain prototypical qualities of the interaction, suggests some level of consensual validation as to what constitute positive or negative attributes in a mother–infant interaction. Certainly, artists for centuries have found mothers engaging in positive types of contact with their infants to be a favorite subject matter, and there seems to be good reason to believe that viewers of these works of art concur with what the respective artists were attempting to depict.

General agreement seems to exist that mother–infant relationships vary considerably and that these relationships forecast important future behaviors and styles of interaction. Yet it is only recently that direct observational studies have been conducted that are aimed at delineating and describing characteristics of mother–infant pairs. Certainly any understanding of the communicative process between mother and infant requires a detailed

171

cataloging of their respective behaviors that either directly or remotely affect one another, as well as a systematic study of the reciprocal changes in behavior that are produced through each other's actions. It would seem that such fundamental information concerning mother–infant interaction could only be achieved through the use of direct observations. These observations thus provide the optimal conditions for determining and describing the development of the communication process in the mother–infant relationship.

In order for communication to occur between mother and infant, certain classes of stimuli or signals need to be emitted by one member of the dyad under conditions where these stimuli can be perceived by the other member of the dyad (pair). These signals, of course, are just the preconditions or elements necessary for communication to take place. The stimuli (signals) provided by one member of the dyad must be perceived by the other member of the dyad, and what is perceived must have the potential of producing a discriminative response. Any indication that either the mother or infant through some action is modifying the behavior of the other, i.e., is influencing learning, is evidence that communication is occurring. According to this criterion, the communication process between mother and infant is initiated during the early days and weeks of life.

Various normative studies have produced data concerning the respective ages at which infants are likely to selectively respond to interpersonal stimuli (and thus be amenable to communication). There is consensus among a number of investigators that "the smile is readily elicited by a human face by approximately two months of age" (Gewirtz, 1965). A fearful response toward strangers is not highly manifest until after 7 or 8 months of age (Tennes and Lampl, 1964). However, this is not to say that the infant does not recognize his own mother much earlier. In a study dealing with the infant's attention to a series of visual stimuli, Carpenter and Stechler (1967) conclude that discrimination of a picture of the mother's face from other stimuli used in their study was manifested as early as 2 weeks of age.

Conditioning studies with infants also provide evidence as to how interactions with the mother might shape continuing changes in the infant's interpersonal responses toward her. Experimental conditioning studies of vocalization (Rheingold et al., 1959), smiling (Brackbill, 1958), and modification of crying (Etzel and Gewirtz, 1967) all illustrate the infant's potential responsiveness to learning contingencies associated with interaction with the mother. Of particular interest to the issue of communication is the fact that in some of these vocalization and smiling studies infants became upset and cried during extinction trials. This behavior suggests that these infants had developed an expectancy for social reinforcements and became frustrated when these reinforcements were no longer forthcoming.

Both mother and infant provide signals toward one another, and each in turn may be influenced by the other's signals. However, in studying the communication process of this dyad it is more difficult to evaluate the origin and meaning of the maternal behaviors, since the mother's actions toward the infant are often colored by previously existing attitudes and culturally prescribed modes of child care. One has to rely, to some degree, on verbal reports from the mother concerning her general orientation in order to assess effectively the meaning of her communicative acts toward her infant. The infant's behavior, on the other hand, tends to be easier to interpret, since it is influenced to a considerably lesser degree by antecedent events and cognitive considerations.

Communication between mother and infant can be conceptualized as occurring at different levels of complexity and can take into account a broad range of behaviors. At the biological level, the let-down reflex, whereby milk spontaneously is secreted from the mammary gland in response to a cry stimulus, represents a form of communication. Similarly, the infant's being comforted or soothed by mild, ambient stimulation can be regarded as an early manifestation of, or a potential basis for, communication with the mother.

Somewhat more complex levels of interaction where communication takes place are instances where the mother receives signals from the infant that reflect a need, a specific orientation, or a change in state that the mother has the potential to react to. When the mother contributes toward satisfying the need, facilitating the orientation, or modulating a nondisruptive state in the infant, she provides evidence that she is responsive or attuned to her infant. What is necessary, then, is for the mother to perceive and correctly interpret the meaning of the signal emitted by the infant. She also should be cognizant of the course of action that is functionally related to dealing with this signal and exhibit a capacity to respond accordingly. For a mother to be attuned to her infant, she need not always be obliged to take a concrete action toward the signals he is displaying. Some signals, indeed, may carry the overtone that the mother should not intervene. Evidence as to the appropriateness and effectiveness of the intervention can, as a rule, only be judged in terms of the outcome.

Crying behavior in the infant provides an illustration of a type of signal in which the mother may have to make the discrimination when or when not to respond. If the infant's crying reflects distress and the mother intervenes to remove the source of distress so that the infant is quieted, it can be assumed that the mother understood and responded appropriately to her infant. There are conditions, however, where the mother might be exhibiting greater sensitivity by not responding immediately to her crying infant. For instance, some infants while shifting from an awake to a sleeping state will cry briefly. In such cases, it appears as if the crying is assisting the infant in making the transition between these states. Mothers who intervene on such occasions may be, in effect, disrupting the infant's functioning. Thus in interpreting the meaning of an infant's cry the mother has to consider the context, duration, and intensity of this behavior. Mothers vary in their ability to make these discriminations, particularly for the more ambiguous signals. They also vary in their desire to respond, as well as in the basis for their response. In attempting to understand and study the communication process between mother and infant, it is necessary to consider that some mothers will attend to a crying infant because of their interest in comforting and providing relief to the infant. Others may respond mainly because they experience the cry as a noxious stimulus and wish to terminate this unpleasantness. In conducting such analyses, attention tends mainly to be focused on the mother in terms of her sensitivity and responsiveness. However, individual differences among infant behaviors also contribute to variability in the interaction. Infants vary in the clarity of the signals they emit. Some infants seem relatively easy to "read" or understand, whereas others tend to be difficult. Also, infants differ greatly in their responsiveness to maternal intervention.

In addition to communications that are based simply on a maternal response to an infant signal, one can observe or infer more complex, interactive communications. An example would be the instances where the infant has acquired an expectancy that his signals evoke differential responses from significant others; e.g., the infant anticipates that his cry may produce a desired effect. Communication at this level demonstrates some degree of learning in the infant. The communication and learning process are naturally combined and under optimal conditions facilitate one another and grow together. The mother who responds to her infant in a clear and predictable manner contributes to the infant's learning opportunities and therefore facilitates higher-order communications.

Over the past number of years at the Child Research Branch of the National Institute of Mental Health, we have conducted several studies on mother–infant interaction during the early months of life. These studies, largely, have consisted of time sampling of mother and infant behaviors in the home. The objective of this research was to obtain a relatively comprehensive picture of the mother–infant interaction so that the precoded categories covered a broad range of variables. Some of the infant behaviors coded were infant state (sleep, awake, and crying time) and the spontaneous occurrences of such responses as smiling, vocalizing, motor activity, and attention to various stimuli in the home environment. Representative maternal behaviors that were coded included caretaking activities and social and physical stimulation of the infant. The variables selected for study were those that seemed particularly germane to the mother–infant interaction process. Thus we hoped to observe how the frequency and patterning of behaviors for the respective members of the dyad were affected, either directly or indirectly, by one another's actions. In addition to the home observations, laboratory studies and interviews to assess maternal attitudes were conducted to identify more clearly some of the factors contributing to the behaviors observed in the home.

Throughout these studies, we have noted that the cry of the human infant has tended to be a potent behavior, woven through many aspects of early mother–infant interaction. We have repeatedly observed that the amount of infant crying was associated with a number of both antecedent and concurrent maternal behaviors. Our thinking concerning the salience of crying behavior for mother–infant interactions is shared by other investigators of early development. The remainder of this chapter will be spent considering some of the research that has been done on infant crying, with the aim of better understanding the relevance and role of this behavior for the interpersonal communication process in the mother–infant interaction. Although we will consider the work of others in attempting to evaluate crying behavior, greater emphasis will be given to the work done in our own laboratory at the National Institute of Mental Health.

Theoretical statements and empirical evidence have focused on the potency of the cry as a determinant of maternal behavior and as a central response linking the mother and infant. Bowlby (1958) regards the cry, along with sucking, clinging, following, and smiling, as one of the five basic responses that tie the infant to the mother and provide the basis for the formation of attachment behavior. He feels that crying and smiling differ from the other three responses in that they "depend for their results on their effect on maternal behavior." He states, "It is my belief that both of them (crying and smiling) act as social releasers of instinctual responses in mothers. As regards crying, there is plentiful evidence from the animal world that this is so: probably in all cases the mother responds promptly and unfailingly to her infant's bleat, call, or cry." Certainly, ethological reports are consistent in reporting that mothers from a large variety of species exhibit discriminative responses to their infants' distress signals. Bell and Ainsworth (1972) consider the cry to be the earliest signal provided by the infant that promotes proximity to the mother. On the basis of their research, they feel that the cry is at first expressive and that it later (by the fourth quarter of the first year) can develop into "a mode of communication directed specifically toward the mother." They base this supposition on their finding that by the fourth quarter of the first year "crying occurs more frequently when an infant is in proximity of his mother than when she is wholly out of sight and earshot." From their point of view, once crying has become focused on a specific person and is goal directed it qualifies as an attachment behavior.

We consider the cry to have communication properties from the beginning of life. Certainly, the communication function of the cry becomes more differentiated, elaborate, and purposeful during the course of normal development. To conceptualize the earliest manifestation of the cry in terms of its communicative function enhances our understanding of the potential and more complex development of this behavior. This developmental viewpoint also facilitates our conceptualizing the mechanisms by which more efficient and sophisticated forms of vocalizing eventually come to replace the cry for the purpose of communicating.

We will now consider some of the existing data on mother–infant interaction in an attempt to evaluate empirically the role and meaning of crying behavior as it contributes to the communication process of this dyad. Some of the basic questions we will attempt to deal with, for which at least partial evidence is available, are as follows:

1. Can the cries emitted by the infant be differentiated in terms of whether they reflect different affective states such as hunger, pain, anger, and frustration? Furthermore, if there is evidence that infant cries do differ, is there any basis for assuming that mothers are capable of discriminating these cries and responding accordingly?
2. Does the cry indeed influence maternal behaviors? If so, what is the nature of these influences and do they vary under different conditions, such as the age of the infant?
3. A reciprocal of the preceding question is whether maternal responsiveness shapes or influences crying behavior. That is, does a consistent and vigilant response on the part of the mother lower the amount of crying behavior that is observed or, the converse, does a nurturant maternal orientation tend to reinforce and enhance crying in the infant? This of course is the notion popularized during the Watsonian era that picking up a crying baby led to "spoiling of the infant."
4. Another issue we will consider is whether attitudinal or personality characteristics among prospective mothers are associated with their later maternal behavior.
5. Finally, we will look at data on sex differences in crying behaviors and maternal responsiveness. In this respect, we are not interested in sex differences, per se, but more in terms of how these differences may help us conceptually in better understanding how crying behavior is related to the communication process between mother and infant.

Wolff (1969) combined the observational and experimental approaches in studying a group of infants in order to determine the underlying stimulus conditions associated with different patterns of crying. Through analysis of spectrographic records and subjective observations, for the neonatal period, he was able to distinguish a rhythmical cry, angry cry, pain cry, and frustration cry. He considers the rhythmical cry to be the basic crying pattern to which the infant eventually shifts from other crying. This is the cry pattern that occasionally is referred to as the "hunger cry" since it often occurs when the infant is hungry. He points out that this term is somewhat a misnomer since there actually is no causal relation between hunger and any particular pattern of crying. The apparent gastrointestinal pain that is symptomatic in "colicky" infants results in cries that are higher pitched, nonrhythmical, and interspersed with irregularly occurring shrill shrieks. The cry of the brain-damaged infant is shrill, piercing, and of higher frequencies than the cry of a normal infant. This cry pattern is particularly distinctive and aversive to adult caretakers. Wolff also observes that by the third week of life infants begin to show a pattern of crying that many mothers regard as attention-seeking behavior rather than reflecting distress. The observation that this cry occurs as early as the third week may seem inconsistent with Bell and Ainsworth's finding that purposeful crying emerges during the fourth quarter of the first year of life. However, they consider this cry as being directed toward a specific person, whereas Wolff regards the earlier attention-seeking cry as being nonspecific as to the identity of the caretaker. That this attention-seeking cry is manifest by the third week supports the view that infants are capable of instrumental communication by quite an early age.

Wolff suggests that mothers are capable of determining the basis for these various cries. However, he has direct experimental evidence only concerning their ability to discriminate and show differential responsiveness between the hunger and the pain cry. Wolff feels that the pain cry elicits an emergency reaction from the mother and states that in response to this cry "most mothers immediately rush into the room looking worried, and once they have made sure the baby is fine they report a sense of relief."

Mothers frequently report that the infants' cry is often a sufficient stimulus to produce a dripping of milk from the lactating breast. A group of Scandinavian scientists (Vuorenkoski *et al.,* 1969) investigated whether this let-down reflex was sensitive to different types of cries. In order to test for this, they assessed temperature changes, using infrared thermography, in the lactating breast to hunger and pain cry stimuli. They produced a tape recording of a hunger cry and a pain cry and played these tapes to a sample of 40 primiparous mothers within the first week after delivery. They then compared the skin temperatures over the breast during the presentation of these two cry stimuli. Their assumption was that the hunger cry would increase breast activity and thus result in an increase of temperature and that the pain cry would have the opposite effect because of the anxiety associated with this type of cry. However, they found that both types of cries produced an increase in temperature. Thus at this biological level there was no difference in maternal response to the hunger and pain cries, at at least for this sample of primiparous mothers.

Some members of this same team of investigators (Valanne *et al.,*

1967) explored whether mothers were able to identify their own newborn's cry during the first week of life. This sample consisted of mothers of second-born infants so that they were somewhat more experienced than the subjects in the previously described study. Tape recordings of a series of hunger cries from nine different infants, including the mother's own, were presented to these subjects. They found that about one-third of the sample were reliably able to identify their own infant's cries.

A few investigators report a high degree of success in utilizing the peculiar characteristics of the cry of the brain-damaged infant for diagnosing this condition. In one study (Partanen *et al.*, 1967), it was demonstrated that a group of adults experienced in child care and pediatrics were able to discriminate pathological cry signals from those of normal babies by listening to a series of prerecorded cries. Although it seems unlikely that the average mother would identify a cry as being characteristic of brain damage, it is reasonable to assume that the high-pitched, shrill, and implacable nature of this form of crying might have a negative effect on the mother in her efforts to communicate and form an attachment to her infant. Indeed, one of the mothers included in our studies (Robson and Moss, 1970) reported very positive feelings toward her baby while still in the hospital. However, when she had been home for a short time she learned that the baby was highly irritable and inconsolable. This mother "reacted violently, wanting nothing to do with this child and feeling 'estranged' and unloved. The baby was subsequently diagnosed as brain damaged."

The evidence for the existence of different types of cries, based on both spectrographic records and subjective observations, suggests that mothers might be able to learn to discriminate among these various cry patterns in developing an initial communication system with their infants and in organizing their caretaking behavior. Unfortunately, few data exist for evaluating the potential connection between the type of cry and the respective maternal response. It would be very difficult to study effectively this relation in the natural setting of the home since it is probable that the great majority of cries that occur naturally are of the basic hunger type with other cries tending to occur infrequently. Also, investigators who have studied the various cries indicate that those cries that often begin as reflecting pain or anger (for example) tend with time to change in character so as to more closely resemble the rhythmical pattern of the basic hunger cry.

Bernal (1972) recently completed a study in which she attempted to determine if mothers monitor their responses in terms of the type of cry exhibited by the infant. She administered a prenatal interview to a sample of mothers of first- and second-borns. She also had these mothers maintain a diary for the first 10 days of life. Her focus for this study was on infant crying and the concomitant maternal behavior during this early period of life. The results of this study showed "that only a small group of mothers in the sample considered the type of cry to be a determinant of their response." The time since the last feeding was the most important determinant of the speed and nature of the maternal response. She also found, contrary to popular belief, that mothers of second-borns respond to crying more quickly than do mothers of first-born infants, and more often by feeding. In response to interview questions, however, the tendency was for multiparous mothers to indicate that they would be more casual and unhurried with the second baby.

In our studies at the Child Research Branch of the National Institute of Mental Health, we have not attempted to distinguish among the various cries. We have been interested mainly in recording the presence of a distress signal from the infant and thus have only coded for fussing or crying. Fussing is defined as low-level, intermittent protest vocalizations similar to a whimper or whine, whereas crying is defined as intense, shrill, and blatant vocalizations reflecting distress. We have found that we are able to distinguish reliably between crying and fussing, although there is a transition point where the discrimination becomes difficult. We have completed three studies over the past number of years involving home observations of mother–infant interactions, and for each of these studies have collected data concerning these distress vocalizations of infants. In some instances, we have coded for and studied cries and fusses separately, whereas in other cases we have combined these two variables into a more inclusive variable that we have labeled as "protesting." The basis for whether we considered cries and fusses separately or pooled these two behaviors (protests) was determined by the type of information we were seeking and the purpose of a particular study.

Our research was not limited to studying protests, but consisted of a general survey of a large number of behavioral variables in order to obtain a comprehensive picture of the salient dimensions of the mother–infant interaction in the natural setting of the home. Examples of some of the other variables included in this research are smiling, vocalizing, visual behavior, and stimulation. In most instances, our subjects were also studied in other projects at the Child Research Branch's longitudinal research program on family development. Thus a sample of husbands and wives first participated in a project aimed at studying early marriage. Once this sample had children they were in turn studied by three additional, independent teams of investigators. First, there was a group studying newborn behavior while the infant was still in the hospital, then our research on mother–infant interaction, and finally a project assessing preschool behavior in a 4-week experimental nursery school. The plan of this research program is to interrelate the data from each of the four respective projects in order to generate a longitudinal design spanning early marriage to the preschool period. The fact that our research on mother–infant interaction occurred in the context of this longitudinal design has shaped our selection of variables as well as influenced our overall research strategy. This summary of the program at the Child Research Branch provides the perspective for our studies on mother–infant interaction.

The three home observation studies we have carried out provide information relevant to some of the questions raised earlier concerning the role of the infant's protest behavior in the communication process (interactions) between mother and infant. Before presenting these results, I will first briefly describe the three studies and the nature of the respective samples. In order to help identify each of the samples, they will be referred to here as cohorts I, II, and III.

All three samples consisted of primiparous mothers. Cohort I involved 30 mother–infant pairs studied by means of direct observations over the first 3 months of life. For this sample, a cluster of three observations was carried out at weekly intervals during the first month of life and a second cluster of three observations around 3 months of age. Each cluster included two 3-hr observations and one 8-hr observation. The 3-hr observations were made with the use of a keyboard that operates in conjunction with a 20-channel Esterline-Angus event recorder. Each of 30 keys represented a maternal or infant behavior, and when a key was depressed it activated one or a combination of pens on the recorder, leaving a trace that showed the total duration of the observed behavior. This technique allows for a continuous record of the total time and the sequence of behavior. For the 8-hr observation, the same behaviors were studied with a modified time-sampling technique. The time-sampled units were 1 min in length, and the observer, using a stenciled form, marked the occurrence of the appropriate behaviors for the time unit in which they occurred. For this sample, we also had ratings of maternal attitudes made from newlywed interviews with the wives that were conducted on an average of about 2 years prior to the birth of the child.

Cohort II consisted of 54 mother–infant pairs studied by means of the modified time-sampling procedure used for cohort I. For this sample, three 6-hr observations were held, two at 1 month of age and one at 3 months. In addition, two interviews dealing with maternal attitudes and behaviors were conducted with the mothers from this cohort. The first interview was carried out during the third trimester of the pregnancy, and the second interview was administered after the completion of the 3-month home observation. At the time of this second interview, the infant and the mother also were studied in our laboratory by means of a few experimental procedures.

The same time-sampling procedure and interview schedule were used with cohort III. However, this sample, which consisted of 121 mother–infant pairs, was observed only at 3 months by means of two closely spaced 6-hr observations. For this sample, in addition to the time-sampling procedure, stopwatches were used for recording the latency of maternal responses to crying episodes and for timing the duration of the cry. For all three cohorts, the time-sampled observations began at approximately 9:00 AM and continued for the scheduled number of hours.

A primary reason for conducting three separate studies on mother–infant interaction was to enable us progressively to develop and sharpen our concepts as well as to refine our methodology. Thus although there is a great deal of overlap in variables and methods used among these three studies, there are also a number of distinct differences. Changes in the research design also were influenced by considerations associated with the larger longitudinal design of our Branch research program. Most of the changes that occurred, across studies, were in the direction of more efficient and economical methods, larger samples, redefining variables, wherever possible substituting dyadic for individual variables, and adding experimental procedures, in order to cross-validate some of the findings obtained from the home observations. Thus this series of studies allowed us both to replicate some of our previous findings and to do new analyses that built on the results of preceding studies, which extended our information concerning the various phenomena we were studying.

Cohort I provides information concerning sex differences, the extent to which protesting influences maternal behavior, and the fact that personality characteristics of the wives assessed from the newlywed interviews were predictive 2 years later of their maternal responsiveness in regard to their infants' protesting during the home observations. These findings are based on the two 8-hr time-sampled observations.

The male infants fussed and cried more than the female infants for both the 3-week and 3-month observation. However, these differences were statistically significant at both ages only for the scores on fussing. In turn, the mothers had much more interaction with the male infants. They held, attended, stimulated, and looked at the male more than the female infants. These sex differences were statistically significant only at 3 weeks, but the same trends were observed for the 3-month observation. This suggests that maternal behavior is under greater control of the infant's state at a younger age and that this influence attenuates as the infant becomes older. This assumption is supported by other data we have collected showing that maternal attitudes are more associated with maternal behavior at the older age.

The fact that these sex differences in maternal behavior may have been a function of the greater irritability observed among the male infants was tested by means of an analysis of covariance. In this case, the mean scores for the sexes on these maternal variables were again compared after controlling for the variance associated with fussing and crying. When infant protesting was controlled for by this means, most of the sex differences disappeared. The exceptions were that the t values became greater, after this analysis, for the variables "mother stimulates/arouses infant" and "mother imitates infant." The higher score for "stimulates/arouses" was obtained for the males and the higher score for "imitates" for the females.

To further clarify the relation between infant irritability and maternal behavior, correlations were computed between the infant's protest score and the degree of maternal contact. The maternal contact variable is based on the sum of the time of holding and attending with the time devoted to feeding behaviors subtracted out. The correlations between infant protests and maternal contact were statistically significant for both the 3-week ($r=0.52$, $p<0.01$ level) and 3-month ($r=0.37$, $p<0.10$ level) observations.

These findings do not provide direct causal evidence for the direction of the effects, but it seems most likely that it is the infant's crying that is determining the maternal treatment. "Mothers describe the cry as a signal that the infant needs attention and they often report their nurturant actions in response to the cry. Furthermore, the cry is a noxious and often painful stimulus that probably has biological utility for the infant, propelling the mother into action for her own comfort as well as out of concern for the infant. Ethological reports confirm the proposition that the cry functions as a 'releaser' of maternal behavior." Later, in presenting some of our findings from cohort II we will provide evidence supporting the hypothesis that the correlations we obtained do indeed reflect a causal sequence in which the cry elicits the maternal behavior.

Although we maintain that infant protesting influences maternal treatment, considerable variability remains as to how responsive different mothers are to their infants' fussing and crying. This variability probably reflects differences in maternal attitudes. Women who express positive feelings about babies and who consider the well-being of the infant to be of essential importance should tend to be more responsive to signals of distress from the infant than women who exhibit negative maternal attitudes. In order to test this assumption, we first derived a score for measuring maternal responsiveness. This score was obtained through a regression analysis in which the expected maternal contact score on the basis of her infant's irritability (fussing and crying) was subtracted from the mother's actual contact score. The difference was used as the measure of maternal responsiveness. This score was obtained separately for the 3-week and 3-month observations.

One should be cautioned not to equate extreme responsiveness with maternal sensitivity since a mother who receives a high score on this measure is intervening more than would be expected in terms of her infant's protest behavior. Such extreme responsiveness might just as easily be interpreted as intrusive or overprotective behavior. Newlywed material was available for 23 of the mothers in this sample. A set of interview variables and factor scores for four factors, based on the complete marital assessment data,[1] were correlated with the 3-week and 3-month responsivity scores. The marital data were collected an average of 2 years before the birth of the infants. The newlywed interview rating that dealt with the degree to which the wife exhibited a positive perception of and nurturant orientation toward babies was significantly correlated with both the 3-week ($r = 0.38$, $p < 0.10$ level) and the 3-month ($r = 0.44$, $p < 0.05$ level) maternal responsiveness scores.

The four marriage factors were generated for couples rather than individuals and were based on specific information from interviews, questionnaires, and behavior in experimental situations. The descriptive labels for these four factors are Closeness to Husband's Family, Traditional Role Orientation, Marital Complaints, and Closeness to Wife's Family. Factor scores were derived for each of these factors, and these scores were, in turn, correlated with maternal responsiveness at 3 weeks and 3 months of age. The correlations of the factor scores with maternal responsiveness at 3 weeks of age yielded negligible results. However, factors 1 and 2 correlated 0.54 and 0.51 ($p < 0.05$ level), respectively, with responsiveness at 3 months. Based on an inspection of the items with high loadings, the first factor seems to reflect a tendency on the part of the couple to maintain closeness with the husband's family, whereas the second factor largely involves traditional role behavior on the part of the husband and wife. Traditional role behavior in this case pertains to the husband's and wife's respective involvement in occupational and household activities. This shows that wives from couples wanting closeness to the husband's family and with a traditional role orientation tended to be more responsive toward their 3-month-old infants.

These results thus indicate that, in addition to the characteristics of the wife herself, marital variables are also predictive of maternal responsiveness. These findings were only suggestive when the infants were 3 weeks of age but became clear by 3 months. This is in keeping with our earlier interpretation that at the younger age the infant's state or crying behavior is more dominant in the interaction process, while at the later age characteristics of the mother begin to prevail.

The 3-hr home observations, for which the event recorder was used in order to obtain continuous data, also yielded information concerning maternal behavior in relation to infant protesting.[2] For this analysis, protest episodes (duration of crying and fussing time) were classified as

---

[1] The marriage study was directed by Dr. Robert Ryder, who carried out the factor analysis and derived the scores employed in this analysis.
[2] This analysis is part of some unpublished work done in collaboration with Dr. Sandra Jones.

to (1) the mother being present at the time the protesting began (mother present or MP episodes), (2) the mother not present but responding during the duration of the episode (maternal response or MR episodes), or (3) the mother not present and not responding during the episode (nonmaternal response or NMR episodes). The two 3-hr observations that occurred within the first month were pooled as were the two that took place at 3 months, just as in the case of the time-sampled observations.

These data showed that the MR episodes occurred with much greater frequency than either the NMR or MP episodes. Thus the modus operandi was for the mothers to respond after the infant began protesting. The MP episodes were more frequent at the younger age period and also occurred more often for male than for female infants at both ages. This finding suggests that the mothers were more likely to hover over the younger infants and the males, anticipating but not effectively intercepting the cry before it actually occurred. This explanation for MP episodes seems plausible since infants often exhibit premonitory signs of approaching fussiness or irritability before they actually commence protesting. We also found from these data that mothers took longer to quiet younger infants and males at both 1 and 3 months of age. Thus the greater difficulty the mothers apparently experienced in terminating protest behavior in these infants may, in part, account for the greater vigilance they showed toward them.

On the other hand, the NMR episodes occurred much more often for the female than the male subjects during the earlier observations. An additional finding that helps to clarify this sex difference is that those protest episodes when the mother did not respond (NMR episodes) proved to be of much shorter duration than those episodes where she did respond (MR episodes). Thus the female infants had more of the short protest episodes for which the mother was less likely to respond. Apparently, one of the criteria mothers use in determining whether or not to respond is the length of time the infant is protesting. It may very well be that responding too quickly, on certain occasions, may have more of a disruptive than a salutory effect.

For cohort I as well as cohort II, cries and fusses were positively correlated and showed comparable correlational patterns with other variables. However, with both these samples the frequency of fusses was greater and fusses showed stronger and more consistent associations with maternal behavior. Therefore, for the purpose of presenting results from cohort II, fusses are used as our index of protest behaviors.

An assumption we make in interpreting much of our correlational data is that it is the protest behavior of the infant that elicits maternal behavior and not, as a rule, the maternal behavior producing the protests. To document this assumption, all the instances for cohort II where the infant protested during the 1- and 3-month observations were studied in terms of whether the protests preceded or followed a maternal response. Altogether 2461 episodes were studied. For 77% of these episodes, the protests were followed by a maternal response, whereas for 6% of the episodes the mother's contact with the infant preceded the protest. For the remaining episodes, the mother failed to respond altogether. Therefore, it seems justifiable to interpret the correlations between infant fusses and maternal behavior as interactions reflecting the infant's effect on the mother.

The cohort II maternal observational variables, for both the 1- and 3-month observations, were correlated with the infant fusses scores in order to ascertain the degree and pattern of this infant effect on the mother. The maternal variables generally could be divided into two broad classes of behavior. One class dealt with caretaking activities and the other involved social and physical stimulation of the infant. A number of maternal variables were significantly associated with the infant fusses for the 1-month data. These maternal variables were mother attends infant, holds the infant close, burps the infant, talks to the infant, imitates vocalizations, engages in mutual visual regard, and rocks using a rocking chair. Thus infant's fusses at this age did seem to evoke a number of maternal responses aimed at soothing the infant.

In the 3-month data, there was a general decrease in the extent to which the caretaking activities were correlated with protesting, but the social and physical stimulation of the infant remained highly associated with infant fusses. There is also a trend at 3 months for the fussing scores to be related to different maternal responses for the sexes, unlike the 1-month data in which the correlations for the males and females tended to be comparable. For the females, fussing is apparently responded to through social stimulation (e.g., talking to the infant, imitating her vocalizations, engaging in mutual visual regard) and through the use of distant caretaking activities (attending the infant and using a pacifier). For the male infants, at 3 months of age, fussing is related to stimulation of the distance receptors (auditory and visual) and to close physical contact with the mother. Vigorous tactile stimulation was correlated with the protest scores for both sexes.

The fact that stimulation emerged as the more prominent mode for responding to fusses at 3 months suggests that the developmental needs of the infant are satisfied more at the older age through the provision of stimulation than by routine caretaking activities. This developmental trend may also reflect the mother's having learned which responses are most effective in quieting an irritable infant. The sex differences in the variables associated with fussing at 3 months of age may reflect different developmental rates for males and females. There is some evidence that female infants mature earlier in their social responsiveness than males, and therefore the females may be more effectively quieted by social stimulation (Moss and Robson, 1968). Also, in the 3-month data males fussed significantly more than females ($Z = 1.86$, $p < 0.05$), and this might be a factor that influenced differential responses from the mother for the sexes. This sex difference in fussing replicates what was found for the cohort I sample.

Learning theory suggests that contingent maternal responses to fussing would be reinforcing and thus lead to an increase in this infant behavior. This possibility was investigated by assessing whether mothers who, on the basis of their pregnancy interview ratings, were more likely to be contingent in their responsiveness to the infant's fusses had infants who fussed more at 1 and 3 months of age. We found that mothers who were rated as being more confident about their maternal skills, invested and positive in their orientation toward infants, and who indicated the intention to behave contingently in responding to infants had infants who fussed more at 1 and 3 months of age. Since the mothers who were judged from the interview ratings to be contingent and positive about the maternal role would seem to be the ones who would be more likely to respond quickly to and thus reinforce protesting, these results are regarded as suggestive of the effects of learning on infant fussing.

An additional analysis was conducted to determine more directly whether contingent maternal responsiveness to the infant's protests led to a higher rate in fussing. All the protest episodes that occurred at 1 month of age were studied in terms of the latency of the mother's response to these protests. Average latency scores derived from stopwatch data for each mother during the 1-month observations were correlated with the amount of fussing that occurred for the infant at 3 months. A low but statistically significant correlation was obtained ($r = -0.29$, $p < 0.05$ level, total sample; $r = -0.38$, $p < 0.05$ level, females; $r = -0.25$, nonsignificant, males). That is, the mothers who responded more rapidly at 1 month tended to have infants who fussed more at 3 months.

The finding that infant protest responses are subject to the laws of learning and can be either strengthened or weakened through an appropriate reinforcement schedule is partially supported by the research of others. Etzel and Gewirtz (1967) showed that they were able to extinguish crying in two infants who ordinarily were reinforced for this behavior, by means of nonreinforcement of crying responses combined with the reinforcement of an incompatible response (smiling). Also, Hoffman *et al.* (1966) demonstrated that ducklings which previously had been imprinted to a moving stimulus showed an increase in distress calls after a series of trials in which the appearance of the imprinted stimulus was contingently associated with these calls. On the other hand, Bell and Ainsworth (1972), in their study of crying behavior, found the opposite pattern. That is, nonresponsive mothers had infants who cried more. The available data do not readily suggest any resolution to this difference in findings. Perhaps both responsiveness and nonresponsiveness under different conditions can lead to increased crying behavior, and what may be needed in order to clarify the unique variance associated with each of these disparate findings is better specification of the conditions relating to the observed protest behavior and consideration of differences in the conceptualization of variables from the respective studies. The fact that our results concerning the effect of maternal responsiveness on infant protesting were based on events during the first 3 months of life, whereas Bell and Ainsworth's findings pertained to the last three quarters of the first year, could be the basis for the difference in results between these two projects.

If one utilizes learning theory for predicting the effect of maternal responsiveness on crying, then it becomes necessary to explain why crying behavior eventually subsides, even under reinforcing conditions. The assumption we make in order to explain this apparent paradox is that "maternal behavior initially tends to be under the control of the stimulus and reinforcing conditions provided by the young infant. As the infant gets older, the mother, if she has behaved contingently toward his signals, gradually acquires reinforcement value which in turn increases her efficacy in regulating infant behavior. Concurrently, the earlier control asserted by the infant becomes less functional and diminishes. Thus, at first the mother is shaped by the infant and this later facilitates her shaping the behavior of the infant" (Moss, 1967). This explanation is in keeping with our findings that the correlations for the earlier observations tend to be dominated by characteristics of the infant, whereas interactions during the 3-month observations begin to more strongly reflect maternal predispositions. The reduction in crying with age could also be related to the infant's increased skill, through both learning and maturity, in attaining more efficient methods than crying for seeking the mother's attention and communicating his needs.

A mother's motives for responding to her crying infant may be varied. An important distinction is whether she responds mainly from a sympathetic desire to soothe and comfort the infant or more from a desire to terminate an auditory stimulus that she finds aversive and intolerable in terms of her own well-being. It is virtually impossible, however, to determine the underlying motivational basis for these maternal acts from direct home observations. When the cohort II infants were $3\frac{1}{2}$ months of age, they were studied in a laboratory situation, while the mothers were interviewed and administered questionnaires elsewhere in the building. At the beginning of the interview, the mothers were shown a panel of lights and were told that a particular light would be turned on if her baby fussed or cried. She was given the option to check her infant any time during the procedure. The light signal was turned on according to a prearranged schedule. This provided an opportunity to determine the mother's responsiveness to her infant's protesting in the absence of any noxious auditory input. Scores derived from the mother's responses to the light signal were correlated with her response times to the 1-month protest episodes. A significant correlation was obtained between the responses to the light signals and the 1-month latency scores for the mothers of the male infants ($r+0.49$, $p < 0.05$ level), whereas these two variables were unrelated for the mothers of females. Thus we have some experimental evidence suggesting that maternal responsiveness is at least partially motivated by nurturant concerns. We already have reported that male infants tend to be more irritable, less consolable, and likely to evoke more vigilant behavior from mothers. On the basis of these findings, we might assume that those mothers who were more responsive toward their male infants in the home may have felt that the experimenters would have greater difficulty comforting these infants in the laboratory and therefore were more likely to be responsive toward them when the light signal was turned on. This interpretation could account for our finding a significant correlation between responsiveness to the light signals and the 1-month maternal latency scores to crying only for the male infants.

The data analysis for the cohort III sample has not yet been completed. Basically, the cohort III data will be used to determine if findings from some of our previous studies replicate. One of the things we have learned from our preliminary analyses of data for this sample is that the pattern of correlations between maternal behaviors and infant protesting corresponds with what we already observed for cohorts I and II. Table I shows intercorrelations between the infant and maternal behaviors for corresponding variables for the three samples studied. On the other hand, the cohort III data show no sex differences in protesting behavior. There are a few factors that may help explain our failure to replicate this finding. For one, with cohort III we combined both fusses and cries in our protest category, and it was fussing behavior in the earlier two samples that showed a consistent significantly higher rate for males. Also, about halfway through the data collection for cohort III we learned that the use of medication to quiet irritable infants was evidently becoming much more fashionable among local pediatricians. Many more mothers in this sample reported their infants being put on these prescriptions than seemed to be the case for our earlier samples.

The higher rate of irritable behavior that we generally have observed in males may not be directly a function of the sex of the infant, but may relate more to a greater vulnerability among males. There is some evidence that other factors interact with the sex of the infant in producing this sex difference. Bell and Ainsworth (1972) did not find a sex difference in crying

Table I. Intercorrelations between Infant Fusses (Protests for Cohort III) and Maternal Behaviors Studied in All Three Cohorts

	Cohort I		Cohort II		Cohort III
	3 weeks fusses	3 months fusses	1 month fusses	3 months fusses	3 months protests
Talks to infant					
Males	−0.35	−0.17	0.65 [a]	0.26	0.25 [b]
Females	0.68 [a]	0.43	0.57 [a]	0.64 [a]	0.34 [a]
Pooled	0.34	0.14	0.61 [a]	0.39 [a]	0.28 [a]
Holds infant close					
Males	0.03	−0.01	0.48 [a]	0.45 [b]	0.32 [a]
Females	0.68 [a]	−0.19	0.33	0.10	−0.02
Pooled	0.51 [a]	0.08	0.40 [a]	0.31 [b]	0.18 [b]
Attends infant					
Males	−0.12	0.03	0.47 [b]	0.20	0.17
Females	0.78 [a]	0.70 [a]	0.39 [b]	0.37 [b]	0.53 [a]
Pooled	0.51 [a]	0.48	0.42 [b]	0.27 [b]	0.32 [a]
Vis-à-vis [c]					
Males	−0.08	−0.04	0.45 [b]	0.20	0.15
Females	0.75 [a]	0.58 [b]	0.52 [a]	0.54 [a]	0.23
Pooled	0.54 [a]	0.37 [b]	0.49 [a]	0.32 [b]	0.18
Feeds bottle					
Males	0.11	0.09	0.27	0.08	0.08
Females	0.52 [b]	−0.26	0.03	0.21	0.19
Pooled	0.28	0.06	0.14	0.12	0.12
Burp (gentle)					
Males	−0.06	0.24	0.18	0.06	0.12
Females	−0.06	0.16	0.44 [b]	0.20	−0.08
Pooled	−0.05	0.25	0.34	0.10	0.04
Pacifier					
Males	0.12	−0.20	0.17	−0.13	0.32 [a]
Females	0.51 [b]	0.51 [b]	−0.05	0.40 [b]	0.27 [b]
Pooled	0.32	0.10	0.04	0.11	0.28 [a]

[a] $p < 0.01$ level.
[b] $p < 0.05$ level.
[c] For cohort I, this variable was limited to mother looks at infant.

when they pooled their sample of first- and later-born infants, but did observe more crying for the first-born males in their study. For a study in our laboratory, we asked parents to administer a series of tests to their infants and compared infant and parent behaviors for infant subsamples of males and females, first- and second-born, and those of working-class or middle-class parents. For this study, we found a significantly greater amount of crying behavior only for first-born males of working-class parents. Thus those males who were born to less experienced parents where the pre- and postnatal care may have been less adequate showed more irritable behavior.

In this chapter, I have traced the developmental role of crying behavior, during the early months of life, as a manifestation of the communication process between mother and infant. An attempt has been made to demonstrate the limits and the possibilities in which crying might contribute to this process. The fact that the cry is the earliest and clearest signal available in the infant's repertoire of responses in which he can make both his presence felt and his need communicated causes this behavior to have a pervasive and central role in structuring mother–infant interactions. Information has been presented that demonstrates that different types of cries can be discriminated, but we assert that this factor, within normal limits, has no major consequences for the mother–infant relationship on a day-to-day basis. On the other hand, the general effect of crying on maternal behavior, differences in maternal responsiveness to cries, and the mother's potential for shaping crying behavior seem to be important and prepotent factors that reflect both the structure and the growth of this early communication system.

References

Bell, S. M., and Ainsworth, M. D., 1972, Infant crying and maternal responsiveness, *Child Develop.* **43**: 1171–1190.

Bernal, J., 1972, Crying during the first ten days of life, and maternal responses, *Develop. Med. Child Neurol.* **14**: 362–372.

Bowlby, J., 1958, The nature of the child's tie to his mother, *Internat. J. Psychoanal.* **39**: 350–373.

Brackbill, Y., 1958, Extinction of the smiling response in infants as a function of reinforcement schedule, *Child Develop.* **29**: 115–124.

Carpenter, G. C., and Stechler, G., 1967, Selective attention to mother's face from week 1 through week 8, in: *Proceedings of the 75th Annual Convention, APA,* pp. 153–154.

Etzel, B. C., and Gewirtz, J. L., 1967, Experimental modification of caretaker-maintained high-rate operant crying in a 6- and a 20-week old infant (Infans Tyrannotearus): Extinction of crying with reinforcement or eye contact and smiling, *J. Exptl. Child Psychol.* **5**: 303–317.

Gewirtz, J. L., 1965, The course of infant smiling in four child-rearing environments in Israel. in: *Determinants of Infant Behavior,* Vol. III (B. M. Foss, ed.), pp. 205–248, Methuen, London.

Hoffman, H. S., Schiff, D., Adams, J., and Searle, J. L., 1966, Enhanced distress vocalization through selective reinforcement, *Science* **151**: 352–354.

Moss, H. A., 1967, Sex, age, and state as determinants of mother–infant interaction, *Merrill-Palmer Quart. Behav. Develop.* **13**: 19–36.

Moss, H. A., and Robson, K. S., 1968, Maternal influences in early social visual behavior, *Child Develop.* **39**: 401–408.

Partanen, T. J., Wasz-Höckert, O., Vuorenkoski, V., Theorell, K., Valanne, E. H., and Lind, J., 1967, Auditory indentification of pain cry signals of young infants in pathological conditions and its sound spectrographic basis, *Ann. Paediat. Fenn.* **13**: 56–63.

Rheingold, H., Gewirtz, J. L., and Ross, H., 1959, Social conditioning of vocalizations in the infant, *J. Comp. Physiol. Psychol.* **52**: 68–73.

Robson, K. S., and Moss, H. A., 1970, Patterns and determinants of maternal attachment, *J. Pediat.* **77**: 976–985.

Tennes, K. H., and Lampl, E. E., 1964, Stranger and separation anxiety, *J. Nerv. Ment. Dis.* **139**: 247–254.

Valanne, E. H., Vuorenkoski, V., Partanen, T. J., Lind, J., and Wasz-Höckert, O., 1967, The ability of human mothers to identify the hunger cry signals of their own newborn infants during the lying-in period, *Experientia* **23**: 768–769.

Vuorenkoski, V., Wasz-Höckert, O., Koivisto, E., and Lind, J., 1969, The effect of cry stimulus on the temperature of the lactating breast of primipara: A thermographic study, *Experientia* **25**: 1286–1287.

Wolff, P. H., 1969, The natural history of crying and other vocalizations in early infancy, in: *Determinants of Infant Behavior,* Vol. IV (B. M. Foss, ed.), pp. 81–109, Methuen, London.

CHAPTER 8

The Communication of Affect Among Rodents Through Mother–Young Interactions

Victor H. Denenberg

Department of Biobehavioral Sciences
University of Connecticut
Storrs, Connecticut

I shall discuss a number of experiments we have done over the last 15 years or so revolving around infantile experiences and mother–young interactions. In this context, we have found that affective or emotional behavior is drastically modified by the manipulations we have introduced in the early life of an animal. To start with, I shall describe a series of studies involving mice, and then turn to research with rats. I will show that the same principles apply in both sets of experiments, thus enhancing the generality of these principles.

Studies of Mice Reared with Rat Mothers or Rat Aunts

There are many ways of manipulating the maternal variable to see what influence this has on the behavior of offspring. One method that we have been using for a number of years is to cross-foster newborn mice pups to a lactating rat mother (Denenberg *et al.*, 1964). We have found that a rat mother will care for mouse pups in a competent maternal fashion, and over the past 10 years we have carried out an extensive series of studies using this basic preparation. We have manipulated such variables as preweaning peer group composition (involving varying combinations of mouse and rat pups), postweaning social interactions (mice and rat pups reared together, mouse pups reared together, mouse pups reared singly), and whether the rat living with the mouse pups was a lactating mother or an "aunt" (the rat-aunt preparation will be described later). These studies have been reviewed in detail recently (Denenberg, 1970), and the reader is referred to that paper for methodological details. In this chapter, I shall be concerned only with the major findings of these studies.

Three major dependent variables we have examined have been spontaneous fighting behavior, open-field activity, and the plasma corticosterone response to a novel stimulus. In these studies, we have used the C57BL/10J inbred mouse and the Rockland Swiss albino mouse, which has been maintained by random breeding within our closed colony. Let me now describe how these behavioral and biological end points are influenced when the infant mouse is raised by a lactating rat mother or in the presence of a rat aunt.

Effects on Fighting Behavior

Our procedure for studying fighting behavior is to take two male adult mice and place them into separate halves of a "fighting box." This is an 11.75-by 15- by 16.25-inch plywood box divided into two equal-sized compartments via a removable plywood guillotine door. Wood shavings are on the floor, and each compartment is covered by a fiberglass top having externally fillable food and water supplies. Each mouse is placed into a separate compartment, where he remains alone for several days. After this, testing begins by removing the partition between the compartments, thus allowing the animals to interact with each other. This continues for a 6-min period unless a fight occurs, in which case the session is terminated 5 sec after the fight starts. The animals are then separated in their individual compartments and the partition is restored. This procedure is continued for 7 days. The presence or absence of fighting is recorded for each testing session.

Our control group in our first set of studies consisted of C57BL/10J mice reared in the usual fashion by a mouse mother. When tested for aggression in the manner described above, approximately 45% of the pairs of animals will engage in one or more fights over the 7-day interval. This statistic is based on well over 100 pairs of animals, and thus is quite stable. In marked contrast to this, however, we find that C57BL/10J mice reared by a rat mother have a fighting incidence of approximately 3–5%.

This was a very dramatic finding. When one studies aggression, one is working with a variable that has a strong genetic basis and an important evolutionary history. Aggression has survival value in that the animal which is more successful in attacking and in defending himself is more liable to survive and to pass his genes on to the next generation. For these reasons, one would expect that aggressive behavior would be a highly invariant trait that would be very well buffered from environmental influences. This has certainly been the interpretation put forth by several popular writers on animal behavior. However, our results say otherwise: if we change one variable, albeit a very profound variable—the nature of the mother—we can turn off this species-specific genetically determined evolutionary phenomenon. Because of the exciting and profound nature of these results, we have pursued this research intensively, and I will tell you of some of the experiments we have done.

One question that came up immediately was: Why do the mice not fight? Is there some reason that being raised by a rat mother makes them unable to fight? Or is it that they no longer are adequate stimuli, or effective releasers, to elicit the fighting response from a conspecific? To answer that question, we paired together a mouse raised by a rat mother with a mouse raised by a mouse mother. (In all previous experiments, mice raised by mouse mothers were paired with each other, and mice raised by rat mothers were paired together.) We had 36 pairs of animals in which one member was mouse-reared and the other was rat-reared. Of the 36 pairs, 16 fought, and in each instance the fight was initiated by the animal raised by a mouse mother. Therefore, the mouse raised by the rat mother is certainly an adequate stimulus to elicit fighting behavior. Our next question was: What happens when a fight starts? Initially, the rat-reared animal will not fight back. However, he is capable of fighting, because if he is pursued and nipped on the flanks he will eventually turn and fight. In terms of a hierarchy of behavior, fighting is much lower in the rat-reared mouse than it is in the control animal.

Effects on Open-Field Performance

Another variable which we were studying at the same time that we were examining fighting behavior was activity in an open-field. The field is an open box with a 32-inch plywood floor marked off into 64 4-inch squares. The animal is placed in the field and observed for 3 minutes. The number of squares entered is recorded. We have consistently found that mice reared by a lactating rat mother are less active in the open field than are control mice.

Effects Upon Plasma Corticosterone

The differences in fighting behavior and open-field activity suggested to to us the possibility that the hypothalamic–pituitary–adrenal axis could be involved as part of the mechanism underlying these major behavioral changes. Therefore, we decided to study the plasma corticosterone response of our control and experimental animals to see whether there were any differences in adrenal reactivity to a novel stimulus situation. For a number of reasons, it was more convenient to use the Swiss albino mouse for the corticosterone studies than to work with the C57BL/10J mouse.

Since we were shifting end point as well as mouse strain, there was no common element relating the two sets of studies. To establish a common link, we conducted an experiment in which Swiss albino pups were reared by a lactating rat mother, and we studied their open-field activity at the time of weaning. We found that the rat-reared mice were less active in the open field than were control Swiss albino animals. This finding, identical to the result we had obtained with the C57BL/10J mouse, established that our rat-mother preparation had generality beyond one particular inbred strain of mouse, and so we proceeded to examine the corticosterone response of the Swiss albino mice reared by mouse mothers or by rat mothers. Our major result was that mice reared by rat mothers had less corticosterone in their blood when exposed to a novel environment than did control mice (Denenberg *et al.,* 1968*b*).

Seeking the Causes of the Differences

The Milk Factor. So here was another exciting finding: in addition to virtually shutting out fighting behavior, the rat mother also dampened the adrenal reactivity of the mice. A very interesting phenomenon having been isolated, the question then becomes: What is the cause of this? As a psychologist, I hoped that the cause was the behavior of the rat mother toward the mouse pups, but there are other possibilities as well. One that comes to mind immediately is the nature of the milk. We know that the quality of rat milk is quite different than that of mouse milk, and these biochemical differences could be important in influencing the animal's later performance. To solve the milk problem, we developed our rat-"aunt" preparation. It is known that the rat does not have to be pregnant and give birth in order to get turned on maternally. All that one has to do is expose an adult virgin to infants for approximately a week (Rosenblatt, 1967). After that, the rat will become very maternal. She will retrieve pups, build a nest for them, hover over them, and engage in all the appropriate forms of maternal behavior except that she will not nurse the pups because she does not have any milk. Therefore, what we did was place together an adult virgin rat and a pregnant mouse. We again worked with the Swiss albino strain, and we were delighted to find that mice raised in the presence of a rat aunt were less active in the open field and had a lesser corticoid response to a novel situation than did control mice (Denenberg *et al.,* 1969*b*). This finding was verified in a second experiment (Denenberg *et al.,* 1969*c*).

Distance Cues from the Rat. These experiments rather conclusively eliminated the milk factor as the determining cause of the difference between the experimental and control mice. In our next experiment, we concerned ourselves with whether distance cues such as the odor from the rat aunt or her visual or auditory signals could have influenced the pups

(Denenberg *et al.,* 1969*a*). Experimental mice were born and reared in a cage where an aunt was present, except that in this instance the aunt was separated from the mice by a double wire mesh wall. Under these conditions, the young mice could smell the rat aunt, hear her, and see her, but no physical contact was possible. Control mice were reared similarly in the presence of an adult nonlactating mouse. At weaning, we tested both groups of animals for their corticosterone response to a novel stimulus, since we had previously found that both the rat-mother preparation and the rat-aunt preparation were sensitive to this measure. We found absolutely no evidence of an effect here, from which we may conclude that olfactory, auditory, and visual cues are not involved in mediating this phenomenon.

The Behavioral Interaction Hypothesis. Since we had eliminated the distance cues and the variable of the milk factor, this made it very reasonable to infer that the differences between the experimental and control mice were due to the behavioral interactions of the rat aunt or rat mother with the mouse pups. However, this is a form of negative inference. That is, having eliminated the most reasonable alternative explanations, we now accept the hypothesis that we favored in the first place.

This is a common way of proceeding in science, and often is the best one can do. However, if it is possible to make a positive test of one's hypothesis this is certainly more conclusive proof than the procedure of attempting to eliminate all alternative explanations. Our hypothesis was that the physical interaction of the rat aunt with the mouse pups was the cause of their behavioral and biological changes. In order to test this hypothesis directly, it is necessary to have one group of rat aunts which are maximally interactive with mouse pups and a second group of rat aunts which are much less interactive. Along with this, it is wise to have a control group of mice reared by mouse mothers to be used as a comparative reference with the other experiments in this series.

One way to maximize the maternal behavior of an aunt is to remove her nipples (technically, to thelectomize her) so that she is unable to nurse, then mate her, let her deliver her young, remove the young at birth, and use her as one type of rat aunt. Our control aunts were thelectomized females that were not mated. The third group was the usual one of mice reared by mouse mothers (Rosenberg *et al.,* 1970).

In this experiment, we made the assumption that the thelectomized group of rat aunts which had given birth to a litter would act more maternally toward mouse pups than would the group of thelectomized aunts which did not become pregnant. To test this assumption, we took daily observations of maternal involvement between the two groups of rat aunts and the pups. Consistent with our expectations, those females which had given birth to a litter of rat pups acted significantly more maternally toward the mouse young than did the other group of rat aunts.

At weaning, some of the mice from each litter were tested for activity in the open field, while others were tested for their corticosterone reponse to a novel environment. The corticosterone data revealed that those animals raised in the presence of a postpartum thelectomized aunt gave the least response to the novel stimulus, followed by the nonpregnant thelectomized aunt group, with mice reared by mouse mothers alone giving the greatest response. The activity data revealed that the control mice were the most active, followed by those reared by nonparturient thelectomized aunts, with the mice by postpartum thelectomized aunts being the least affected.

Comparison of Swiss Albino and C57BL/10J Mice. These experiments yielded positive evidence that it is the behavioral interaction between the rat aunt and the mouse pups that is the cause of the change in adrenal reactivity and open-field performance. But these data are based on the Swiss albino mouse, while we started our experiments examining fighting behavior in the C57BL/10J mouse. Having traveled this far down our experimental path, it was now time to circle back to our starting point to see whether we could integrate our various findings. And so we carried out an extensive experiment involving the C57BL/10J mouse and the Swiss albino mouse using both a rat-mother and a rat-aunt preparation and examining several behavioral end points including open-field activity and fighting Paschke *et al.,* 1971). In this study, we found that 82% of 17 pairs of control C57BL/10J mice fought as compared to 17% ($N = 12$ pairs) of mice reared by rat mothers and 36% ($N = 11$ pairs) of mice reared in the presence of rat aunts. The latter two groups did not differ significantly from each other, but both were significantly different from the control group. As expected, both experimental groups of C57BL/10J mice were less active in the open field than were mice reared by mouse mothers.

This finding of reduced open-field activity was also obtained with the experimental Swiss albino mice. However, being reared by a rat mother or in the presence of a rat aunt had no effect on the aggression of the Swiss albino strains. Approximately 82% of each of the three groups fought in our standard fighting box situation. In a more recent study, we have determined that the fighting behavior of F_1 hybrids between the C57BL/10J and Swiss albino mice is also not affected by either the rat mother or rat aunt (Denenberg *et al.,* 1973).

Here, then, is a good example of genetic–environmental interaction, since a particular environmental condition—the nature of the maternal variable—was able to influence the genes affecting aggression in one strain of mouse, but not in another strain. On the other hand, this same maternal variable had an equal influence on open-field activity in both mouse strains.

It is obvious from these data that the behavior of a mother or mother surrogate during an animal's early development profoundly influences its later behavioral and biological capabilities. One of our next objectives in this research program is to isolate those behavior patterns of the mother that bring about these several changes in the mouse offspring.

Effects of Postweaning Social Interactions between Mice and Rats

I mentioned earlier that in some of our experiments we placed mice with rats at the time of weaning and let them live together until adulthood. When this was done, we never had an instance in which a mouse was killed by a rat, although it is well known that a certain percentage of rats in any colony are mouse killers. This suggested the possibility that the early social interactions between mice and rats were sufficient to inhibit this response, and so we conducted an experiment to investigate this hypothesis (Denenberg *et al.*, 1968*a*).

At the time of weaning (21 days), experimental rats were placed with weanling C57BL/10J mice into cages where they remained until 57 days of age, when the rats were removed and placed into a rat colony. Control rats of the same age had spent their whole life in the rat colony. At 90 days of age, each rat was placed separately in a cage, and either a C57BL/10J mouse or a Swiss albino mouse was put into the cage with it. The next day, a mouse of the opposite strain was placed in the same cage. None of the 20 experimental rats which had been reared with black mice killed any of the mice in adulthood. However, 18 out of 40 control rats killed both black and white mice.

We see from this study that early socialization between rats and mice will prevent the killing response from occurring. In addition, since the experimental rats had been exposed only to black mice during early life and killed neither black nor white mice in adulthood, it is clear that there is a large generalization gradient for the inhibition of the killing response.

Special attention should be paid to the control group in this experiment. This group had never seen a mouse prior to 90 days of age, and yet 45% of them killed one or both mice. The control group meets all the requirements set down for the "isolation experiment" that has been used as a major criterion for the definition of an instinctive behavior (Lorenz, 1965). Since some of the rats did kill mice, one could call this an instinctive response. However, that would be a very naive conclusion because it is apparent that if we add to our experimental design the experience of social interraction between rats and mice, the behavior pattern disappears. To conclude that mouse killing is instinctive while not-killing is environmentally determined gets us into all sorts of logical silliness. Rather than try to classify behavior into arbitrary categories, such as innate and learned, it is more sensible to view any behavioral act from a developmental perspective, taking into account both the biological potential of the organism and its experiential history.

Effects of Maternal Emotionality in the Rat on the Offspring's Emotionality

Let me now turn to some research involving rats (Ottinger *et al.*, 1963). In all this work, the open field has been our end point. With the rat, open-field behavior has been shown to be a measure of emotional reactivity: the lower the activity and the greater the defecation, the more emotional is the animal (Denenberg, 1969*b*; Whimbey and Denenberg, 1967).

This research started when a young graduate student in child-clinical psychology at Purdue University came to me and said that, from his observations in the clinic, he thought that disturbed children had parents who were highly inconsistent in the ways they behaved toward their children. For example, the child might do the same thing on two different days; one day the mother would positively reinforce this behavior, and on the other day she would either ignore the child or punish him for doing the same thing. This student was interested in developing a model of inconsistency with rats. After a lot of thought and discussion, we finally worked out the procedure that follows.

An Experimental Procedure for Maternal Inconsistency

We know there are marked individual differences among rat mothers in the way they care for their young (Seitz, 1954, 1958). Therefore, if a particular rat litter is cared for by its own mother for one 24-hr period and is then cared for by a different mother for a second 24-hr interval, the maternal behavior pattern that the litter is exposed to during the second 24 hr would not be the same as the behavior pattern they experience during the first 24-hr period. In that sense, the litter of pups is in an inconsistent mothering situation. Experimentally, what we did was to pair up litters of pups born on the same day. The natural mothers took care of their young for the first 24 hr; then the cage doors were opened, and the mothers were removed and placed in the cages containing the other's pups. Twenty-four hours later, this was reversed so that each mother was again taking care of her own young. The mothers of control pups were also removed from their cages daily, held for a few moments, then returned to the same cage.

An Individual Difference Measure of Maternal Emotionality

In addition to this experimentally manipulated variable of inconsistency, which we expected to influence the emotionality of the offspring, we were also interested in an individual difference variable of emotionality, namely, the emotionality of the mothers of our experimental animals. In order to obtain an estimate of the females' emotionality, we tested all of them in the open field prior to mating. Based on the activity and defecation data, we classified the females into three groups: high emotionality (low activity and high defecation scores), low emotionality (high activity and low defecation scores), and medium emotionality (intermediate scores). Within each of these three groups, we randomly assigned our experimental variable of rotating mothers from one cage to another.

It is important to note that our manipulations were imposed on the mothers of our subjects and that the pups themselves were not disturbed (we waited until the mothers were not nursing or otherwise in contact with their pups before removing them from the cages). Therefore, any differences that are found in the behavior of pups must be the function of (1) the experimental manipulations imposed on the mother and/or (2) the individual differences in emotionality as measured by the open-field test given the females prior to pregnancy.

Effects on Emotionality

All pups were weaned at 21 days and maintained under standard laboratory conditions until 50 days of age, at which time they were given the open-field test. The results came out as predicted. Those rats which had been reared alternately by their own mother and by another mother were significantly less active in the open field than the rats which had been reared only by their own mother. Hence the procedure of rotating mothers, which was used as an experimental technique to produce inconsistency, resulted in animals with higher emotional reactivity. We also found a direct relationship between the prepregnancy open-field performance of the mothers and of their pups at 50 days of age: pups born of and reared by mothers classified as having high emotionality were the least active in the open field, followed by those of medium emotionality, while the most active group were the offspring of the low-emotionality mothers.

Further Analyses of the Individual Difference Variable

The finding relating maternal emotionality to offspring emotionality is difficult to interpret because it could be due to (1) a genetic effect, (2) some prenatal influence, or (3) a postnatal maternal effect. We carried out two experiments to investigate these possibilities. In our previous experiment, our rotation had been done within an emotionality level. Thus two high-emotionality females were rotated every 24 hr, and the same was done within the medium- and low-emotionality classifications. In our second experiment, we paired high-emotionality and low-emotionality females and rotated them so that the pups were exposed for one 24-hr period to a high-emotionality mother and during the subsequent 24-hr period to a low-emotionality mother. When we tested the open-field activity of these pups at 50 days, we found that their scores were intermediate between those of pups which were consistently with either low-emotionality or high-emotionality mothers. Thus we draw the inference from these data that postnatal emotionality levels significantly affect the offspring's emotionality level.

The final experiment in this series separated the genetic and prenatal effects from the postnatal ones by cross-fostering at birth. Based on pre-pregnancy open-field scores, adult females were classified as having high or low emotionality. At birth, pups were cross-fostered so that low-emotionality mothers reared pups born either of low- or high-emotionality mothers, and the same was true for the high-emotionality females. Again, we tested open-field performances at 50 days. We found both a significant prenatal and postnatal effect: in both instances, the less emotional the natural or foster mother, the less emotional were their young. We interpret the prenatal effect as probably reflecting a genetic variable since it is well known that there is a large genetic component to open-field performance. The postnatal influence must clearly be a function of the behavior of the mothers toward their foster young between birth and weaning.

Nongenetic Communication of Affect Across Generations

We have seen from the studies described above that maternal behavior patterns influence and change some important behavioral and biological characteristics of the offspring. Thus one important class of early experience variable is that called "maternal behavior." A very different class of early stimulation that has also been shown to have profound effects on an animal is that called "handling" (Denenberg, 1969c). Essentially, this procedure involves removing the pups from the nest box and placing each individually into a container with shavings. The pups remain in this container for 3 min and are then returned to the nest box. This seemingly innocuous technique has been shown to profoundly affect many performance parameters of rodents, including emotional reactivity (for a review, see Denenberg, 1969c).

We see, then, that we have two quite different forms of manipulation in infancy that will modify the animal's later emotionality, namely, maternal behavior and the technique of handling. We may then ask the question: Can handling in infancy so change the behavioral and biological characteristics of female rats that their offspring's behavior will be changed? The following experiment was designed to answer that question (Denenberg and Whimbey, 1963).

In infancy, a large number of rats were either handled or not handled from birth until weaning at 21 days. At that time, the females were placed into group cages and maintained under standard laboratory conditions until adulthood, when they were mated. When the handled and nonhandled females gave birth, some of the pups were fostered so that some mothers which had been handled in infancy reared foster pups born of either handled or nonhandled mothers, while other females which had not been manipulated in infancy also reared foster pups born of handled or nonhandled mothers. In addition, one group of mothers which had been handled in infancy did not have their pups fostered; this was also done for one group of nonhandled mothers. For this discussion, we are interested only in the four groups which were fostered.

After fostering on the first day of life, the litters were not disturbed until weaning, at which time the pups were placed in laboratory cages and maintained under standard conditions until 50 days of age, when they were tested in the open field. Note that in this experiment the experimental manipulation was done to the mothers of our subjects during their infancy. The pups were not differentially treated at all during the experiment. Thus any differences obtained in the pups' behavior can be related back to the experiences that their mothers had when they were infants. Table I presents the open-field activity findings of this experiment.

We see one group which stands out as being clearly different from the

Table I. Mean Open-Field Activity Scores of Rat Offspring as a Function of the Infantile Experiences of Their Natural Mother and Their Rearing Mother.[a]

Infantile experience of prenatal mother:	Not handled		Handled	
Infantile experience of postnatal mother:	Not handled	Handled	Not handled	Handled
Mean open-field activity of offspring:	114.9	188.4	139.6	121.5

From Denenberg and Whimbey (1963).
[a]All animals were fostered at birth.

other three groups. It is the group of pups whose natural mothers were non-handled controls and which were reared by handled mothers (mean 188.4). Their activity scores are significantly higher than those of the other groups. Since the nature of the experimental design randomizes the genetic differences among groups. we conclude that the effects of stimulating the females in infancy was to bring about a set of physiological changes that expressed itself during the prenatal period and also brought about a set of behavioral changes expressing itself during the postnatal period. The joint interaction of these two factors resulted in the increased activity score of the second group in Table I.

How far can such results be extended? Is it possible to demonstrate a grandmother effect? That is, can we show that experiences in infancy of females can be projected ahead two generations to influence the grandoffspring of these females? Our next experiment investigated this question (Denenberg and Rosenberg, 1967). The experimental design and results are given in Table II.

We started out with female rats which were handled or not handled in infancy. They were maintained in maternity cages and laboratory cages until adulthood and were then mated. When pregnant, these animals were placed in either maternity cages or free-environment boxes, and the animals which were born in these units became the mothers of our experimental subjects. At the time of weaning, the female pups were placed in laboratory cages or into free-environment boxes, where they remained until they were 50 days old. At that time, all animals were placed in laboratory cages, where they remained until mature, when they were mated. All animals gave birth to

Table II. Mean Open-Field Activity Scores as a Function of Grandmother's Infantile Experience and Mother's Rearing Habitats[a]

Grandmother's experience	Mother's preweaning housing	Mother's postweaning housing	Mean activity of grandpups
NH	MC	LC	32.0
NH	MC	FE	44.3
NH	FE	LC	22.4
NH	FE	FE	27.1
H	MC	LC	29.7
H	MC	FE	35.5
H	FE	LC	49.8
H	FE	FE	28.8

From Denenberg and Rosenberg (1967).
[a] NH, not handled; H, handled; MC, maternity cage; FE, free environment; LC, laboratory cage.

their offspring in standard maternity cages. At weaning, these pups (which were the grandchildren of the original handled and nonhandled mothers of the study) were given 1 day of testing in the open field. Their activity scores are presented in Table II. The following interactions were found to be significant: grandmother handling × mother preweaning housing, grandmother handling × mother postweaning housing, and preweaning housing × postweaning housing. Some understanding of the nature of these interactions can be gleaned by looking at the third and seventh groups of Table II. Both of these groups are animals whose mothers were raised under the same laboratory housing conditions, but the handling experience of their grandmothers differed, and this resulted in a large difference in the open-field behavior of the grandpups.

Therefore, we may conclude that the experiences during one's infancy may be visited on one's descendants two generations away.

Conclusions

We see that in the rodent world there is remarkably clear evidence of communication of affective behavior between the mother and her natural or foster offspring. The mechanisms that bring about these changes are at present unknown, but they rather clearly reside within the behavior patterns of the mother and of the infants. Indeed, we have here a truly interactional situation since we know that the mother's behavior influences the offspring and that the offspring's behavior feeds back to modify the mother (Denenberg, 1963; Hudgens *et al.*, 1972). In order to understand these mechanisms, it is necessary to carry out detailed behavioral observations of mother–young interactions in a manner similar to that which Dr. Moss describes in Chapter 7 of this volume. We are now conducting such studies.

In conclusion, let me state a personal belief that I have expressed elsewhere (Denenberg, 1969a), namely, that I am convinced that we will make the greatest progress toward understanding the influence of early experience and developmental processes if those of us doing animal research and those doing human research can work together, carrying out analogous experiments and freely moving back and forth from the animal laboratory to the infant nursery. Another way that we can advance our knowledge rapidly is for the animal researcher and human researcher to get together at more conferences.

Acknowledgments

The research described in this chapter was supported, in part, by research grants MH 19716, from the National Institute of Mental Health, and GB 27511X, from the National Science Foundation.

References

Denenberg, V. H., 1963, Early experience and emotional development, *Sci. Am.* **208**: 138–146.

Denenberg, V. H., 1969a, Animal studies of early experience: Some principles which have implications for human development, in: *Minnesota Symposia on Child Psychology* (J. P. Hill, ed.), pp. 31–45, University of Minnesota Press, Minneapolis.

Denenberg, V. H., 1969b, Open-field behavior in the rat: What does it mean? *Ann. N.Y. Acad. Sci.* **159**: 852–859.

Denenberg, V. H., 1969c, The effects of early experience, in: *The Behaviour of Domestic Animals* (E. S. E. Hafez, ed.), pp. 95–130, Bailliere, Tindal, and Cassell, London.

Denenberg, V. H., 1970, The mother as a motivator, in: *Nebraska Symposium on Motivation: 1970* (W. J. Arnold and M. M. Page, eds.), pp. 69–93, University of Nebraska Press, Lincoln, Neb.

Denenberg, V. H., and Rosenberg, K. M., 1967, Nongenetic transmission of information, *Nature* **216**: 549–550.

Denenberg, V. H., and Whimbey, A. E., 1963, Behavior of adult rats is modified by the experiences their mothers had as infants, *Science* **142**: 1192–1193.

Denenberg, V. H., Hudgens, G. A., and Zarrow, M. X., 1964, Mice reared with rats: Modification of behavior by early experience with another species, *Science* **143**: 380–381.

Denenberg, V. H., Paschke, R. E., and Zarrow, M. X., 1968a, Killing of mice by rats prevented by early experience between the two species, *Psychon. Sci.* **11**: 39.

Denenberg, V. H., Rosenberg, K. M., Paschke, R. E., Hess, J. L., Zarrow, M. X., and Levine, S., 1968b, Plasma corticosterone levels as a function of cross-species fostering and species differences, *Endocrinology* **38**: 900–902.

Denenberg, V. H., Paschke, R. E., Zarrow, M. X., and Rosenberg, K. M., 1969a, Mice reared with rats: Elimination of odors, vision, and audition as significant stimulus sources, *Develop. Psychobiol.* **2**: 26–28.

Denenberg, V. H., Rosenberg, K. M., Paschke, R. E., and Zarrow, M. X., 1969b, Mice reared with rat aunts: Effects on plasma corticosterone and open-field activity, *Nature* **221**: 73–74.

Denenberg, V. H., Rosenberg, K. M., and Zarrow, M. X.,1969c, Mice reared with rat aunts: Effects in adulthood upon plasma corticosterone and open-field activity, *Physiol. Behav.* **4**: 705–707.

Denenberg, V. H., Paschke, R. E., and Zarrow, M. X., 1973, Mice reared with rats: Effects of prenatal and postnatal maternal environments upon hybrid offspring of C57BL/10J and Swiss albino mice, *Develop. Psychobiol.* **6**: 21–31.

Hudgens, G. A., Chilgren, J. D., and Palardy, D. D., 1972, Mother–infant interactions: Effects of early handling of offspring on rat mothers' open-field behavior, *Develop. Psychobiol.* **5**: 61–70.

Lorenz, K., 1965, *Evolution and Modification of Behavior*, University of Chicago Press, Chicago.

Ottinger, D. R. Denenberg, V. H., and Stephens, M. W., 1963, Maternal emotionality, multiple mothering, and emotionality in maturity, *J. Comp. Physiol. Psychol.* **56**: 313–317.

Paschke, R. E., Denenberg, V. H., and Zarrow, M. X., 1971, Mice reared with rats: An interstrain comparison of mother and "aunt" effects, *Behaviour* **38**: 315–331.

Rosenberg, K. M., Denenberg, V. H., and Zarrow, M. X., 1970, Mice (*Mus musculus*) reared with rat aunts: The role of rat–mouse contact in mediating behavioral and physiological changes in the mouse, *Anim. Behav.* **18**: 138–143.

Rosenblatt, J., 1967, Non-hormonal basis of maternal behavior in the rat, *Science* **156**: 1512–1514.

Seitz, P. F. D., 1954, The effect of infantile experience upon adult behavior in animal subjects. I. Effects of litter size during infancy upon adult behavior in the rat, *Am. J. Psychiat.* **110**: 916–927.

Seitz, P. F. D., 1958, The maternal instinct in animal subjects. I, *Psychosom. Med.* **20**: 215–226.

Whimbey, A. E., and Denenberg, V. H., 1967, Experimental programming of life histories: The factor structure underlying experimentally created individual differences, *Behaviour* **29**: 296–314.

Index

Rocking 185

Scala Naturae 56, 60
Semanticity 53
Semantics
  in animals 34-36
Sex differences 176, 181, 184, 188
  in crying behaviors 176
  in maternal responsiveness 176
Sidman avoidance 19
Signals 53
  acoustical 52, 53, 55, 63, 65
  alarm call 41
  as manifestation of emotional state 42-44
  auditory 32, 37
  begging call 41
  chemical 32, 33, 52, 58, 64, 67
  electrical 32, 33
  graded 36, 37
  learning of 44
  olfactory 33, 35, 55
  sematic properties of 53
  separation of context and noise from 60
  sexual call 41, 42
  specific distinctiveness in 37-38
  specialization 27
  specificity 66
  stereotype of 36
  synthetic 38-40
  tactile 52, 55, 58, 67
  uses of 40-42
  visual 32, 35, 37, 52, 55, 58, 63
Smiling 174, 175, 179
Social behavior 59, 67
Social communication
  monkey 92

Social insects 30, 63, 64, 65
  ants 31, 53, 56, 64
  bees 30
  honeybee 31
Social interactions
  post-weaning 194, 199, 200
Social isolation 10
Socialization 199
Sources of pheromonal sex attractants in
    rats 118-119
  anatomical sources 119
Speech
  human 53, 54
Stress 10
Sucking 175

Taxes 67
Teleology 134-135
Territorial marking 10

Urine 14, 16

Vocalizing 174, 176, 179

Wasps 59
Weaning 198, 203, 205
Whales 35, 66
Wisconsin general test apparatus 86
Wolves 30, 54

Zeigarnik effect 118